M000318140

Selling Worship

Selling Worship

How what we sing has changed
the church

Pete Ward

PATERNOSTER

Copyright 2005 Pete Ward

First published in 2005 by
Paternoster Press

Reprinted 2005
11 10 09 08 07 06 05 8 7 6 5 4 3 2

Paternoster Press is an imprint of Authentic Media,
9 Holdom Avenue, Bletchley, Milton Keynes MK1 1QR, UK
And 129 Mobilization Drive, Waynesboro, GA 30830-4575, USA

www.authenticmedia.co.uk/paternoster

The right of Pete Ward to be identified
as the Author of this Work has been asserted by him in
accordance with the Copyright, Designs and
Patents Act 1988.

*All rights reserved. No part of this publication may be reproduced,
stored in a retrieval system, or transmitted in any form or by any means,
electronic, mechanical, photocopying, recording or otherwise, without the
prior permission of the publisher or a licence permitting restricted copying.
In the UK such licences are issued by the Copyright Licensing Agency,
90 Tottenham Court Road, London W1P 9HE.*

British Library Cataloguing in Publication Data
A catalogue record for this book is available from the British Library

ISBN 1-84227-270-5

Cover Design by FourNineZero
Typeset by Textype, Cambridge
Print Management by Adare Carwin
Printed and Bound by J. H. Haynes & Co. Ltd, Sparkford

To
Chris and Belinda

Contents

List of Abbreviations   x

Introduction   1
'Hungry'   2
The Worship Story   4
My Story   6

Part One – The Story of the Songs

1. Means and the Early Days: *Youth Praise* and MGO   11
The Characteristics of the Movement   13
Evangelical Cultures of Religious Production: 16
   The USA and England
Youth Music and Evangelism: *Youth Praise*   23
MGO and *Buzz* Magazine   28
MGO, Gospel Beat and *Youth Praise*   31

2. The Jesus Movement Has Landed   35
Turned on to Jesus: The Jesus Movement in the USA   36
Youth Culture and Renewal   40
The Festival of Light: The Jesus Movement Arrives in the UK 43

3. The Spreading Culture of Worship   49
Worship Can Be Hip   50
Greenbelt: The Beginnings   53
Sound of Living Waters   56

4. The Shift to Worship   61
Youth for Christ and the Big Tour   62
The End of MGO   65
Songs of Fellowship   67
Spring Harvest   70
Make Way and The March for Jesus   72

5. The Growing Market   75
The Economic Context of Worship   76
Publishing and Recording   78
The Christian Copyright Licensing Scheme   81
The Mediation of Worship   88
Economics and Technology: The Worship Scene   95

6. Merchandising, Mergers, and Ministry   97
Wimber and the Renewal of Renewal   98
Alpha   101
New Wine and Soul Survivor   103
Vineyard and the Toronto Blessing   107
Consolidation and Alliance   111
Making it in America – Delirious?   114
Enter the Web   116
Selling Worship   118

Part Two – Singing the Story

7. Teaching to Worship: *Youth Praise* and   121
Sound of Living Waters
Youth Praise Book One   122
Sound of Living Waters   127

8. Marching to Intimacy: *Songs of Fellowship*, Graham 135
Kendrick and *Songs of the Vineyard*
Songs of Fellowship Volume 1   136
The Graham Kendrick Songbook Volume 2   141
Songs of the Vineyard Volume 1   145

9. The Heart of Worship: *The Survivor Songbook*   151
Heart   152
Giving Praise as a Sacrifice of Love   155
The Way of the Cross   157
Intimacy, Place, Coming Before and Now   159
Jesus Christ, Lover of the Soul   161

Part Three – Worship: A Critical Appreciation

10. Worship and Culture   165
Faithful and Relevant   166
Changing the Content and Form of Worship   168
The Contradictions of Culture   169
Adapting the Culture   175
Selling Out to the Culture   179

11. Participation: From Folk to Fan   183
Participation and Renewal: Folk Art   184
Participation in a Media-generated Worship Culture   187
Being a Fan: Investment in Worship   189
Participation and Production in Contemporary Worship   191
The Worship Apparatus   192

12. Songs as Narratives of Encounter   197
Songs in Charismatic Worship   198
Charismatic Renewal and Encounter with God   200
Narratives of Encounter   202
Mission and Encounter   205
Singing about Singing; From Objective to Reflexive Worship   206

Bibliography   211
Songs Index   225
Author Index   231
General Index   233

Abbreviations

BYFC	British Youth For Christ
CSSM	Children's Special Service Mission
GK	*Graham Kendrick Songbook Volume 2*
ICC	International Christian Communications (Recording Studios)
MGO	Music Gospel Outreach
SF	*Songs of Fellowship*
SLW	*Sound of Living Waters*
SS	*The Survivor Songbook*
SV	*Songs of the Vineyard Volume 1*
YP	*Youth Praise*
YP2	*Youth Praise 2*

Introduction

Charismatic worship has become the default setting in most evangelical churches in Britain. This was not always the case. The worship of the1950s and early 1960s was a world away from the guitar-based folk and rock music of the present day. At its most basic this change in the style of worship may simply relate to a shift in culture. As one generation has given way to another, so a more youth-orientated music has been adopted by the church. From the perspective of the present, it may seem quite natural or even self-evident that popular forms of music should form part of the worship of the church. We have become used to the idea that changes in the church will reflect the gradual move towards a youth-dominated culture in the wider society. Yet the story of how evangelical faith has come to be expressed within the cultural forms of popular culture has been neither obvious nor natural. This change has come about because of the activities of a relatively small number of key individuals, and the organisations and companies they have created. The consideration of the growth and significance of contemporary worship takes us straight into a world of religious entrepreneurs, evangelical businesses and spiritual marketing. In short, through a variety of means – be it Christian bookstores, or festivals such as Spring Harvest and Soul Survivor or publishing and record companies like Kingsway and Thankyou Music – evangelicals have been engaged in selling worship.

Selling in this context is not necessarily negative. Selling indicates a means of communication and exchange.

Selling suggests a process where a product or a service is offered and how that service or product is appropriated. In the context of worship, this is perhaps best illustrated in relation to an individual worship song: the Vineyard song, 'Be the Centre'.[1]

'Hungry'

'Be the Centre' was written by the worship leader Michael Frye in 1995, but I first came across it on a visit to South Africa in the winter of 2000. I was leading a series of workshops exploring new forms of worship. The sessions combined charismatic worship with visuals and more liturgical elements drawn from alternative worship.

My host collected me from Johannesburg airport. In the car, he announced that he could not wait to play me the 'latest thing', the *Hungry* CD, published by Vineyard Music. Throughout my trip, despite my efforts to play ambient dance music to set the scene for the seminar, I would invariably find that at some point the local sound engineer would replace my CD with *Hungry*. Putting aside my mild irritation, I eventually bought the album as a memento of my trip and on arriving home I was particularly struck by the song, 'Be the Centre'. It is something of an irony that I had to go all the way to South Africa to be introduced to a CD which has the subtitle, 'Live from London'. Interestingly, the blurb on the back says that it is, 'Distributed in South Africa by Vineyard Music Group of South Africa'; however, the recording and the songs are both copyright Vineyard Songs (UK/Eire). These brief notes indicate the extent and the sophistication of the evangelical communication culture.

It was a few months later that I set about trying to use 'Be the Centre' in a worship service in my local church. Not being particularly gifted at working out guitar parts from recordings, I was pleased to find that the latest edition of

---

[1] *SS* 82.

the *The Survivor Songbook* had a version of the song, with both the guitar chords and lyrics reproduced.[2] So, I set about learning the song. After a week or so, I was just about able to use the song at a worship service in the church. It was a real encouragement, not simply for me but also for the church. Somehow, at that time, the song summed up where we were at in the early days of what was a new church project. For a year or so, the song was sung regularly at church, and then almost overnight it felt tired and dated. For us, as a church, it felt as if it had had its day. Although I still very much like 'Be the Centre', if I were to lead worship at that church today I would hesitate to use it because the feeling was so strong.

The first observation I would draw from this story relates to selling. Had I not bought the CD, I would not have been aware of the song. I certainly would not have set about using it in the worship at my church if I had not purchased and listened to the recording of the song. Also, I might never have mastered the song without the helpful chord diagrams in the *The Survivor Songbook*.

It is possible to continue making these kinds of observations. The album represents the commitment of the Vineyard churches to write songs and record them. There is a long line of writers, performers, recording engineers, producers, designers, printers, business people, copyright specialists, distributors, and so on, in the network of Vineyard music companies around the world. Most of these people will be evangelical Christians and they are all involved in one way or another with selling worship.

Selling in this sense cannot be reduced to something 'commercial' or materialistic. We misrepresent 'Be the Centre' if we follow these kind of simplistic critiques of consumer culture. The point here is that the value of the song might be said to lie in its content and its use in the worship of the church, but we cannot separate these aspects of its use and meaning from the ways in which the

---

[2] *SS* 82.

song has been transmitted. Even the way that the song became a significant part of worship and then fell out of use in my local church is related to selling. We see here the way that selling makes songs widely available, but the culture of selling has begun to influence the culture and practice of the church.

There have always been fashions in music, and hymns are no exception to this but what we are seeing in the contemporary worship scene is a much more temporary and transitory hymnology.[3] What this means is that the worship scene is subject to trends, enthusiasms and fashions in much the same way as the wider culture. Songs, including worship songs, are experienced as being 'in' and then they are 'out'. This aspect of charismatic culture is evident at the various Christian festivals as well as in the local church. These personal or social aspects of the worship culture are also related to the way that popular music is marketed and sold.

The Worship Story

Selling Worship sets out to explain how evangelical Christians in Britain came to embrace popular music, and how this has affected the practice and theology of worship. Part One explores the story of contemporary worship and the connections that emerge from the various streams of youth work, the charismatic movement and popular music. At the heart of this story lies the desire to reach out to young people in evangelism. The pop culture of the 1960s was taken up for evangelistic ends by groups such as MGO and Youth For Christ, who began to pioneer the use of contemporary gospel music in coffee-bar evangelism. As the 1960s gave way to the 1970s, a new impetus was given to these groups by the introduction of the style and music of the Jesus Movement from the USA. This cocktail of

---

[3] See L. Adey, *Hymns and the Christian Myth* and *Class and Idol in the English Hymn.*

evangelical Christianity and a new youth style was mixed with the spreading charismatic movement. As these streams flowed together, contemporary worship was born.

In Part Two, 'Singing the Story', I concentrate on the changing lyrical content of worship songs. From *Youth Praise* to *The Survivor Songbook*, the shifting patterns in metaphor and imagery common in worship songs reveal a gradual theological development. The observation that the theology of the church is being changed through the songs that we sing is very significant. If we add to this the realisation that the changing patterns in theology are related to the way that popular music markets and sells itself, then some important and perhaps less than positive observations can begin to be made.

This is where Part Three takes up the argument. This section sets out to develop a critical appreciation of charismatic worship. A number of theological and cultural issues that have emerged from the study are explored and suggestions for the future direction in worship are set out.

Selling Worship has grown from my work for an earlier book. *Growing Up Evangelical*[4] was basically a study of evangelical youth work which included a chapter on songbooks that were used in worship. The book was also divided into three sections. The first was a series of historical studies into Christian work among young people. In these studies, I argued that evangelical subculture was generated as evangelicals sought to reach out in the universities and the public schools. The final section of the book explored the nature of present-day evangelical subculture in relation to issues of risk and safety in youth work. The middle section analysed the lyrical content of songbooks used within evangelicalism. This material has been revised and greatly expanded to form the second section of *Selling Worship*.

The central argument in *Growing Up Evangelical* was that

---

[4] P. Ward, *Growing Up Evangelical: Youthwork and the Making of a Subculture.*

it was youth work that generated evangelical subculture. Looking back, this is an argument, with which I remain in general agreement, but it also seems clear that a further examination of the relationship between worship songs, styles of youth work and evangelical subculture is able to reveal a more dynamic link than was first suggested. In *Growing Up Evangelical* I located the culture of English evangelicalism in the context of student or young people's membership groups. Moreover, the character and sensibilities of these membership groups were closely related to the privileged environment of English public schools and Oxbridge from which they emerged. It now seems clear that it is hard to locate either the present-day subculture of evangelicalism, or the songs used in evangelical and charismatic worship, within this establishment and rather elite culture. The present-day worship scene suggests that evangelicalism in this country has embraced contemporary popular culture and, in particular, popular music in ways that are hard to relate to the previous ethos which emerged from Oxbridge and the public schoolboys camps of Scripture Union and Children's Special Service Mission (CSSM). (It is perhaps worth observing that some of the conflicts in contemporary evangelicalism may have more cultural and social roots than are generally acknowledged. My own feeling is that a great deal of light can be shed on the differences between groups such as Reform and charismatic evangelicals through a more cultural theology. *Selling Worship* may go some way to help this analysis take place.) How this came about is the focus of attention in the next section, but before I explore these developments, I want to make a few more personal comments.

My Story

The changes in the musical style and the theological content of worship described in *Selling Worship* have not taken place in a vacuum. Many of us have lived through these changes. I certainly am not excluded from this. In the early 1970s, I joined the youth group at my local Anglican Church. We used the *Youth Praise* songbook. As the charismatic renewal started to spread, I was part of the choir in my hometown that produced the worship-based musical *Come Together*. Largely through the popularity of *Come Together*, my local church introduced *Sound of Living Waters*. This new, guitar-friendly songbook meant that, even as a fledgling guitarist, I could play a few tunes for the youth group. By my student days *Songs of Fellowship* had appeared on the scene and when I became a youth worker in Oxford we used the combined *Songs and Hymns of Fellowship* at my church. In more recent times, I have occasionally led worship using *The Survivor Songbook*. In my various careers as musician, youth leader and lecturer I have been involved in Greenbelt, Soul Survivor and other events around the country. I say all this because I feel that, in many ways, the worship story is my story.

I have sung the songs in worship and lived through the changes in evangelical culture. I am not simply a disinterested academic. Charismatic worship has shaped my spiritual life. There are times when worship has kept me afloat. As the song says, 'You are my Rock in times of trouble'.[5] That said, my relationship with the worship scene has gone through phases. Perhaps I should admit I am something of an inhibited charismatic. I deeply appreciate the atmosphere and experience of charismatic worship but my hands have generally stayed firmly in my pockets. However, I have never had any objection to my next-door neighbour letting it all hang out as they praise God: each to their own. At the same time, I have from the start appreciated a wide range of worship styles. I like the traditional evensong from the Anglican prayer book and I also enjoy alternative worship. Yet, ever since my youth group days, the songs of renewal have been a regular feature of my spiritual life.

---

[5] 'Faithful One', Brian Doerkson. Copyright 1989. Mercy/Vineyard Publishing/Music Services.

I say this by way of introduction because I want it to be clear that I appreciate charismatic forms of worship and spirituality. I feel the positive contribution of the movement has been very much for the good in the church. At its most elemental, I feel that the charismatic movement has focused attention on a more immediate experience of God. This has generated considerable energy in the church in Britain. The gradual development of styles of worship and the evolution in the lyrical content of songs have been right at the heart of these developments. At the same time, I have to admit that there are aspects of the worship scene which have made me uncomfortable. In fact, there have been periods in the worship story where I have been left cold by the songs I have been singing and, occasionally, I have even felt alienated by the music and some of the lyrics. I suppose what I am saying is that I am a worshipper, but I am also a critical worshipper. It is this spirit of commitment and comment, belief and analysis that I have tried to bring to this study of worship.

Part One

The Story of the Songs

One

'Means' and the Early Days: *Youth Praise* and MGO

Evangelical religion has always been attracted by selling. It has long been argued that there are close links between the culture of Protestantism and the development of capitalist markets.[1] While Weber's thesis locates these links in the theology of Calvinism there are more practical links between evangelicals and the marketplace. At a very obvious level the desire to communicate faith has many parallels with commerce. These common interests and concerns have led to various crossovers between the world of selling and the world of the church. In the present day, 'church growth' models draw quite openly from business management theories. From a historical perspective, it is clear that the methods of evangelism used by evangelicals have also been influenced by commercial models. Interestingly, the traffic has not always been one way. There are also examples of evangelical innovations in communication and organisation being adopted by the business community.[2]

In the 1950s, evangelicals in Britain began to focus their activities on communicating the gospel to young people. Through ministry in universities and public schools new

---

[1] See M. Weber, *The Protestant Ethic and the Spirit of Capitalism*.
[2] L.I. Sweet (ed.), *Communication and Change in American Religious History*.

patterns of activity evolved. While these were never commercial in the strictest sense, they were adapted to forms of communication that were appropriate in these particular and distinct environments. A 'culture' of religious practice and sensibility evolved. This grew from these educational worlds and the informal culture developed by privileged young people within them. Evangelicals used the patterns of university societies, lectures, seminars, study groups and term cards to create a particular contextualisation of faith.[3] By the late 1960s, evangelical involvement in youth ministry had spread from the universities and public schools to parishes, youth fellowships and youth clubs all around the country.[4] The desire to reach out to a wider range of social groups meant that evangelicals had to make connections to the developing youth culture of the day.

Music was obviously the key to reaching young people. For the Anglican editors of *Youth Praise*, the use of popular forms of music in youth groups became a matter of urgency. Soon these songs were being used in the regular worship of Anglican churches as they developed family services. At the same time, the desire to evangelise youth led to the formation of 'gospel beat groups'. Linked through MGO and its magazine *Buzz*, these groups were playing at youth clubs and coffee bars all over the country. Christian beat groups were to develop forms of music which combined a distinctively evangelical expression with a youth-orientated pop or folk music. Communication in this musical culture was not just a matter of using guitars or writing in particular musical forms. Popular culture was produced by a number of media related activities. In the 1960s, this included record companies, magazines and the various media technologies such as radio and TV. More recently, we are aware of the way that the internet has affected the way that we access and use popular music.

Through shows such as *Pop Idol* and *Fame Academy* we

---

[3] For more on this see Ward, *Growing Up Evangelical*.
[4] Ward, *Growing Up Evangelical*.

have become more aware of the way that stars are packaged and produced. Behind the pop sensation we now know that there are record companies, producers, publishing contracts and a whole jungle of financial deals and royalties. As evangelicals sought to share Christ with young people, they began to construct parallel worlds of Christian record companies, festivals and organisations. At the heart of this was the desire to communicate Christ in the youth culture of the day. Popular culture was and is a commercially orientated consumer culture. This means that to relate you have to 'sell' but at the same time you are nothing if the consumer does not 'buy'. Buying and selling, production and consumption shape our consumer culture.

When evangelicals made the connection between the gospel, youth culture, popular music and worship they inevitably were drawn into this consumer and media world. It is important to note right at the start that developments were not necessarily a 'sell out' of the faith for evangelicals. The desire to connect with people and express the gospel in contemporary terms is driven by a theology which goes to the heart of the evangelical expression of the faith. From the earliest times evangelicals have used 'means' to communicate the faith.

The Characteristics of the Movement

Historians generally date evangelicalism from the early eighteenth-century.[5] It is:

> . . . a fairly discrete network of Protestant Christian movements arising during the eighteenth century in Great Britain and its colonies.[6]

---

[5] See A. McGrath, *Evangelicalism and the Future of Christianity*, 11ff.;
D. Tidball, *Who are the Evangelicals?: Tracing the Roots of Today's Movements*, 11ff.; M. Saward, *Evangelicals on the Move*, 7ff.; M. Noll, D.W. Bebbington and G.A. Rawlyk, *Evangelicalism: Comparative Studies of Popular Protestantism in North America, the British Isles and Beyond*, 9.
[6] Noll et al., *Evangelicalism*, 6.

... a popular Protestant movement that has existed in Britain since the 1730s. It is not to be equated with any single Christian denomination, for it influenced the existing churches during the eighteenth century and generated many more in subsequent years. It has found expression in a variety of institutional forms. A wine that has been poured into many bottles.[7]

This discrete religious movement has a history and a particular culture. Bebbington identifies four main qualities that have shaped evangelicalism: conversionism, activism, biblicism and crucicentrism. Conversionism refers to a belief that people's lives need to be changed; activism to the expression of the gospel through effort; biblicism to 'a particular regard for the bible'; and, crucicentrism focuses on the centrality of the sacrifice of Christ on the cross. Together these form the distinctive 'marks' of evangelical religion.[8] This cocktail of distinctives gives rise to a particular form of church life where theological convictions shape, and are shaped by, patterns of communication. So, desire to see people's lives change through conversion led to a stress on particular forms of activity within the movement. Bebbington recounts how evangelicals were immediately busy in the development of new social forms to fulfil their mission, for example, Finney's development of a technology of revivals,[9] the formation of missionary societies in the eighteenth century,[10] and the creation of particular societies and classes for new converts.[11] In addition, Bebbington argues that eighteenth-century evangelicalism was, 'permeated by enlightenment influences'.[12] In

---

[7] D.W. Bebbington, *Evangelicalism in Modern Britain: A History from 1730s to the 1980s*, 1.

[8] Bebbington, *Evangelicalism*, 2.

[9] Bebbington, *Evangelicalism*, 8; see also C.G. Finney, *Lectures on Revival*, and C.E. Hambrick-Stowe, *Charles G. Finney and the Spirit of American Evangelicalism*.

[10] Bebbington, *Evangelicalism*, 12; see also J. Butler, *Awash on a Sea of Faith: Christianizing the American People*, 278.

[11] Bebbington, *Evangelicalism*, 24.

[12] Bebbington, *Evangelicalism*, 57; see also M. Noll, *A History of Christianity in the United States and Canada*, 154–7.

particular, it paralleled aspects of the Enlightenment in what he describes as 'pragmatism', 'empiricism' and 'optimism'.

> The spirit of the age – flexible, tolerant, utilitarian – affected evangelicals as much in practice as in thought. Field preaching, an activity that lay near the heart of the revival, was an embodiment of the pragmatic temper. If the people would not come to church, they must be won for Christ in the open air.[13]

Pragmatism was also seen in the willingness to co-operate across denominational boundaries in creating voluntary organisations, for example, the London Missionary Society or the British and Foreign Bible Society.[14] Such links 'exemplified an abandonment of exclusive denominationalism, a certain practical empiricism'.[15] Also linked to the Enlightenment empiricism was an emphasis upon experience. Evangelicals saw true Christianity as being located in 'experimental religion' (i.e. it must be tried in order that it may be experienced).[16] There was therefore a significant articulation between Enlightenment empiricism and conversionism. Revivalism also connected with Enlightenment optimism in that its millennial expectation encouraged a belief in gradual improvement.[17] Enlightenment empiricism, optimism and pragmatism fuelled evangelical activity. This activism represented a discontinuity with previous forms of Protestantism in the way the new movement placed an emphasis upon mission. This was commonly expressed by the use of the term 'means': 'Means was the key word signifying the whole apparatus of human agency.'[18]

Most significantly, evangelicals were interested in finding the means of expressing the gospel relevant to the

---

[13] Bebbington, *Evangelicalism*, 65.
[14] Bebbington, *Evangelicalism*, 66.
[15] Bebbington, *Evangelicalism*, 66.
[16] Bebbington, *Evangelicalism*, 57.
[17] Bebbington, *Evangelicalism*, 62.
[18] Bebbington, *Evangelicalism*, 41.

society and culture of their own day. Human creativity and a variety of communication technologies have been used by evangelicals but always with an emphasis upon the priority of theological aims and perspectives. The effect of this has been that as evangelicals have adopted different forms of expression and communication they located their expression of the faith in relation to wider cultural movements. Through adopting and adapting various approaches to communication and media a distinctive evangelical culture can be seen to have developed. By the use of 'means' evangelicals have become cultural producers as well as consumers.

Evangelical Cultures of Religious Production: The USA and England

During the 1920s evangelicalism on both sides of the Atlantic was in significant decline, but as the 1940s gave way to the 1950s a substantial resurgence was to take place in the USA and in the UK.[19] Bebbington argues that the renewal of evangelical religion in the USA and in England has followed roughly similar and parallel trajectories.[20] Despite similarities he also identifies three differences between evangelicalism in the USA and in Britain. First, American evangelicals tended towards ecclesiastical separation, whereas in England the movement has been primarily within existing denominations, in particular within the Anglican Church. Secondly, in the USA fundamentalism marked a key phase in the development of the movement; this was not the case in England.[21] Thirdly, he identifies what he calls a 'secular tendency' in American evangelicalism. He describes this as, 'A mixture of populism, individualism, democratisation, and market-making has recently been defined as the essence of the

---

[19] D.W. Bebbington, 'Evangelicalism in its Settings: The British and American Movements since 1940', in Noll et al., *Evangelicalism*, 368.
[20] Bebbington, 'Evangelicalism in its Settings', 368.
[21] Bebbington, 'Evangelicalism in its Settings', 371.

American way of shaping religion.'[22]

Bebbington is drawing upon a growing body of research into the relationship between American evangelicalism and the market.[23] Butler argues that following the American Revolution and the passing of the First Amendment to the Federal Constitution in 1791 the legal privilege of religion was removed.[24] The result was that churches in the United States began to compete in an open marketplace, not simply with each other, but also against the goods and technology of the wider society.[25] Hatch describes how in the nineteenth century, through the market and competition, American Protestantism in general, and evangelicalism in particular, embraced what he calls a, 'democratised populism'.[26] It is the adoption of forms of communication and religious life associated with popular culture that has brought this about: 'The democratisation of Christianity, then, has less to do with the specifics of polity and governance and more with the

---

[22] Bebbington, 'Evangelicalism in its Settings', 373. Populism and the use of contemporary media were to some extent a characteristic of classical Pentecostalism and the Salvation Army in England. see A. Hastings, *A History of English Christianity 1920–1990*, 265; W.J. Hollenweger, *The Pentecostals;*, H. Cox, *Fire From Heaven: The Rise of Pentecostal Spirituality and the Reshaping of Religion in the Twenty First Century*; F. Coutts, *The Weapons of Good Will: The History of the Salvation Army 1946–1977*. Bebbington, however, makes no mention of these groups, perhaps because he is giving a more broad brush treatment of developments within evangelicalism as a whole.

[23] See M. Marty, *Pilgrims in their Own Land: 500 Years of Religion in America*; 410ff.; J.A. Carpenter, *Revive Us Again: The Reawakening of American Fundamentalism*; G.M. Marsden, *Reforming Fundamentalism: Fuller Seminary and the New Evangelicalism*; Hambrick-Stowe, *Finney*; Sweet (ed.), *Communication*; Butler, *Awash on a Sea of Faith*; H. Stout, *The Divine Dramatist: George Whitefield and the Rise of Modern Evangelicalism*; R.L. Moore, *Selling God: American Religion in the Marketplace of Culture*; D.F. Wells, *No Place for Truth or Whatever Happened to Evangelical Theology?*; N.O. Hatch, *The Democratization of American Christianity*; L.W. Dorsett, *Billy Sunday and the Redemption of America*; L.W. Dorsett, *A Passion for Souls: The Life of D.L. Moody*.

[24] Butler, *Awash on a Sea of Faith*, 268.

[25] Butler, *Awash on a Sea of Faith*, 275.

[26] Hatch, *Democratization*, 5.

incarnation of the faith in popular culture.'[27]

During the early nineteenth-century, the activities of Christian entrepreneurs led to a remarkable series of innovations in religious culture. Competition led to the development of revivalist camp meetings that were characterised by vernacular, popular styles of preaching, publishing and the creation of a mass religious market. In particular, Hatch notes the development of new styles of spiritual songs based on folk tunes.[28] It was evangelicals who were most successful in adapting to this new arena of innovation and competition in a religious marketplace: 'evangelical religion prospered largely because the price was right and the streets were filled with vendors.'[29]

The historical relationship between American evangelicals and a culture based on the marketplace may not be the only reason for its significance. The size of the American religious market as compared to the UK should not be underestimated. This is not simply related to the difference in populations, it is also the fact that a significantly higher proportion of the population in the USA maintain church affiliations. For instance, in a Gallop Poll taken in 1976, 34 per cent of Americans described themselves as being 'born again'. In 1980 the same question was answered positively by 40 per cent.[30] Moreover, this substantial proportion of the population was in the regular habit of making significant financial donations to religious causes. In 1985, 72 per cent of all individual giving went to religious institutions. The habit of giving meant that religious groups, including evangelicals, had access to staggering economic resources. For example, Bebbington recounts: 'In the years immediately after the war American religious organisations, taken together, actually enjoyed a higher annual income than the whole budget of the British Government.'[31]

---

[27] Hatch, *Democratization*, 9.
[28] Hatch, *Democratization*, 125ff.
[29] Hatch, *Democratization*, 15.
[30] Bebbington, 'Evangelicalism in its Settings', 377.
[31] Bebbington, 'Evangelicalism in its Settings', 378.

Even when it is acknowledged that a significant number of wealthy individuals were Jewish and unlikely to give to evangelical groups, these figures are highly significant. The size of the American market enabled a market-orientated culture to develop and to thrive.[32] This was not the case in the much smaller world of English evangelicalism. The evangelical resurgence in England was not based around a market pattern of religious production and consumption. The cultural economy of English evangelicalism relied less on market capitalism and more on the voluntary association or student membership groups. Evangelical resurgence grew out of ministry among public schoolboys and students.[33] The chief pattern of contextualisation and cultural production was the youth fellowship or student Christian Union. Innovative patterns of Christian evangelism, discipleship and worship were first developed in the context of educational institutions and the conventions of public school and Oxbridge life, and they were then transported into parish life by leaders nurtured in these youth movements. This is what Bebbington describes as the 'grand strategy' of conservative evangelicals in their fight against the spread of liberalism during the 1920s.

---

[32] There is some evidence that during the eighteenth and nineteenth centuries the culture of religious production within evangelicalism on both sides of the Atlantic was largely based on a market pattern. An example of this would be the ministry of George Whitefield (for Whitefield's use of publicity and the Press see H. Stout, 'Religion, Communications and the Career of George Whitefield', in Sweet (ed.), *Communication*; see also Stout, *Divine Dramatist*) A further example would be the ministry of D.L. Moody (see Dorsett, *Passion for Souls*; G.M. Marsden, *Fundamentalism and American Culture: The Shaping of Twentieth-Century Evangelicalism 1870–1925*, 34; for impact in the UK see K. Hylson-Smith, *Evangelicals in the Church of England 1734–1984*, 173–7). After World War II it would appear that the USA and England no longer shared a culture based on the marketplace and the use of contemporary media. Evidence of this can be seen in the reaction to Billy Graham's use of advertising and publicity during the 1954 Harringay Crusade (W. Martin, *The Billy Graham Story: A Prophet with Honour*, 174; Hastings, English Christianity, 454–5).

[33] Ward, *Growing Up Evangelical*.

If the liberals had gained the ascendancy in certain areas in the present, the conservatives adopted a grand strategy designed to give them control in the future. Mission to youth was a priority, often the overriding priority. 'Concentrate on young people,' said Bishop Taylor Smith, 'they will bring you in the highest dividends'.[34]

The renewal of evangelicalism in Britain has been widely attributed to this strategy.[35] In the immediate post-war period and into the early 1970s, five distinctively British factors came together to bring about the evangelical resurgence in England:

1. The public school camps started by Eric Nash (or Bash as he was known by the campers). Linked to Scripture Union it was through these camps that a whole generation of (mainly Anglican) evangelical clergy were to be brought to faith and then trained in Christian evangelism and discipleship.[36]
2. The growing ministry of the Inter-Varsity Fellowship and related groups – the Tyndale Fellowship for biblical research and Inter-Varsity Press. The Christian Union Movement gave many young Christians their first taste of leadership and initiated them into evangelical theology.[37]
3. The work of the Crusaders Union of Bible Classes and the spread of the Anglican Pathfinders and Church Youth Fellowships Association. Work amongst mainly middle-class young people in parishes or Bible classes provided a steady flow of committed evangelicals into the universities.[38]

---

[34] Bebbington, *Evangelicalism*, 225.
[35] See McGrath, *Future of Christianity*, 35; Saward, *Evangelicals on the Move*, 31; and also Ward, *Growing Up Evangelical*, 6ff.
[36] See J. Eddison (ed.), *Bash: A Study in Spiritual Power*.
[37] See D. Johnson, *Contending for The Faith: A History of the Evangelical Movement in the Universities and Colleges* and McGrath, *Future of Christianity*, 35.
[38] See Ward, *Growing Up Evangelical*, 23–62.

4. The growing influence of the Brethren and the Pentecostal churches.[39]
5. The example of John Stott in his steady commitment to parish ministry within the Anglican Church was an inspiration to many.[40]

On being made Rector of All Souls, Langham Place in 1950, Stott set about applying to an Anglican parish the lessons he had learned in student ministry during his time at Cambridge in the Cambridge Inter-Collegiate Christian Union and from his many years working with public schoolboys at the Bash Camps held at Iwerne Minster. These were places where the culture of evangelicalism was being formed and Stott realised that he had learned a great deal. Now he was consciously setting out to use the lessons he had learned to shape the ministry at All Souls. Dudley-Smith makes this very clear:

> John Stott at this stage of his life knew himself to be a 'product of Iwerne and the Cambridge Inter-Collegiate Christian Union, having learned from them whatever I knew of evangelistic and pastoral work'. Faced with this awesome opportunity, he was itching to apply their well-tried principles, which he had seen God use and honour to the realities of a Church of England parish.[41]

A similar testimony was given by David Watson in his autobiography.[42] Watson was clear that involvement in the Iwerne Minster Bash Camps over five years was the 'most formative influence on my faith'. He goes on to say that the camps taught him the basics of evangelism, Christian nurture, prayer, Bible reading and pastoral work with individuals and with groups.[43] Stott and Watson each had an international dimension to their work but they were

---

[39] O. Barclay, *Evangelicalism in Britain 1935–1995: A Personal Sketch*, 24; Hastings, *English Christianity*, 265; Bebbington, *Evangelicalism*, 196.
[40] McGrath, *Future of Christianity*, 35.
[41] T. Dudley-Smith, *John Stott: The Making of a Leader*, 251.
[42] D. Watson, *You Are My God*, 39.
[43] Watson, *You Are My God*, 39.

also very much rooted in parish ministry within the Anglican Church. Their careers reflect a distinctive pattern in evangelical life in England. In the USA itinerant, evangelistic organisations routinely operated very like businesses. In England the 'culture of production' was somewhat different. While organisations such as the Inter-Varsity Fellowship, Scripture Union, and Banner of Truth may have been involved in publishing books, music and bible reading notes (in the case of Scripture Union even running a network of bookshops), these activities arose from an ethos based on membership and charitable status.[44] So these commercial ventures, and similarly the ministries of Stott (and to some extent Watson) required a wider framework for support than that which was usual in the USA where the market was large enough to sustain businesslike ventures. The size of the market, however, may not be the only explanation for the differences.

An evangelical culture nurtured on public schoolboy camps and at Cambridge Inter-Collegiate Christian Union was perhaps less likely to be sympathetic to the 'vulgarities' of commerce and media culture. The influence of the Anglican Church within post-war evangelicalism is also of significance, because its established nature may have militated against competition and the market pattern of cultural production. At the same time, it seems clear that one of the major factors in limiting the spread of a commodified, media-orientated evangelical religion in England was the size of the market rather than any refined sensibilities. Stott was one of the main supporters of Harringay Crusade and he appears to have defended the methods adopted by Graham. Evangelical pragmatism and a concern to see people converted to Christ perhaps overcame other sensibilities.[45] As the 1950s gave way

---

[44] For Scripture Union, see Eddison, *Bash*; J.C. Pollock, *The Good Seed: The Story of the Children's Special Service Mission and the Scripture Union*. For the Inter-Varsity Fellowship, see Johnson, *Contending*; Barclay, *Evangelicalism in Britain*. For Banner of Truth, see I.H. Murray, *D. Martyn Lloyd-Jones: The Fight of Faith 1939–1981*, 356ff.

[45] Dudley-Smith, *John Stott*, 295ff.

to the 1960s and the 1960s to the 1970s, evangelicals increasingly began to utilise popular culture in their efforts to communicate the gospel. As a result, the dominant culture of production began to change.

Youth Music and Evangelism: *Youth Praise*

The emphasis upon young people within evangelicalism was fundamental to its rise in the post-war period.[46] A culture of production based on student membership shaped its character during this period. The emphasis upon young people, however, was eventually to change the culture of evangelical religious production reshaping it around a mediated popular culture. As the culture of young people began to change, so the style, and eventually the nature, of evangelical religion itself would have to change. The chief agent of this contextualised evolution was to be the spiritual song.

The singing of hymns has been a characteristic of evangelical religion.[47] Evangelical work among children and young people inherited this tradition but adapted it to the generational and cultural needs of young people. Starting with *Golden Bells or Hymns for Children* which was published by CSSM in 1890 and then with the *CSSM Chorus Book*, which was published in 1921, a tradition of Christian songs for children became common place. According to Pollock, the chorus from this point on became a recognised aspect of evangelical work amongst young people and children, not only in the United Kingdom but also around the world.[48]

The *CSSM Chorus Book* was important because it

---

[46] Some material in this section has been revised from Ward, *Growing Up Evangelical*.

[47] A. Dunstan, 'Hymnody in Christian Worship', in C. Jones, G. Wainwright, E. Yarnold (eds.), *The Study of Liturgy*.

[48] Pollock, *Good Seed*, 83. CSSM eventually became more widely known as Scripture Union, see N. Sylvester, *God's Word in a Young World: The Story of Scripture Union*, 159.

encouraged the development of a distinctive style of worship for children. The same principle was soon to be applied to young people. The crucial difference, however, was that young people during the 1960s were perceived as having their own 'youth culture'. As work among young people and children grew in the 1950s and on into the 1960s, the limitations of the CSSM choruses became evident. It was soon clear that there was a need for a youth-related songbook for use in the many youth fellowships attached to churches. During this period a new generation of evangelical Anglican clergy were starting their ministries in churches around the country.[49] Through the work of the evangelical Anglican youth organisations Pathfinders and the Church Youth Fellowships Association these young clergy were to look for innovative ways to involve young people in the life of the church and in evangelical Christianity.[50]

> There can have been very few Anglican evangelical leaders who did not sharpen their skills by helping at a Churches Youth Fellowship Association or Pathfinder Venture. In this way, a whole host of leaders arose from this ministry including Michael Baughen, Michael Saward, Gavin Reid, George Hoffman, John Goldingay, Richard Bewes, David Huggett, Garth Hewitt, David Gillett and many others.[51]

The *CSSM Chorus Book* was a little limited in its appeal and somewhat dated. Saward recounts that in the early 1960s a number of these clergy started to compose songs and choruses for use in youth groups.[52] In order to use the songs with groups home-produced songbooks were developed. Michael Baughen, who was at this time a curate at Hyson-Green, entitled his song book *Zing Sing*. By the time he had moved on to Reigate he had started to compose his own

---

[49] Bebbington, *Evangelicalism*, 257.
[50] Ward, *Growing Up Evangelical*, 48–54.
[51] Ward, *Growing Up Evangelical*, 54.
[52] Saward, *Evangelicals on the Move*, 53.

songs and he had produced *Zing Sing 5*.[53] The burgeoning youth work scene meant that there was considerable demand for material. Baughen recounts that his *Zing Sing* books, 'Went round like wildfire'.[54] *Youth Praise* was therefore born out of this lively grass-roots concern for outreach amongst young people.

Youth Praise was published in 1966 by Falcon Books for The Church Pastoral Aid Society (CPAS). Containing 150 hymns, songs, choruses and spirituals, the songbook was edited by Michael Baughen; he was assisted by Richard Bewes and David Wilson.[55] The introduction makes clear the provenance and purpose of the *Youth Praise*:

> This book has been compiled to try to meet the evident need for a composite youth music book in Christian youth groups of many kinds. Its purpose is not to provide 'musical entertainment with a religious flavour', but the provision of words and tunes, in adequate number and variety, to allow contemporary expression of youth praise and prayer and worship.[56]

Whilst Baughen eventually compiled the material a committee was responsible for the early stages of the work. This group, which reads like a list of *Who's Who* in evangelical Anglicanism included: Michael Botting, Kenneth Habershon, John Perry, Gavin Reid, Tom Walker, David Watson, John Stott and Timothy Dudley-Smith.[57] Given the profile of those involved, perhaps unsurprisingly, *Youth Praise* reflects the values of 1960s evangelicalism. The songs are seen as an aid to the Bible teaching, which was characteristic of youth groups such as Churches Youth Fellowship Association and Crusaders.[58] The material is organised under a series of headings that

---

[53] Ward, *Growing Up Evangelical*, 111.
[54] Baughen, quoted in Ward, *Growing Up Evangelical*, 111.
[55] R. Leaver, *A Hymn Book Survey 1962–80*, 15.
[56] *Youth Praise Book 1*, v.
[57] *Youth Praise Book 1*, vi.
[58] See Ward, *Growing Up Evangelical*, Chapter 1.

either indicate their function within a youth work program, for example, 'At the Beginning of a Meeting' or 'Challenge' or under doctrinal headings e.g. 'God's Love and Grace' or 'The Mission of the Church'.[59] The editors urge that the songs should not be used 'just for the sake of singing', but rather they should be used 'purposefully'.[60]

Youth Praise was firmly located in a culture of production that is linked to student or youth membership associations. The songbook was produced and marketed to serve the needs of the various youth and student groups that were gaining in numbers and strength at the time. The structure and the identity of the book as a product arose from the pre-existing pattern of cultural production and consumption associated with evangelicalism of this period. The songbook was bought and used because it served the needs of this culture of production. A similar observation could be made of the CSSM chorus books that emerged from the children's ministry and beach mission of the CSSM.

Whilst both the *CSSM Chorus Book* and *Youth Praise* were clearly products which were marketed and consumed, both production and consumption were shaped by the dominant paradigm of cultural production within evangelicalism, i.e. the membership group. In the case of *Youth Praise*, consumption was structured by identity and membership, rather than identity emerging from consumption. Having said this, whilst being consistent with a particular flavour of evangelical Anglicanism, *Youth Praise* was also a self-conscious attempt to connect with the prevailing youth culture. Perhaps for this reason the book was not universally welcomed. Routley dismissed it as 'that highly unmeritable collection'.[61] Bebbington observes that *Youth Praise* was designed to appeal to, '. . . the burgeoning pop culture'.[62] *Youth Praise* was one of the first

---

[59] *YP*, iii.
[60] *YP*, v.
[61] Routley quoted in Leaver, *Hymn Book Survey*, 15.
[62] Bebbington, *Evangelicalism*, 258.

English collections of worship songs to be arranged not only for the piano but also for the guitar. At this time, says Everrett, for the British teenager it was the guitar which was the object of desire and the cause of many a shredded finger.[63]

Youth Praise reflects the way that evangelical youth work was characterised by the steady adoption of this 1960s youth culture. The Christian youth work scene had started to spawn its own version of 'beat music'. Two of these groups contributed material to *Youth Praise*. The Venturers arranged 'Can it be true?'[64] and they also wrote 'Jesus is the Saviour'.[65] This song is based on the twelve bar structure common in blues and rock 'n' roll. Another group, The Followers, wrote 'The King of Love'.[66]

The evangelistic imperative of evangelicalism and the emphasis upon youth meant that the desire to reach young people with the gospel involved negotiation with contemporary youth culture. In *Youth Praise* the first stages of an articulation between a youth orientated popular music and Christian worship can be seen to be emerging. This articulation involved a cultural logic of media related production and consumption that was to change the dominant cultural pattern within evangelicalism. The evidence of Christian beat groups within *Youth Praise* indicates the means by which the new pattern was to be brought into play. These groups, along with many others, were part of a wider subculture within evangelicalism. From the Christian beat group scene an organisation emerged which was to play a key role within the development of mediated religious culture, MGO.

---

[63] P. Everett, *You'll Never be 16 Again: An Illustrated History of the British Teenager*, 26.
[64] *YP* 36.
[65] *YP* 61.
[66] *YP* 63.

MGO and *Buzz* Magazine

MGO grew out of a conference held for gospel beat groups on 5 December 1964 in Ealing.[67] The resulting organisation, which was eventually formed in 1965, was conceived as a catalyst to help in the development of gospel beat. According to Payne, '. . . there was a need for a central organisation to speed up the links between groups and to provide the necessary practical help required'.[68] David Payne was the chairman of the new organisation, Geoff Shearn was in charge of training and Peter Meadows was the editor of the new MGO magazine *Buzz*. All three of these people were to play formative roles in the development of the emerging pattern of cultural production within the evangelical subculture. The story of mediated religious culture within charismatic evangelicalism is to a large extent the story of the creativity, ingenuity and survival of these three people.

The gospel beat scene in the early 1960s was generated by the proliferation of coffee-bar outreach by churches and Christian groups around the country. Coffee bars were characteristic of teenage consumption of the late 1950s and early 1960s.

> The continental coffee bar was taking over from the drab egg-on-toast 'cafe' with its steaming urns and its tin ashtrays; it was also replacing the clattering tea-shop – the Lyons or Kardomah, where permed ladies kept their coats on and nibbled fancy cakes – and it was a welcome alternative to the pub as a place to sit and chat.[69]

Coffee bars, unlike pubs, were accessible to teenagers. Soon with thumping juke-boxes they became a favourite hang out for young people. For evangelical youth organisations the coffee bar became a means to attract large groups of young people. Many of these outreach projects were given

---

[67] David Payne 'You Catalysts and 1966' in *Buzz* January 1966, 2.
[68] David Payne 'You Catalysts and 1966' *Buzz* January 1966, 2.
[69] Everett, *You'll Never be 16 Again*, 31.

'hip' names: 'Top Gear', 'Bar None', 'Mad Pad', 'The Hideout', 'Nu-Kreetcha' and 'Studio Y'. Central to the evangelistic strategy were the growing number of gospel beat groups. The first issue of *Buzz* lists a number of coffee-bar events that featured gospel beat groups – these included The Chanells at Strethan Mission Church; The Evangelairs at Brentwood, Maidenhead and St Albans; The Word Bringers in Chalfont St Peter; The Pilgrims at Catford; The Ribbonettes in Acocks Green; The Envoys at the Cellar Club in Kingston; and The Unfettered in Rickmansworth. In addition, the DJ, Dave Eastwood, was reopening the Catacombs Coffee Bar in Manchester.[70]

Buzz was to prove to be a powerful advocate of the use of contemporary youth culture in evangelism. Payne's article in the very first *Buzz* argues that this kind of activity is nothing new. According to Payne, Paul and Silas used music to great effect when they were staying in one of the 'worst dives out – a jail house'.[71] Payne argued that, all kinds of music could be used in evangelism. As he puts it:

> The fact remains that beat, folk, jazz music, etc., can be employed by dedicated Christians in bringing Christ to others. Many are engaged in the work and God is blessing. The standards are high and the task exacting, but we have a great God who can carry us through.[72]

Buzz reflects the activities of 1960s evangelical youth who were busy expressing their faith by means of contemporary media. This generated a wide range of activities. As well as beat concerts, and *Buzz* magazine, many of the groups were starting to record their music. The first *Buzz* includes two reviews of recordings: The Soul Seekers' single 'Beyond the Bridge/Where Could I Go' (Evangelical Recordings) and The Joystrings', 'He Cares/All Alone (Regal-Zonaphone).[73] In 1967 Elim Bible College used the

---

[70] News item, *Buzz* October 1965, 4.
[71] David Payne 'It's Not Unusual' *Buzz* October 1965, 1.
[72] David Payne 'It's Not Unusual' *Buzz* October 1965, 1.
[73] *Buzz* October 1965, 2.

pages of *Buzz* to advertise its new fully equipped recording studio as available for use.[74] In the same year, *Buzz* started 'Mail Disc', its mail order service. *Buzz* acknowledged the possibility for profit in this activity explaining to the reader: 'By the way, we'll probably make a bit of profit. At least we hope so. This will go towards the administration and improving of the general work of MGO.'[75]

Record labels specialising in gospel bands were starting to take off. In 1967 Pilgrim Records took out the first full-page advert in *Buzz* for records and songbooks, including, The Cross Beats' *Crazy, Mixed Up Generation*.[76] By 1968 the American Record Company, Word, had started its UK operation under the name Word UK. Their first advertisement in *Buzz* featured a number of artists from the USA including an album by The Jimmy Owens Singers.[77] Jimmy Owens, along with his wife Carol, was to play a significant role in spreading the charismatic movement among young people through his musical, *Come Together*.[78] The same issue of *Buzz* announced the start of MGO's own record label, Key. 'Suddenly Christian records are exciting,' says the advertisement, which features the first release on the new Key label by a group called The Forerunners.[79] Training events for bands were to be a regular feature of MGO's work. In 1966 around one hundred people attended one of the first of these gatherings, where practical music tuition was offered. The event also featured a session on coffee-bar evangelism. Alongside the other activities, MGO also started to advertise a series of holidays. The first of these took twelve people to the Filey Bible Week in 1966.[80] By 1969 groups from MGO were also off to Spain.[81]

---

[74] Advert, *Buzz* March 1967, 2.
[75] Advert, *Buzz* July 1967, 5.
[76] Advert, *Buzz* December 1967, 8.
[77] Advert, *Buzz* November 1968, 9.
[78] See below.
[79] Advert, *Buzz* November 1968, 12.
[80] News Item, *Buzz* May 1966, 8.
[81] News Item, *Buzz* September 1969, 3.

The advertising, marketing, and other activities recorded by *Buzz*, gives evidence of a developing scene within evangelicalism. The use of popular, youth-orientated music to communicate the gospel involved a dynamic of production and also consumption. The desire to reach out to young people through relevant evangelism meant the assimilation of practices associated with popular music into the culture of evangelicalism. Consumption and production gradually began to lose their close association with any clearly defined membership group. The culture of religious production therefore started to shift away from student associations towards a market-based production and consumption of mediated religious product. In the early days of MGO, these changes were embryonic. Two factors limited their growth. The first was the size of the market. The second was the emphasis upon evangelism itself. In the early days, *Buzz* had a preference for evangelism and performance over participation and worship.

MGO, Gospel Beat and *Youth Praise*

During the 1960s there is some indication that, for those involved in producing *Buzz*, 'praise' music was less than fashionable. A review of an EP by Terry Dene dismissed the track 'Down with his glory' sung to the tune of 'O Sole Mio' as 'merely a song of praise'.[82] In 1968 The Glorylanders recorded 'If I tried', a Judy MacKenzie song that was arranged by Norman Warren and included in *Youth Praise Book 2*.[83] According to *Buzz*, this is a 'strum along type number which doesn't impress me too much simply because the tune [was] not memorable'.[84] In 1969 Mike Leher from the worship organisation 'Reflection' described his work as focusing upon worship in the local

---

[82] Review, *Buzz* February 1967, 10.
[83] *YP2* 245.
[84] Review, *Buzz* August 1968, 7.

churches. Perhaps reflecting the general emphasis of the *Buzz* readership he admits that, 'This for a lot of Christians is a big let-down.'[85]

Youth Praise was, however, hugely successful: two years after it was published it had sold 50,000 copies.[86] Soon the editors of *Youth Praise* were planning to publish a new volume that was to be entitled, *Youth Praise Book 2*. As early as 1967 the readers of *Buzz* were being asked to contribute songs for possible inclusion in the new volume. The emphasis, however, was to be on material which was 'designed for community singing'.[87] There is some evidence that material from the various gospel beat groups was actually included in the volume. The successful Liverpool band, The Cross Beats, for instance, contributed 'Crazy Mixed Up Generation'.[88] Songs written by artists such as, Judy MacKenzie, Gerry McClelland, Cliff Richard and Chris Burns were also included.[89]

To coincide with the publication of *Youth Praise 2*, a recording of the songs was released on the MGO label Key. The album, *A Tribute to Youth Praise*, was recorded by thirty young people from The Elim Church in Portsmouth. They called themselves The Crusaders. The album also featured tracks by a gospel beat group called The Navigators. *Buzz* was enthusiastic about the project, but it also appeared to be highly critical of the style of singing in most youth groups. *Buzz* expressed some frustration with worship. 'Oh those wasted "Do Lord" sessions which meant absolutely nothing! You see I do find it hard to get enthusiastic about "Give me Oil in my lamp"', said *Buzz*.[90] The first *Youth Praise* songbook was an improvement. According to *Buzz*, this new book, and the album, would go a long way to making a difference: singing songs in the youth group

[85] Mike Leher, 'Reflection', *Buzz* August 1969, 10.
[86] News Item, *Buzz* July 1968, 7.
[87] News Item, *Buzz* December 1967.
[88] *YP2* 272.
[89] News Item, *Buzz* November 1969, 1.
[90] *Buzz* November 1969, 1.

should be 'enjoyed' rather than 'endured'.[91]

The evangelical leaders who initiated *Youth Praise* can be seen as representing the evangelical establishment within the Anglican Church. Stott, Baughen, Bewes and the others involved in the project were the emerging leadership of the movement and they were all shaped by the culture of student and public school membership groups. At the same time, there seems to have been a take up on this material by Pentecostal churches, particularly groups connected to Elim. The emerging relationship between *Youth Praise* and the gospel beat groups, MGO, Key Records and *Buzz*, is evidence of how, by the end of the 1960s, a media-generated religious culture starts to gain considerable ground within evangelicalism. It is also significant that the main vehicles for this development were the practices, behaviours, and conventions associated with the production and consumption of popular music. It is possibly this adoption of popular culture that brings common ground between Anglicans and Pentecostal groups. At the time, however, contemporary music was marginal within the social world of evangelicalism. Significant changes took place during the early 1970s. These were to change all of this and locate popular music culture in the mainstream of evangelical life. These changes are brought about through the influence of two closely related religious movements within evangelicalism: the Jesus Movement and the charismatic movement.

---

[91] *Buzz* November 1969, 1.

Two

The Jesus Movement Has Landed

In youth fellowships and coffee bars around Britain evangelicals were starting to use pop culture as a means to connect with young people. The desire to lead young people to Christ in turn led evangelicals into a media-related world. Soon there was a new breed of Christian producers and a growing culture of Christian consumers. The catalyst which turned the modest youth fellowship and coffee-bar evangelism into something, which was to have a much wider impact, was to come from the USA.

In the late 1960s and early 1970s, the Jesus Movement began to impact the lives of thousands of young people as it swept through North America. As they 'turned on' to Jesus young people began to create a 'hip' Christianity. This combined with a Pentecostal spirituality and new styles of worship became a heady mix.

It was this mix that was imported into Britain with the support of some of the major figures in the charismatic renewal. MGO and others who were already active in youth evangelism were caught up in the flood of this new style and as they were swept along they too experienced the 'baptism in the Spirit'. Suddenly, a creative synergy was to develop between the various 'means' of communication and charismatic worship in this country.

Turned on to Jesus: The Jesus Movement in the USA

As the 1960s gave way to the 1970s in America young people were 'turning on to Jesus' in what was known as the Jesus Movement or Jesus Revolution. The movement started on the West Coast of America where large numbers of middle-class American young people were discovering a 'hip' Jesus.[1] The Jesus People, according to Ford, were indistinguishable in their style of dress and the way they wore their hair from the other groups of young people in his home town of Berkley.[2] A similar observation is made by Enroth, Ericson and Peters:

> Fundamentalists will be confused because the Jesus people say the right things in the wrong language. Besides, they are long-haired, hippie-looking, and alienated from the established churches. Theologically, the Jesus People are fundamentalists, sociologically, they are not.[3]

They argue that the Jesus Movement was part of a general turning towards religion by young people in the USA. The Jesus People were distinctive because instead of practising Eastern mysticism or Native American spirituality they embraced the 'simple message of the gospel'.[4] As the hippie movement became more disorientated, young people were looking for an escape from bad drug experiences, destructive relationships and alienation from society as whole. For these young people the Jesus Movement became a means to 'restore some sort of order, stability, and meaning to their lives'.[5]

> The Jesus Movement should be regarded sociologically as a social movement because it was composed of various disconnected sub-

---

[1] Green in R.C. Palms, *The Jesus Kids*, 7.
[2] C. Ford *Jesus and the Street People: A First-hand Report from Berkley*, 26.
[3] R.M. Enroth, E.E. Ericson and C.B. Peters, *The Story of the Jesus People: A Factual Survey*, 17.
[4] Enroth et al., *Jesus People*, 227.
[5] Enroth et al., *Jesus People*, 228.

groups. These groups remained outside any formal organisation, they did, however, share common values and concerns.[6]

The movement gave birth to a number of leaders and ministries that served as cultural producers and mediated the culture of the movement.

The Jesus Movement was significant because it linked evangelicalism with the style, behaviours, music and values of the hippie movement. This incorporation of youth cultures into evangelicalism was a central ingredient of the developments in the USA.

A wide variety of Jesus-branded consumer materials accompanied the movement. According to McDannell, fashion and consumer goods became an important aspect of this new religious culture: 'Jesus people did not merely want to read about Christianity. Some of the Jesus People expressed their sentiments by producing their own unique arts and handmade merchandise.'[7] McDannell indicates how quickly evangelical marketing companies seized upon this grass-roots trend among young people. Within a very short period of time, the style of the Jesus Movement was being copied by commercial companies such as Warner Press.

> Companies realised that young people eagerly wore Christian symbols in order to publicise their newfound religious beliefs. At the same time, these 'new' Christians – like generations of Christians before them – wanted symbols that harmonised with the fashion and the mood of the times.[8]

Popular music was the most distinctive consumer product offered by the new movement.

Larry Norman is generally acknowledged as the central figure in the new 'Jesus Music'. Enroth, Ericson and Peters call him the 'poet laureate' of the movement.[9] His music

---

[6] Enroth et al., *Jesus People*, 232.
[7] C. McDannell, *Material Christianity*, 248.
[8] McDannell, *Material Christianity*, 249.
[9] Enroth et al., *Jesus People*, 80.

combined a rock-music style with a clear evangelical message. Central to his appeal, however, was his image. Jaspers points out that Norman managed to conform to the media image of a 'Jesus freak' with his long, blond hair and patched Levi's, in a way that Arthur Blessitt (author of *Turned on the Jesus*) and Duane Pederson (editor of *The Hollywood Free Press*) did not.[10]

Plowman has surveyed the musical activities of the Jesus People in the USA. During the 1970s a number of musicians were engaged in producing Christian rock music. Some of those involved were musicians before they became converted: they just carried on with the same style of performance and music. Their purpose had now become evangelism and their message was about Jesus.[11] In the early 1970s, Plowman is clear that a significant musical and cultural shift is taking place in American evangelicalism: 'a Christian music revolution is in full swing today. Coffee houses, Jesus festivals, campus events, youth meetings, record shops, park concerts, Top 40 music stations: the sound of folk, rock, and mod Gospel are all around.'[12]

Through its music, the movement started to affect traditional churches, says Plowman.[13] He identifies two factors that acted together in this 'revolution'. The first he calls the 'God-search mood' of popular culture, a search that tends to become commercialised. The second factor was the musicians themselves who came from the 'street culture' and who, 'unconditioned and uninhibited by church taboos – [were] inclined to worship and to proclaim the Gospel in the idiom of the scene they [knew] so well'.[14] For Leech, these kinds of developments were superficial, a matter of style rather than theology.[15] Writing from a British

[10] T. Jaspers, *Jesus and the Christian in a Pop Culture*, 97.
[11] E.E. Plowman, *The Jesus Movement*, 103.
[12] Plowman, *Jesus Movement*, 98.
[13] Plowman, *Jesus Movement*, 98.
[14] Plowman, *Jesus Movement*, 99.
[15] K. Leech, *Youthquake Spirituality and the Growth of a Counter-Culture*, 117.

perspective, Leech is perhaps a little hasty in this judgement. While the young people within the Jesus Movement generated a new youth-orientated evangelical style, they also managed to combine it with an overt Pentecostal/charismatic spirituality.

For the most part, the Jesus Movement adopted and advocated a charismatic spirituality. Graham is clear that a characteristic of the movement was a renewed emphasis on the Holy Spirit.[16] In fact, one contemporary commentator was clear that most of the leaders of the movement placed significant stress upon the Holy Spirit. In particular, they appeared to connect the experience of the Spirit directly to speaking in tongues. Tongues were also seen as being related to true acceptance of Christ.[17] This particular emphasis indicates the relationship between the Jesus Movement and classical Pentecostal theology. For Enroth, Ericson and Peterson, involvement in what they term, the 'Pentecostal scene' is one of the distinctives of the movement.[18] At the same time, they are clear that many of the Jesus People were ambivalent about the Pentecostal label and critical of many who they regarded as classical Pentecostalists.

> A number of the Jesus People disavow any association with the label 'Pentecostal', however. Some of the Jesus People are quite aware of the excesses that have characterised much of classical Pentecostalism, and they are attempting to avoid a repetition of these.[19]

The significance of the Jesus Movement is that it articulated a middle-class youth hippie style and Pentecostal spirituality. It did this in a way that was largely outside of the formally organised church. Pentecostal spirituality merged with the new hip style was now mediated through relationships of production and consumption. New sites

---

[16] B. Graham, *The Jesus Generation*, 11.
[17] Palms, *Jesus Kids*, 73.
[18] Enroth et al., *Jesus People*, 195.
[19] Enroth et al., *Jesus People*, 195.

for cultural circulation began to emerge – rock festivals, magazines, bumper stickers, etc. It is this media-related religious culture with its Pentecostal/charismatic emphasis that was to have a significant impact as it was transported to the UK.

Youth Culture and Renewal

Charismatic renewal, as it was called, began to spread in the USA, the UK and around the world.[20] Before this time speaking in tongues or glossolalia had been confined to Pentecostal churches. The term charismatic (as opposed to Pentecostal) was first used in the USA – it originates from charisma, or gift of the Spirit.[21]

Hastings argues that the origins of the modern charismatic movement, or neo-Pentecostalism, as he calls it, are to be found in California in 1959.[22] During the early 1960s a number of evangelical Anglican clergy were influenced by the charismatic movement.[23] Among their number was Michael Harper, who, in 1963, was curate at All Souls, Langham Place. In 1964 Harper resigned his curacy and set up The Fountain Trust to promote charismatic renewal within the denominational churches in Great Britain.[24] This emphasis upon 'renewal' within the existing churches and denominations was a major distinctive of those associated with the Fountain Trust.

Walker uses the term renewal to identify this strand within the charismatic movement from both Pentecostalism and what he calls restorationism.[25] In the early days of the

---

[20] Bebbington, *Evangelicalism*, 229.
[21] Bebbington, *Evangelicalism*, 229.
[22] Hastings, *English Christianity*, 557.
[23] General Synod of the Church of England, *The Charismatic Movement and the Church of England*, 8.
[24] Bebbington, *Evangelicalism*, 230.
[25] A. Walker, *Restoring the Kingdom: The Radical Christianity of the House Church Movement*, 57; for an account of the relationship between Pentecostalism, renewal, restorationism and Wimber see D.E. Albrecht, *Rites in the Spirit: A Ritual Approach to Pentecostal/ Charismatic Spirituality*, 27ff.

charismatic movement, says Walker, the attention was mainly focused on those who were actively committed to the mainstream denominations. At the same time, however, a number of more radical separatist groups were beginning to emerge. During the 1960s, he says,

> The stage was taken by Renewalists, and the emphasis was on co-operation, ecumenism and being one in the Spirit while accepting differences in doctrine. But while everyone's eyes were up front watching the performance of the big denominations, slowly but surely house churches began to appear through out the country. The members of these churches were primarily from sectarian backgrounds. They were suspicious of the mainstream success, yet at the same time benefited from it.[26]

These separatist groups came from a variety of backgrounds, including Brethren, classical Pentecostal, evangelical Free Baptists, Salvation Army and various non-aligned churches. It was from these groups that restorationism was to emerge.[27] Walker argues that at this time renewal and restoration shared many aspects of charismatic subculture. This was particularly the case with styles of worship and individual worship songs. Renewalists also attended restoration-linked festivals such as the Downs and the Dales Bible Weeks. By the end of the 1970s the restorationist song, 'Bind us together, Lord', could be heard in every type of British charismatic church.[28] Common styles of expression in worship and, in particular, the increasing use of popular music in worship indicate how the charismatic movement in both restoration and renewal were shaped by wider cultural developments of the 1960s and early 1970s.

Bebbington argues that the charismatic movement was 'most powerfully moulded' by this wider context: 'Young people in the 1960s, in Britain as in America, were turning

---

[26] Walker, *Restoring the Kingdom*, 59.

[27] Walker, *Restoring the Kingdom*, 59–64.

[28] Walker, *Restoring the Kingdom*, 60.

in large numbers to a counter-culture, the world of hippies and drop-outs, drugs and flower power. "Make love not war" was the slogan of the day.'[29]

The counter-culture was characterised, says Bebbington, by a turning away from good taste and a turning to pop art and rock music. The values of the counter-culture entered mainstream society and emerged as a rejection of a 'techno-cratic society dominated by scientific rationality. The traditional, the institutional, the bureaucratic were rejected for the sake of individual self-expression and idealised community.'[30] Walker suggests that the 1960s should be seen as a revolution in 'experience'. The charismatic move-ment, he argues, should been seen in parallel to these developments: 'The Charismatic Movement in the churches reflected the idealism, the heightened experience, and the hedonism of this counter-culture even though ideologically they were opposed to each other.'[31]

The Anglican report, *The Charismatic Movement in the Church of England*, also links the movement to the counter-culture. It does not argue that there is a causal link between the secular phenomena and the charismatic movement; rather, it sees the two as developing in parallel. It identifies the charismatic movement as a kind of 'Christianised existentialism'.[32]

The close connection between the counter-culture and the charismatic movement is paralleled by similar con-nections in the Jesus Movement. Leech argues that there are direct links between the two movements.[33] This

---

[29] Bebbington, *Evangelicalism*, 232.

[30] Bebbington, *Evangelicalism*, 233.

[31] A. Walker, 'Thoroughly Modern: Sociological Reflections on the Charismatic Movement from the End of the Twentieth Century', in S. Hunt, M. Hamilton and T. Walter (eds.), *Charismatic: Christianity Sociological Perspectives*, 30.

[32] General Synod, *Charismatic Movement*, 42. This term is not explained by the report. It possibly refers to an emphasis upon an experiential, encounter with God within the movement.

[33] Leech, *Youthquake Spirituality*, 125. I have been told by one or two people that Jean Darnell encouraged the invitation to Arthur Blessitt and Larry Norman because she saw them as giving new life to a flagging Fountain Trust. Unfortunately, I have been unable to substantiate this insight.

judgement may simplify what was a complex relationship. There is evidence, however, that the arrival of the Jesus Movement in the UK did a great deal to boost the spread of the charismatic movement, particularly among the young. This connection was also to spawn a growth in mediated religious culture as the commodified popular music of the Jesus Movement stimulated the indigenous developments associated with MGO and the worship styles of both restorationist and renewalist wings of the charismatic movement.

The impact of these developments on evangelicalism in England was substantial. The style of worship, and the distinctive religious culture that was to emerge, gradually spread and became the dominant culture within evangelicalism in England. An example of the way these elements converged within evangelicalism can be seen clearly in what was called The Festival of Light, where charismatic worship, the activities of MGO, and the Jesus Movement from America combined forces for the first time.

The Festival of Light: The Jesus Movement Arrives in the UK

It was the visit of Arthur Blessitt to the UK in 1971 that first brought the Jesus Movement to the public's attention.[34] News of the 'Jesus Revolution' was first carried in the June 1971 edition of *Buzz*:

> Will the Jesus revolution strike in Britain? I believe it already has, though in a less outward and spectacular way. Gospel Rock Bands and Jesus folk singers have been saying their bit here for several years now. But British Christianity is more tolerant than its USA counterpart. There has been no need to take refuge in communes.[35]

---

[34] Leech, *Youthquake Spirituality*, 117. I recall myself as a young teenager seeing Arthur Blessitt interviewed on the BBC's nationwide at this time.

[35] 'The Jesus Revolution', *Buzz* June 1971, 3.

MGO was clearly anxious to identify itself with this next wave of activity among Christian young people. For the next few months, the pages of *Buzz* carried story after story about the Jesus People, Larry Norman and Arthur Blessitt.[36]

Buzz was interested in three main characteristics of the movement. First, the style: in an article speculating on the possibility of 'Jesus Culture' crossing the Atlantic, *Buzz*, can see the attraction of a new way of dressing.[37] Secondly, and not surprisingly, the musical culture of the American Jesus Movement was very attractive to *Buzz* magazine. Finally, it is clear that along with a new subcultural style the Jesus Movement injected considerable momentum into the spread of charismatic experience among evangelicals in the UK. *Buzz* welcomed the impetus for young people to get involved in 'exuberant praise'.[38] In August 1971 a Festival of Jesus Rock was organised by Guildford Baptist Church. A news item covering the event in *Buzz* included a picture of young people dressed in t-shirts and patched jeans with arms raised in the air, heads on one side in a pose characteristic of charismatic worship.[39] The Jesus Movement was clearly starting to connect with Christian young people. Subcultural style and consumption was seen as being combined with charismatic experience. All of these factors were to the fore at the Festival of Light.

The Festival of Light, which was held on 25 September 1971, was the initiative of Peter Hill, a returned missionary who was shocked at the amount of pornography available in the Britain. Hill had a vision of large numbers of people marching in protest at the availability of this material and so he gathered a group of individuals around him to help bring this vision into reality. Prominent supporters included Malcolm Muggeridge, Lord Longford and Mary

---

[36] *Buzz* August 1971; Sept 1971; January, February, May, June, July and December 1972.

[37] 'Will the Jesus Movement Reach Britain', *Buzz* August 1971, 11.

[38] 'Will the Jesus Movement reach Britain', *Buzz* August 1971.

[39] News Item, *Buzz* October 1971, 18.

Whitehouse.[40] The style and music of the Jesus Revolution was much in evidence. Arthur Blessitt addressed the crowds in Trafalgar Square and Judy MacKenzie led them in singing her song written for the event which was called: 'Let there be light'.[41] During the day, it was the charismatic worship and actions of many of those in the crowd which drew attention: 'An imported version of the culture of the American Jesus People was much in evidence throughout the day giving the enthusiastic crowd plenty of opportunity for action in "Jesus chanting", singing and "one way" finger pointing.'[42]

Walker argues that it was this aspect of the Festival of Light that acted as a catalyst to the hitherto disparate groups that made up the embryonic house church or restoration churches. Through such exuberant behaviour, says Walker, group members were able to experience just how many charismatics there were on the ground.[43] The festival was also a considerable encouragement to those closely involved with charismatic renewal within the denominations such as the Fountain Trust. According to Jean Darnell, this was 'just the beginning'.[44] In August and September 1972 a follow-up event was organised by MGO, with events throughout London eventually culminating in a huge rally in Hyde Park. Once again, Jesus music was very much to the fore with Larry Norman, Gordon Giltrap, Roger and Jan, Graham Kendrick and Cliff Richard all performing. The theme song for the event was 'Light up the fire', recorded by the Liverpool-based folk group, Parchment. *Buzz* launched a campaign to encourage Christians to buy the single and get it into the charts and thus on to national radio. Unfortunately, the song only reached number thirty in the charts and so narrowly missed a regular airplay spot on BBC Radio 1.[45]

---

[40] Leech, *Youthquake Spirituality*, 128.
[41] News Item, *Buzz*, November 1971, 9.
[42] News Item, *Buzz* November 1971, 9.
[43] Walker, *Restoring the Kingdom*, 69.
[44] News Item, *Buzz* November 1971, 11.
[45] Jaspers, *Pop Culture*, 147–8.

MGO produced a songbook to accompany the event. *Songs for Jesus*[46] was printed in an informal handwritten style, as if it was personally written by Judy MacKenzie. The songbook was offered by *Buzz* as songs for 'you and your youth group to sing'[47] and included songs by Larry Norman, Malcolm and Alwyn, Parchment, Randy Stonehill, Graham Kendrick, as well as Judy MacKenzie. Kendrick's 'Long as I Live', with its references to raised hands in praise, shows signs of the charismatic influence that was spreading in Britain.[48] There was, however, a connection between the production of the songbook and the release of records by MGO. Judy MacKenzie, in introducing the book, said that the material had been presented in 'keys which are easy to play on the guitar' but she pointed out that probably the best way to learn them is to listen to the relevant recordings. There is evidence here of connected interests within *Buzz*/MGO. MGO organised the events, managed most of the artists, released the records of the artists and published the songbook. *Buzz* (an MGO publication) promoted the events, advertised the records and the books, and then reported on the event as news. All of these activities meant that, at the time, those behind MGO, such as Meadows and Shearn, were starting to be at the centre of an interconnecting web of Christian media.

Despite its marketing, *Songs For Jesus* was not really a worship songbook; rather, it reflected the culture of Christian performance and evangelism which was characteristic of MGO at the time. This emphasis also seems to have been shared by the Jesus Movement in the USA. Larry Norman, for instance, was never really a worship leader. His songs and albums were meant for evangelistic performance rather than corporate worship.

The importance of the convergence seen in the Festival of

---

[46] MGO 1972.
[47] Advert, *Buzz* June 1972, 8.
[48] Graham Kendrick, 'Long as I live', MGO 1972.

Light – and later on the Festival for Jesus – is that, over time, worship increasingly adopted the style and the means of cultural production of the Jesus rock artists. This link to charismatic worship was forged within the newly energised charismatic movement. Through the house church movement and, later, through festivals such as Spring Harvest, contemporary styles of worship were to spread throughout the country.

Three

The Spreading Culture of Worship

The Jesus Movement made hip Christianity acceptable – at least for Christian young people in Britain. MGO and others were excited by the Jesus Movement and the developments that went with it and although it was not often at the centre of these events, *Buzz* generally welcomed the arrival of the Jesus musicals and Christian rock festivals, such as Greenbelt. Most of these activities, however, though influenced by the charismatic movement did not tend to focus on worship or on worship music. One of the reasons for this was that the first generation of Jesus rock and folk singers were primarily interested with the way that the gospel message could be expressed evangelistically in the forms of popular culture. This meant that, in the initial stages, interest was focused on the style and music of the Jesus People and what it could do for evangelism. Organisations like MGO saw a direct link between the music of people like Larry Norman and their own gospel beat scene. At the same time, however, more mainstream charismatics were starting to see the potential of popular forms of music for the expression of worship.

Again, links between America and Britain were central to these developments. When the American charismatic musical *Come Together* started to sweep the nation, it was clear that something special was starting to happen. *Come Together* encouraged the link between recording, music publishing, large-scale events and tours, and charismatic worship. Suddenly, popular media was seen to be spreading a style of worship within the church. *Come Together* and worship events run by MGO were followed by the songbook *Sound of Living Waters*. Born out of the mainstream charismatic renewal, *Sound of Living Waters* spread the music and with it a style of worship to the adult church.

Worship Can Be Hip

During the early 1970s evangelicals began to explore the possibilities of 'worship' as a subcultural activity. In the first instance, the move towards praise and worship as a 'hip' youth event was brought about by the behaviour and values of those involved with the Jesus Movement in the USA and the charismatic movement in the UK. MGO was soon to catch the mood.

One of the main events organised by MGO was a New Year concert at the Albert Hall. In previous years, the names of bands were highlighted in the advertising. In 1973 the Albert Hall 'Start the New Year with Jesus' concert was advertised with the headline 'Come Worship the King'. While Malcolm and Alwyn, and other artists, continued to be on the bill, this was the first major worship concert publicised in the pages of *Buzz*.[1] The event drew a crowd of 10,000, divided between two concerts.[2] In the same year, the September and October issues of *Buzz* featured a double length article by W.T.H. Thomas on baptism in the Spirit. In part cautionary, Thomas advocated a balanced endorsement of the charismatic experience.[3]

Charismatic renewal also affected the way that the editor and writers of *Buzz* reported events. In 1973 the Billy

---

[1] Advert, *Buzz* August 1973.
[2] News Item, *Buzz* February 1974.
[3] W.T.H. Thomas, 'There are some vital lessons to be learned on the Baptism in the Spirit', *Buzz* September 1973, 8–9; 'More Vital Lessons on the Baptism in the Spirit', *Buzz* October 1973, 27.

Graham Organisation ran Spree '73. Worship at the event was led by Dave Pope and Graham Kendrick. The Swedish choir, Choralerna, also made an appearance. Despite some reservations about the organisation of the event, *Buzz* reported that, 'God stepped in and ministered to those who came. He did something new and special in the lives of so many who were there.' When faced with the demand to go out on the streets and witness, we are told, 'some discovered the resources available in the Holy Spirit; others found God meeting them and filling their hearts with worship and praise'.[4] The language used by *Buzz* is, perhaps, an indication of the spreading influence of the charismatic movement in the magazine's priorities.

In September, Jimmy and Carol Owens' musical *Come Together* arrived in the UK. The event, which featured the American pop star, Pat Boone, toured the country, playing in major concert halls in Edinburgh, Birmingham, Liverpool, Belfast, Coventry and London. Many of these venues were sold out and hundreds were turned away from performances.[5] *Come Together* was brought to Britain and administered by two prominent charismatics – Jean Darnell, who was closely involved with renewal, and Gerald Coates, from the restoration group of churches. Coates hosted the first performance of *Come Together* in Westminster Central Hall, London.[6] The musical was overtly charismatic, but it did not advocate a clearly identified denominational or Pentecostal line. The *Come Together* booklet, which accompanied the event, made this clear: 'Throughout the world today, God is doing a unifying work among his people. To those Christians who will heed His voice, the Holy Spirit is saying, "Come together! Agree! Love One Another!"'[7]

The musical emphasised what it called 'ministry to the Lord'. This was seen as a personal involvement in worship,

---

[4] 'Spree '73: God did something special', *Buzz* October 1973, 8.
[5] 'Come Together', *Buzz* October 1973, 29.
[6] G. Coates, *An Intelligent Fire*, 93.
[7] Jimmy and Carol Owens, *Come Together*, 1972, 1.

as opposed to passive attendance at church.[8] Public praise
was advocated as a powerful witness to the world around
of the love and authority of God.[9] Worship should be
expressive 'Lifting Holy Hands to God'. For the inhibited,
advice was on hand from the *Come Together* booklet, 'If you
can't quite accept the freedom to lift your hands high in
praise and blessing to the Lord, try cupping them in front
of you like a vessel ready to receive an outpouring of living
water from the Lord.'[10]

Central to *Come Together* was the exercise of ministry to
one another. This involved praying in small groups for
each other: those participating were invited to confess their
sins to one another, and receive forgiveness.

The musical was a great success. 'The result has been
Christians of many denominations experiencing a freedom
of worship they had not known before', said *Buzz*.[11] As well
as the nationwide tour, *Come Together* was also made
available on record and as a songbook published by Word
UK. These materials, plus the central administration of the
continuing work of the musical, meant that local church
groups were able to stage their own *Come Together*
musicals. In June 1974 *Buzz* reported on thirty-four such
local *Come Together* musicals. These were held in significant
venues, including St Alban's Cathedral, Bath Abbey,
Canterbury Cathedral and Cheltenham Town Hall.[12] By
August of the same year, *Buzz* summed up what was
happening around the country: 'Just twelve months ago
Come Together was little more than a gleam in the spiritual
eyes of a few. Now it is fast becoming a heart experience of
thousands of Christians across the United Kingdom.'[13]

Come Together made a significant impact on the
evangelical scene, but it was also a massive financial

---

[8] Jimmy and Carol Owens, *Come Together*, 1972, 9.
[9] Jimmy and Carol Owens, *Come Together*, 1972, 11.
[10] Jimmy and Carol Owens, *Come Together*, 1972, 13.
[11] 'Come Together', *Buzz* October 1973, 29.
[12] News Item, *Buzz* June 1974, 31.
[13] News Item, *Buzz* August 1974, 10.

success. In three years, Word Records reported that the accumulated sales of the *Come Together* album were 57,869 copies. This made it the all-time best selling Christian album in Britain. Moreover, according to *Buzz*, this probably meant that it had sold double the number of its nearest rival.[14] Jimmy and Carol Owens followed up the success with another musical worship event called *If My People* that toured twenty towns and cities during 1975.

Come Together was significant because it made charismatic worship much more widely available. The adoption of record releases and concert tours introduced a commodified product that people could consume. At the same time, the music books allowed for a franchising arrangement so that local groups could start to arrange their own events and concerts. *Come Together* therefore represents a significant turning point in the generation of evangelical religious culture in this country. Most importantly, it focused upon a specifically charismatic style of worship and spirituality. The success of this articulation of media generated religious culture with charismatic worship was to be repeated throughout the following years. At the same time, the links between popular music and evangelical Christianity were to be considerably boosted by the emergence of the first Christian arts festival, Greenbelt.

Greenbelt, like the Festival of Light represents a convergent site of cultural production bringing together the Jesus Movement from the USA, indigenous rock and folk bands. In the earliest days Greenbelt also featured charismatic worship.

Greenbelt: The Beginnings

In 1973 a group called The Jesus Family presented a musical, called *Lonesome Stone*, at the Rainbow Theatre.[15]

---

[14] News Item, *Buzz* October 1976, 13.
[15] Jaspers, *Pop Culture*, 116.

The musical featured Larry Norman and was described in its own advertising as, 'The Story of the How the Jesus People Came Alive'.[16] Jim Palosaari, who was the leader of The Jesus Family, was concerned that this event should not just be seen as entertainment for Christians, but also as an evangelistic opportunity.[17]

The Jesus Family originated from an old hippie colony in Milwaukee. The group was brought to England under the leadership of Palosaari and shortly after his arrival he met Kenneth Frampton, an English businessman. Frampton was a Christian and through his Deo Gloria Trust he began to support the work of The Jesus Family. Soon, two communal houses were established in London and *Lonesome Stone* presentations and concerts, by the rock band, The Sheep, began to take place.[18]

Palosaari and The Jesus Family attracted a number of the key figures, who were later to start the new festival, Greenbelt. They included Nick Stone, Steve and Ruth Shaw and Martin Evans.[19] In 1973, when Lonesome Stone was on tour in Suffolk, Palosaari was approached by Richard Holloway, a young Christian and son of a Baptist minister. Holloway was a member of the Christian blues band, All Things New, and he shared his vision with Palosaari for a Christian rock festival. Palosaari's advice was simple, 'Find yourself a field and you've got yourself a festival'.[20]

The first Greenbelt Festival was held on August Bank Holiday weekend at Prospect Farm, Charsfield, in 1974. The new festival was also supported financially by Frampton's Deo Gloria Trust. It was estimated that around 2,000 people attended the first festival, although 400 of these were performing at, or running, the event.[21] The festival featured a number of bands from the UK including,

---

[16] Advertisement, *Buzz* February 1973, 2.
[17] News Item, *Buzz* May 1973, 9.
[18] Ward, *Growing Up Evangelical*, 96.
[19] Ward, *Growing Up Evangelical*, 97.
[20] S. Henderson, *Since the Beginning Greenbelt*, 2.
[21] News Item, *Buzz* October 1974, 7.

The Mighty Flyers, All Things New and After the Fire. In between the acts were speakers such as the evangelist Eric Delve and Jean Darnell. As well as the Jesus Movement musical *Lonesome Stone*, the festival featured a performance of *Come Together*, including a time of breaking bread.[22]

Since 1974 the Greenbelt Festival has been held annually. In 1975 it moved to Odell and the seminar programme exploring the relationship between Christianity and the arts began to evolve.[23] *Buzz* approved of the music at the festival, but the emphasis upon the arts and the lack of explicit evangelism it felt was less than ideal.[24] However, Greenbelt proved to be significant 'marketplace' for a mediated religious culture which was spreading within evangelicalism. Bebbington sees it as one example of the way that, 'the youth culture was married to the gospel during this period'.[25] The festival allowed for communication between groups and individuals within the subculture and also offered an attractive and high-status platform for many bands and speakers, which also stimulated and encouraged the development of record companies, artists, publishing companies, and so on. Through the seminar programme the relationship between evangelical faith and popular culture was kept continually in play.

From the outset it became apparent that the festival represented a serious marketing opportunity. For example, The Jesus Family ran a small bookstall at the first festival. Over the weekend they sold more books than they had during the previous year's activities.[26] They were able to build on this success by starting a mail-order service selling books, records and leather Bible covers.[27]

In 1983, 30,000 people were attending the festival and the

---

[22] Greenbelt 1974 Programme in Henderson, *Greenbelt*.
[23] Greenbelt 1975 Programme in Henderson, *Greenbelt*.
[24] News Item, *Buzz* October 1975, 21.
[25] Bebbington, *Evangelicalism*, 263.
[26] Ward, *Growing Up Evangelical*, 102.
[27] Advertisement, *Buzz* August 1976, 34.

sheer numbers meant 'Greenbelt forced itself upon the general consciousness of music orientated young people. Britain's national pop station Radio 1 brought the festival's story into every home.'[28] Such figures perhaps promised a significant market for contemporary Christian music:

> It is important to see the festival as a catalyst in the Christian Music World: it can show off groups; it aids Christian record sales, and it encourages new writers, singers and musicians to reach towards the best and most certainly to reject any idea that Christian music must necessarily be inferior to the general secular product.[29]

The success of this network of production was dependent on a sustainable market. Within the UK the limitations of the market were to continue to be of significance, both negatively and positively – negatively, in that it inhibited the development of contemporary Christian music; positively, in that companies, artists and publishers were eventually to find a sustainable market in the music for worship.

The growing appeal of the charismatic movement witnessed through events such as *Come Together* and *If my People* allowed for a broadening of the market in worship music. Charismatic worship was able to develop a style and an ethos which connected with young people, but which also appealed to a wide variety of ages. Leading the way in these developments was a new song collection called *Sound of Living Waters*.

Sound of Living Waters

Sound of Living Waters was published by Hodder & Stoughton in 1974. The songbook was given the subtitle, 'Songs of Renewal',[30] which reflected the growing influence

---

[28] Jaspers, *Pop Culture*, 137.
[29] Jaspers, *Pop Culture*, 145.
[30] This subtitle was added because in the same year Celebration Services released an album by the Fisherfolk which was also called *Sound of Living Waters*.

of the charismatic movement within the denominational churches during the early 1970s: 'Here are the fresh sounds which reflect the cascade of joyous praise, of awesome wonder which accompany the Holy Spirit's renewal in the church today.'[31]

The collection of songs was edited by Betty Pulkingham and Jeanne Harper. Betty Pulkingham was married to Graham Pulkingham, an Episcopalian priest notable for his pioneering of renewal at The Church of the Redeemer in Houston, USA.[32] Pulkingham had experienced the baptism in the Spirit through the ministry of the Pentecostal youth minister, David Wilkerson.[33] The Pulkinghams and the worship group from The Church of the Redeemer, The Fisherfolk, toured Britain during the early 1970s, and in 1973 they worked closely with David Watson.[34]

Jeanne Harper was married to Michael Harper, the leader of the UK-based renewal organisation, the Fountain Trust. While the Fountain Trust had, by this time, been in existence for a decade, its effects upon the denominations were limited. A change started around the end of the 1960s and into the 1970s, says Hastings.[35] It was the increasing popularity of musicals such as *Come Together* that made a crucial difference. The material from *Come Together* was, however, limited in its suitability for use in the local church. The music was somewhat complex: the musical score was arranged for large choirs and, perhaps most significantly, the songs were set in keys that were challenging for the average guitarist.

Sound of Living Waters was able to build on the success of *Come Together*, most crucially because it included what was one of the most popular songs from the musical, 'Holy holy'.[36] In addition, the new songbook offered a source of

---

[31] Advertisement, *Buzz* January 1975, 20.
[32] See G.W. Pulkingham, *Gathered for Power* and *They Left Their Nets*.
[33] Pulkingham, *Gathered for Power*, 71–7.
[34] T. Saunders and H. Sansom, *David Watson: A Biography*, 164.
[35] Hastings, *English Christianity*, 557.
[36] *SLW* 19.

music that was much more suitable for congregational singing. That said the songs of the Fisherfolk were less 'pop culture' and more 'folk culture' in orientation. As the introduction to the book makes plain:

> The ocean is deep and wide and so also is the musical scope of this book; it is not confined to youth or content simply with the old. Simply turn the page and it will transport you from Handel to the sound of rock in *Godspell*. We believe the wideness of sounds reflects the wideness of God's mercy – like the wideness of the sea.[37]

The songbook attempts to embrace a wide range of musical material from traditional hymns such as 'Amazing Grace',[38] to pop songs such as 'Morning has broken'.[39] Alongside this material are songs written by and for children. If *Youth Praise* locates itself within the context of the youth group and youth culture, *Sound of Living Waters* addresses itself to the wider church community. As Pulkingham and Harper say, 'The Holy Spirit gives songs as one means of encouraging the body of Christ.'[40] By locating itself within the middle ground of culture, *Sound of Living Waters* made itself accessible to a wide range of churchgoers. It was a perception of gentleness, as well as a sense of depth, combined with a celebration of simplicity and joy which attracted leading figures in the British church, including David Watson, Tom Walker and many others, to the songs of the Fisherfolk.[41]

Sound of Living Waters was supplemented by a further volume, *Fresh Sounds*, in 1977. The Fisherfolk continued to release records and by 1979 their publishing and record company Celebration Service had a catalogue of ten albums and books.[42] The Anglican report, *The Charismatic*

---

[37] *Sound of Living Waters*, Foreword.
[38] *SLW* 5.
[39] *SLW* 9.
[40] *SLW*, Foreword.
[41] Watson, *You Are My God*, 111; T. Walker, *Open to God*, 12.
[42] Advertisement *Buzz* December 1979, 8.

Movement in the Church of England, argues that it was popularising of the music of renewal which allowed the charismatic movement to 'gain force'.[43] *Sound of Living Waters* and *Fresh Sounds* were significant in that they broadened the appeal of charismatic worship. The emphasis upon a gentle, inclusive folk-art style of worship meant that these worship products were taken up by many within the evangelical subculture. Having said this, it is possible to see renewal at that time as being more of a reaction to the surrounding popular culture, rather than a thoroughgoing contextualisation of it. As I argue elsewhere:

> The cultural productivity in the church very soon became disconnected from any reference point in the wider culture. In the shallow pools and sunny backwaters of the churches the evangelical subculture quickly grew. 'Community' and 'folk art' combined to offer a comforting and convenient escape from the harsh realities that characterised the pluralistic urban communities within which many churches were set. *Sound of Living Waters* takes aspects of the counterculture and domesticates it. It was a religion for ex-hippies who now had children and straight jobs.[44]

As such, *Sound of Living Waters* is possibly to be seen as a stepping stone along the path towards a media-related religious culture contextualised within popular music. Yet, as worship developed within the charismatic movement, a much closer relationship was to be forged with popular music and those from within MGO were again to lead the way.

---

[43] General Synod, *Charismatic Movement,* 10.
[44] Ward, *Growing Up Evangelical,* 125–6.

Four

The Shift to Worship

MGO entered the 1970s speculating that their grass-roots activities, which were mainly associated with coffee-bar evangelism, were about to come to an end. While some, such as Doug Barnett, were far from convinced that this method of outreach was over, others recognised that the advent of disco meant that sooner, rather than later, evangelicals would need to find new methods of reaching out to young people.[1] As the decade wore on it, was apparent that small-scale outreach based in coffee bars was slowly starting to fade away. At the same time, the media activities of MGO were to go through a period of unprecedented growth. This growth came in two main directions. First, a culture of large events and tours was to develop and, secondly, through a significant investment in worship music. In the first of these areas of activity MGO acted in partnership with British Youth For Christ (BYFC). This partnership proved to be at its most effective when these two activities were brought together in the creation of a new Christian festival, Spring Harvest. At the same time, another key alliance was to take place between MGO and the publishing company Kingsway. This was to lead to the publication in the 1980s of the hugely successful worship song collection *Songs of Fellowship*. Drawn mainly from the

---

[1] 'The End of the Coffee Bar?', *Buzz* January 1970, 6.

restorationist house churches, this music was to be adopted much more widely through the enormous sales of the songbooks. It was this style of worship that Graham Kendrick was to take on to the streets in a worldwide popular movement of praise marching.

Youth for Christ and the Big Tour

The move towards large concert-type events was a natural progression for MGO. During the late 1960s MGO held a series of larger events. The first, *Sound Vision*, was held at Westminster Central Hall in 1967. The event was a showcase for gospel music and it featured many of the bands that were closely connected with MGO. The intention was to demonstrate what gospel music was about.

> MGO feel that the time for argument is over. Now something positive is needed. Modern gospel music is a truly wonderful medium for bridging the gap between church and young people outside – when it is used in the right way.[2]

Around 2,500 attended *Sound Vision* in 1967.[3] In 1968 an event called *The Why Generation* was staged at Westminster Central Hall; it featured David Winter, George Hoffman and Nigel Goodwin.[4] In the New Year, Cliff Richard and The Settlers filled the Albert Hall for two successive days. The concerts entitled *Help, Hope and Hallelujah* were held in aid of the Evangelical Alliance relief organisation, Tearfund.[5] In 1970 MGO took *Sound Vision* on tour. The event featured Judy MacKenzie, Nigel Goodwin and the rock band, Out of Darkness. In connection with the tour MGO also released a compilation album on Key Records which featured the artists who were on the tour.[6] The

---

[2] News Item, *Buzz* February 1967, 2.
[3] News Item, *Buzz* June 1967, 4.
[4] Advertisement, *Buzz* October 1968, 5.
[5] News Item, *Buzz* February 1969, 5.
[6] Advertisement, *Buzz* March 1970, 21.

London date for *Sound Vision* was a sell out, but in Portsmouth and in Bristol they found it hard to fill the large auditoriums they had booked.[7] At the end of the year, MGO launched their most ambitious tour featuring a newcomer to the scene, Graham Kendrick.

Meadows' admiration of Kendrick was perhaps a little exuberant: 'Someone must have waved a flag for Bob Dylan. I'd like to do the same for Graham Kendrick.'[8] The comparison may have flattered, but Meadows was prophetic in adding, 'and I think you'll be hearing a lot more from Graham Kendrick and his message'.[9] Of course, Meadows was to have more than a little say in fulfilling his own prophecy.

The tour entitled *Soapbox* was to visit premier venues including Bristol's Colston Hall, and Manchester's Free Trade Hall, as well as three performances at Westminster Central Hall in London.[10] Large events were to continue to feature in MGO's activities. In 1973, *Start the New Year With Jesus* drew 10,000 people to hear 'Cliff Richard and Friends' at the Royal Albert Hall.[11]

In 1975 Clive Calver was appointed as the National Director of BYFC.[12] In the early days, *Buzz* had suffered a quite stormy relationship with BYFC. In particular, in 1966 the BYFC magazine *Vista* published a scathing attack on gospel music entitled, 'The Rape of the Ear'. The piece was by Ben Ecclestone, but it was written with the knowledge and support of the BYFC committee.[13] By the following year, the dispute seems to have been settled and an event was organised by BYFC which featured gospel music, and Meadows also spoke about coffee-bar outreach. The fact that the event featured the semi-finals of the Bible knowledge quiz suggests that BYFC had not yet totally

---

[7] News Item, *Buzz* April 1970, 6–7.
[8] P. Meadows in *Buzz*, July 1970, 2.
[9] Meadows in *Buzz*, July 1970, 2.
[10] Advertisement, *Buzz*, July 1970, 8–9.
[11] News Item, *Buzz* February 1973, 7.
[12] New Item, *Buzz* January 1976, 3.
[13] Editorial, *Buzz* June 1966, 1.

embraced popular youth culture.[14]

In 1970, faced with falling sales, *Vista* magazine was forced to close. Ben Ecclestone negotiated a deal between BYFC and *Buzz*. *Buzz* gained the remaining subscribers to *Vista* and in return *Buzz* agreed to regularly cover events and news stories which were linked to BYFC.[15] For the next few years this arrangement worked fairly well, but it was with the arrival of Calver as national Director that the relationship really started to develop.

In September 1977 *Buzz* reported that Calver had given BYFC a 'blood transfusion'.[16] Two aspects are central to the new approach pioneered by Calver within BYFC. First, he encouraged the strategy of creating what were called 'Youth for Christ Centres' in towns and cities around the country. By 1977, BYFC had thirty-eight working centres. Secondly, Calver initiated the establishment of a music department which was to be led by Graham Kendrick.[17] With the already established network of locally based Youth for Christ Centres, the arrangements were in place to support the activities of touring musicians and evangelists.[18] The first major event planned by *Buzz* and BYFC was *An Evening for the King* at the Royal Albert Hall in January 1978. The event featured Graham Kendrick, Eric Delve, Adrian Snell and Dave Pope.[19] During the late 1970s BYFC and *Buzz* co-operated on a series of tours featuring Kendrick and Calver. Invariably, these were based around a particular theme and an album released by Kendrick was linked to the tour. These albums and tours included, *Fighter*, *Our God Reigns* and *Triumph*. The events were all heavily promoted by glossy full-page advertisements in *Buzz*. Following the tours, *Buzz* would also cover the events as a news story.[20]

---

[14] News Item, *Buzz* December 1967, 12.
[15] News Item, *Buzz* February 1970, 2.
[16] News Item, *Buzz* September 1977, 40.
[17] News Item, *Buzz* September 1977, 41.
[18] News Item, *Buzz* September 1977, 43.
[19] Advertisement, *Buzz* September 1977, 60.
[20] See *Buzz* October 1978, 22; January 1979, 63; August 1979, back page; October 1979, 28.

The End of MGO

The link with BYFC seems to have been connected, at least in part, with developments within MGO/*Buzz*. In the early 1970s the activities of Key Records had attracted a number of gospel artists such as Judy MacKenzie, Malcolm and Alwyn, and Graham Kendrick. By 1972 a number of these artists had launched out as full-time professional musicians – these included Parchment, Malcolm and Alwyn, Graham Kendrick, The Glorylanders, The Advocates, Judy MacKenzie and Dave Cooke, and Ishmael and Andy. This was a significant new development for the Christian music scene. As *Buzz* put it: 'Suddenly the Jesus music scene has exploded. A year ago there was hardly anyone in Britain operating full-time in contemporary Christian music. But from this autumn there will be at least 8 full-time soloists and groups.'[21]

In addition to acting as music publisher through its linked company 'Thankyou Music', MGO was also acting as management for the first three of these artists.[22] The music publishing, record company and the artist management side of MGO were all managed by Payne and Shearn, while Meadows continued to edit the magazine *Buzz*. By 1975 these activities were under severe financial strain and MGO announced losses for the financial year of £47,800. While Key Records was making a small profit of £2,260, *Buzz* magazine itself had lost £9,300. As a result, MGO, which was previously a company, announced that it had changed its legal status and had become a charitable trust. The reason for this change was that it made it possible to appeal for donations to fund its activities.[23] Linked to its new charitable status, in July 1975 MGO announced a further change in policy. The strategy previously had been for their record label, Key, to release a small number of quality recordings which would earn their

---

[21] News Item, *Buzz* October 1972, 10–11.
[22] News Item, *Buzz* October 1972, 10–11.
[23] News Item, *Buzz* May 1975, p20–1.

way by large sales. The problem with this, according to *Buzz*, was that it led to an undue emphasis on a small number of artists. In contrite mood *Buzz* confessed: 'Unfortunately this tended towards an over-emphasis on "stars" and the temptation to over promote artists who should have been enjoying a much quieter ministry.'[24]

Subsequently, MGO would seek to follow a new course by endeavouring to support artists, 'who share our belief in the need to be ministers rather than stars'. By 1976 the stresses and strains in the various aspects of MGO's activities led to a split in the organisation. The magazine, *Buzz*, was sold to a small group of Christian businessmen – David Evans from Birmingham, and Derek, Hugh and Colin Saunders.[25] Meadows formally left MGO and joined the new company as one of the directors and he continued to edit *Buzz*. Doug Barnett also joined the new magazine publishing company as one of the directors. Payne left MGO and moved to join the Christian record label Pilgrim Records. Shearn, however, continued with all the MGO activities; these included: concerts, the mail order record business, Mail Disc, the record label Key and the music publishing company, Thankyou Music.[26]

The next few years were to prove to be financially very difficult for Shearn and MGO. By April 1977 MGO were laying-off staff, citing falling record sales and rising administrative costs as the reason for this move.[27] In 1978 MGO sought financial and organisational refuge in a merger with the Christian book publishers, Kingsway Publications, who were based in Eastbourne. Still under Shearn's management, MGO became Kingsway Music. According to the chairman of Kingsway, 'the development can do nothing but good for Christian communication and not only adds a new dimension to Kingsway but gives a greater depth of

---

[24] News Item, *Buzz* July 1975.
[25] News Item, *Buzz* February 1976, 13.
[26] News Item, *Buzz* February 1976.
[27] News Item, *Buzz* April 1977, 14.

support for the work of MGO.'[28] It was in this new guise of Kingsway Music that Shearn and his colleagues were to discover the secret of success, worship music.

Songs of Fellowship

Shearn moved into the Kingsway offices with a small staff of three, including himself. During the early 1970s Thankyou Music had started to publish some of the material associated with the charismatic renewal. The first album of this new generation of worship songs was called *A New Song* and featured The Cobham Fellowship singing material first used at the Capel Bible Weeks. Despite success with these ventures, Kingsway Music was very close to going out of business. All of this was to change when one of Shearn's colleagues, Nigel Coltman, discovered an old song book in the Kingsway warehouse with the title, *Songs of Fellowship*. Coltman said that the book was imported from the USA and it had, for a while, been out of print. It was a comparatively simple task to gain permission to use the title of the book for the new worship series he was at that time planning with Shearn.[29] This new Kingsway Music publication brought together various material already published by Thankyou Music. Tony Cummings records that there was at the time a serious interest in the songs associated with renewal and with the various groupings of the house churches.

> Inadvertently Kingsway had stumbled across a product for which there was a huge demand. The songs of charismatic renewal were just beginning to creep from Britain's pioneering house churches into the mainstream denominational churches and *Songs of Fellowship* quickly became the premier source book.[30]

---

[28] News Item, *Buzz* February 1978, 19.

[29] T. Cummings, 'Songs of Fellowship Story', *Cross Rhythms* August/ September 1991, 31.

[30] Cummings, 'Songs of Fellowship Story', *Cross Rhythms* August/ September 1991, 32.

The first edition of *Songs of Fellowship Book 1* was published in 1979. The book had just fifty-three songs and it was partly financed by a large order from The Crusade for World Revival, the Pentecostal organisation, who paid for 3,000 copies in advance. This was a significant proportion of the original print run of 8,000. To accompany the book, an album – *City of God* – featuring the songs was released. Coltman recalls that the album cost £800 to record. It sold 33,000 copies. 'God gave us that album and from that time the company went from strength to strength.'[31]

Kingsway released *City of God* and *Songs of Fellowship* albums before the original songbook was released. These albums were advertised in *Buzz* a year before *Songs of Fellowship Book 1* was actually made available. The success of the *Songs of Fellowship* led to a new edition in 1981, this time featuring 159 songs. Coltman and Shearn collected this material to expand the book by soliciting sample tapes and by visiting churches and Christian events.[32] One of the main criteria for selecting songs for inclusion in the *Songs of Fellowship* books was that they were currently in use in churches.[33]

> The *Songs of Fellowship* editorial process has both its good and its bad points. Good in that we try to represent what is actually going on at the grass roots, in the churches, bad, in that some of the songs selected, albeit in use in churches did not stand the test of time.[34]

In 1983 *Songs of Fellowship Book 2* was published. In the same year *Buzz* reported that overall sales of *Songs of Fellowship* had reached 90,000. In addition to these direct sales, the material was also being used at Christian events. Festivals such as

---

[31] N. Coltman quoted in Cummings, 'Songs of Fellowship Story', *Cross Rhythms* August/September 1991, 33.
[32] Cummings, 'Songs of Fellowship Story' *Cross Rhythms* August/September 1991, 3.
[33] News Item, *Encore* Winter 1992, 10.
[34] Coltman quoted in News Item, *Encore* Winter 1992, 10.

Spring Harvest, Filey Bible Week, The Banquet, and Prepare the Way would create their own song collections and insert them in the program that was linked to the event.[35] In 1985 *Songs of Fellowship Book 3* was published and in 1987 a collection of Hymns was also published under the title *Hymns of Fellowship*. In 1987 all four volumes were brought together as *Songs and Hymns of Fellowship*. By 1991 this combined edition had sold over one million copies worldwide.[36]

Alongside the success of *Songs of Fellowship*, Kingsway also began to develop a number of other branded lines of worship material. In 1983 they bought the rights to publish the songs associated with David and Dale Garrett from the songbook, *Scripture in Song*. Graham Kendrick's 'Make Way' material, which was used as part of the March for Jesus, was also originally produced by Kingsway. Following the successful visits of John Wimber to this country, Kingsway brought out a series of songbooks and albums featuring the worship songs used by Wimber's Vineyard church in the United States. The first of these, published in 1987, was, *Songs of the Vineyard Volume 1*. Into the 1990s Kingsway have continued to release new editions of their *Songs of Fellowship* series, but they have also made links with Soul Survivor with Thankyou Music, publishing Matt Redman's songs and his albums being released under a special Survivor Label linked to Kingsway.

The growth and development of Kingsway indicates how a switch, from an emphasis on contemporary Christian music performers and recordings, to worship music was a successful strategy. Kingsway led the way in developing a market for charismatic worship. It also pioneered innovative connections between music publishing, recording and promotion of worship leaders. In all of these areas what emerges is a mediated religious culture borrowing from the methods of production associated with the popular music of

---

[35] News Item, *Buzz* June 1983, 39.
[36] Cummings 'Songs of Fellowship Story', *Cross Rhythms* August/ September 1991, 3.

the period. The number of sales of songbooks and recordings indicate the extent to which mediated forms of production were enthusiastically consumed by individual Christians, churches, and organisations within evangelicalism. Whilst firmly located within charismatic evangelicalism, Kingsway managed to establish itself as a business which was not limited by a direct connection to any one denomination or ministry. This enabled it to capitalise on the shifting changes within the evangelical/ charismatic scene. At the same time, it was also able to facilitate these changes by making worship materials from the various artists, producers and charismatic movement more widely available.

All of this marks a significant shift in the developing culture of production of evangelical worship. Kingsway represents the embracing of a culture of production that is based on popular music and the market. Through Kingsway the commodification of worship as product, and the consumption of that product, was increasingly to shape the scene. Alongside the activities of Kingsway, and other music publishers, there was also the development of significant new sites for cultural production. Arguably the most significant of these was Spring Harvest.

Spring Harvest

The link between BYFC and *Buzz* magazine could be said to have come to fruition in the development of Spring Harvest. Three thousand people attended the first Spring Harvest from 7–13 April 1979 at Tower Beach Holiday Village in Prestatyn North Wales.[37] The event featured a number of evangelical speakers, including: Luis Palau, Clive Calver, Eric Delve, Pete Meadows, Doug Barnett and Ian Barclay. Graham Kendrick and Dave Pope led worship at the event. During the 1980s the number of weeks and the venues where the event was held were to multiply. In 1987 *Buzz* reported that 50,000 people had attended.[38] By 1990

---

[37] News Item *Buzz* June 1979, 38.
[38] News Item *Buzz* June 1987, 13.

this number had increased to 80,000.

The impact of Spring Harvest upon the church in the UK has been deeply significant. According to Walker, Spring Harvest has been 'the greatest success of evangelical and Charismatic Christianity in Great Britain since the initial Pentecostal revivals in the first half of this century'.[39]

Central to the impact of Spring Harvest was the way that the event spread charismatic styles of worship around a large number of churches in this country.[40] Spring Harvest was the major showcase for Kendrick's worship songs. Originally a folk/rock musician, Kendrick now started to write worship material for the event. He was encouraged by Shearn to record some of this material and in 1979 Kendrick's first worship album, *Jesus Stand Among Us*, was released on the Kingsway label. It was at Spring Harvest, however, that Kendrick was able to win an accepting audience for his new material and at the same time the focus of his own ministry began to change. Kendrick remembered this as a slow process:

> Spring Harvest started fairly small, just a couple of thousand people, but as it grew and my role within it as worship leader developed, so it became a matter of course for me to present to the selection committee several songs for inclusion in the programme. And that kind of accelerated the process.[41]

The numbers of people attending Spring Harvest meant that it was a significant market, not only for organisations such as Kingsway, but also for Spring Harvest itself and a succession of products were to emerge out of the event. These included live worship albums, tapes from seminars, worship books featuring the songs from each year's event, and books containing the themes used in the seminars. The sales of these products were an indication of the impact

---

[39] Walker, *Restoring the Kingdom*, 307.
[40] News Item *Buzz* April 1983, 38.
[41] G. Kendrick interview with Cummings in *Cross Rhythms* September 1990, 52.

that was made by Spring Harvest on the church in the UK. It also points to the shift of the culture of production within the charismatic movement to the creation and consumption of worship as a product.

With these changes there also came a shift in fortunes within the charismatic movement. Walker argues that the success of Spring Harvest is one of the main reasons for what he sees as a decline in the restoration group of churches. Spring Harvest brought this about, says Walker, primarily by its worship style. Through Spring Harvest individual Christians were able to experience a similar excitement and style of worship to that which was on offer at the Restorationist Dales and Downs Bible Weeks. At Spring Harvest, however, they were able to do so without taking on board the restrictive authority structure, narrower teaching and separatist ecclesiology of restoration.[42] If *Songs of Fellowship* may be read as the high-water mark for restorationism, Spring Harvest can perhaps be seen as the gradual siphoning away of the water. The point is that a mediated religious culture makes the product widely available and once commodified it can be reinterpreted and reshaped by location and context. Spring Harvest offered a significantly different and more open context where the life and energy that originated within restoration could be more widely consumed and re-located within existing denominations and churches. To the extent that it made this possible, Spring Harvest should also be seen as having a reinforcing influence upon renewal. This process of commodification and democratisation of charismatic energy in worship and production is also seen in the development of the March for Jesus.[43]

Make Way and The March for Jesus

In 1988 Graham Kendrick formed his own company called 'Make Way'. A board of directors was appointed and, at the same time, Kendrick moved to join the house church linked

---

[42] Walker, *Restoring the Kingdom*, 309.
[43] G. Kendrick, G. Coates, R. Forster and L. Green, *March For Jesus*, 25.

Ichthus Fellowship.[44] Kendrick soon began to work on a series of worship albums and books that were linked to the idea of marching and public praise. Shortly after moving to Ichthus, Kendrick joined a praise march that was organised by his new church. The praise march took place in the Soho area of London. It was this experience which led him to write a style of material that was specifically designed for this sort of event. Kendrick expresses the need for a new kind of song in these terms, 'Out on the streets you want to declare the truth very precisely, clearly and strongly. We needed specially written songs with a driving rhythm that made it feel it was a momentous occasion.'[45]

The first joint march was organised by a small group of individuals and the charismatic organisations which they led: Gerald Coates from Pioneer, Lynn Green Director of Youth With A Mission, Roger Forster from the Ichthus Fellowships and Graham Kendrick from Make Way. On the 23 May 1987, 12,000 people gathered in Smithfield's Market to march around the City of London.[46] 'The aim was to mobilise Christians to proclaim the name of Jesus in London and to pronounce the defeat of the Spiritual forces entrenched in the capital and the heart of the nation.'[47]

A decision was made to continue with more marches. It was decided to call the initiative March for Jesus and a second march was planned around Westminster in 1988.[48] The police estimated that 55,000 people attended the 1988 march, which passed along the Embankment to Hyde Park, passing, on the way, the Houses of Parliament, and Buckingham Palace.[49]

Kendrick's Make Way songs and books were the visible products of the March for Jesus. The album *Make Way – A Carnival of Praise* was premiered at a large rally at The

---

[44] News Item, *Worship* Winter 1988, 2.
[45] Kendrick et al., *March For Jesus*, 25.
[46] Kendrick et al., *March For Jesus*, 28.
[47] Kendrick et al., *March For Jesus*, 28.
[48] Kendrick et al., *March For Jesus*, 42.
[49] Kendrick et al., *March For Jesus*, 47.

National Exhibition Centre (NEC) in 1988. The album sold
30,000 copies in two years. The follow-up album, *Shine
Jesus Shine* attracted 15,000 to its launch at the NEC. In the
first eight weeks after its release the album sold 25,000
copies.[50] The March for Jesus was copied in towns and cities
across the UK and then around the world. In 1998 it was
estimated that 10 million people would take part in
marches around the world.[51] This remarkable growth was
facilitated by the utilisation of resource-orientated products which were marketed through Make Way. Like
Spring Harvest, March for Jesus has been a major site of
cultural production and distribution within the charismatic
subculture. It is also an indication of the way that charismatic culture has increasingly become a globalised
phenomenon. This globalisation has been enabled by the
commodification of worship as production and as
subcultural consumption.

---

[50] News Item, *Worship* Summer 1988, 9.
[51] *Church of England Newspaper* 29 May 1998, 6.

Five

The Growing Market

The success of charismatic worship music was directly related to specific economic pressures and opportunities. In the first instance, this meant that the evangelistic orientation of the Jesus rock music and MGO's Christian beat groups gave way to more mainstream worship music. The impact of the much smaller British Christian youth scene on the development of evangelical worship culture should not, however, be underestimated. At the same time, worship leaders had a major advantage in that they could be employed directly by churches for the regular weekly worship. The numbers of churches making this commitment to fund a full-time worship leader is a measure of growing significance of charismatic worship at the time. Christian record companies and music publishing companies soon found a new way to support their activities. MGO entrepreneurs, Geoff Shearn and Nigel Coltman, were to lead the way in seeking new sources of revenue to support their activities. The Christian Copyright License was an invention that rewarded artists, record companies and publishing companies who focused on worship music. The importance of a range of publishing opportunities for individual songs and the complexity of the global worship market led to initiatives such as CopyCare which managed all aspects of royalties for song writers and publishers in the Christian scene. This kind of exploitation of varied streams of funding was a major factor in the success of charismatic worship.

The Economic Context of Worship

The Christian music scene in Britain was shaped by its size. The limits of the Christian market acted to privilege worship music over contemporary Christian music. This meant that, despite the efforts of MGO and the activities of Youth for Christ and the existence of festivals such as Greenbelt, very few Christian musicians have been able to make a living as professional artists in the UK. In 1979 Norman Miller, at the time one of the largest promoters of Christian artists, was very clear on this fact. 'Britain is just not big enough to support full-time gospel artists. Some of our artists are literally living on the bread line.'[1] Cummings points out that in 1972 the average contemporary Christian music album would sell around 2,500 copies. In the 1980s albums sales were still roughly the same.[2] Cummings reveals the extent of sales was very low even with what might be widely regarded as a successful record: 'Christian music hits sell between 3,000 and 6,000 and anything over 6,000 sales in the UK is both a mega hit and a rarity.'[3]

This meant that contemporary Christian music could not be supported through the usual sources of record sales and touring. This was a market-based reality. That worship leaders were able to develop a larger and more viable market for their records was also a market reality. In the 1980s Spring Harvest were able to increase their impact through the sale of worship books and recordings. Between 1984 and 1989 Word Records sold 100,000 units linked to Spring Harvest. In addition to these sales, the Spring Harvest 1989 Celebration Album sold 20,000 copies.[4]

---

[1] News Item, *Buzz* January 1979, 4.
[2] T. Cummings, '5 Years: British CCM's Past, Present and Future', *Cross Rhythms* April/May 1995, 24.
[3] Cummings, '5 Years: British CCM's Past, Present and Future', 24.
[4] News Item, *Worship* Autumn 1989, 14.

These kinds of sales made the activities of Christian music companies just about viable in this country. What they did not do was support the worship leaders themselves. Graham Kendrick is one of the few exceptions to this. As a gospel artist, Kendrick made a fairly modest and perhaps precarious living. He was essentially a missionary being supported by the charitable funding of BYFC. When he began to focus upon worship, this situation changed and he was able to support not only himself but also his whole organisation, Make Way, on the basis of record sales and income from publishing. Kendrick's success as a worship leader made this level of activity and income possible.[5] That said, Kendrick was something of an exception in being able to support himself in this way.

For the majority of worship artists, a wide range of diverse activities were required if they were to be able to earn a realistic living – chief among them was a salaried post, working with local congregations. As well as being based in churches, worship leaders were also employed full-time by evangelists, preachers and Christian organisations. While Christian musicians who specialised in performance and evangelism tended to suffer financially, those involved in worship were able to develop relatively secure careers by receiving regular financial support from these kinds of relationships. In the 1980s Andrew Maries was one of the first of these new breed of worship leader to be employed by an Anglican Church. He was supported in this ministry by David Watson's church, St Michael le Belfry in York. In the 1990s, when he was still a teenager, Matt Redman was employed as worship leader by St Andrew's, Chorley Wood, where David Pytches was the vicar. From there he was able to develop his ministry by working with Mike Pilavachi of Soul Survivor.

Gradually, worship leaders became a regular fixture in charismatic churches throughout the country. For many of

---

[5] T. Cummings, 'Marching to a Different Drum', *Cross Rhythms* July/August 1992, 52.

these artists, a regular income from the local church, supplemented by fees for appearances at other events, made the full-time worship leader a realistic, if somewhat modest possibility. As well as working for the church, a number of worship leaders have been linked with the ministry of a particular preacher or evangelist, for example, Dave Fellingham and Terry Virgo, Noel Richards and Gerald Coates, Matt Redman and Mike Pilavachi and in the early days, Graham Kendrick and Clive Calver.[6] These relationships were significant because they provided a way for new songs and styles of worship to become known more widely.

Publishing and Recording

For companies such as Kingsway and Thankyou Music, the developing worship scene involved a varied range of activities. While the sales of contemporary Christian music were extremely modest, sales from products associated with worship were relatively successful. The commodification of worship songs, however, also led to the slow development of a number of other opportunities to create income. These developments are a key distinctive of the economics of worship music and they are a major factor in the ability of companies and artists to sustain their activities in the British evangelical subculture.

In the area of record sales, Kingsway Music and others were able to develop sales strategies that maximised income from both artists and from individual songs. Within the developing genre of the worship album, four main categories emerged. First, there were albums that were branded and linked to particular worship books. The *Songs of Fellowship* albums would be an example of this kind of recording, where the record was linked by a brand name to a particular collection of songs published in a

---

[6] D. Fellingham, *Cross Rhythms* July 1990, 13; N. Richards, *Worship Together* Autumn 1988, 16.

songbook. Secondly, there were worship albums that were made by live recordings at particular events. The *Spring Harvest Live* worship albums would be an example of this type of recording. These kind of albums benefit from the branding of the event and they have a sense of integrity that comes from this association. Thirdly, there were albums that were recordings, usually made in a studio, by an individual worship artist or band. Kendrick's various albums would be an example of this kind of recording. These albums represented the latest offering from the artist offering a collection of their work at that time. Finally, record companies found that they were able to draw upon all of this material to produce compilation albums. The development of these different kinds of recordings meant that a successful worship song or artist might be packaged and sold in at least four different ways.

A similar strategy to maximise the way that songs were made available can be seen to have developed in the area of music publishing. Following the success of *Songs of Fellowship* a number of publishers brought out collections of worship songs and songbook series. Physically, Graham Kendrick was not able to be the worship leader in every charismatic church in the country, but in the mid-1980s there was a very high probability that his songs would have made an appearance. This was made possible because his songs were made available in a number of different songbooks. Basic to the use of songs in churches, therefore, was their publication in these songbook collections. Kingsway had their *Songs of Fellowship* series, but there were a number of other publications from which churches might choose.

The main competitor to *Songs of Fellowship* was the *Mission Praise* series published by HarperCollins. The first *Mission Praise* book was published in 1984 as a songbook linked to the visit of Billy Graham for Mission England. The explicit aim of the book was to produce a collection of songs that reflected the breadth of evangelical worship. Thus it included a number of standard hymns alongside worship material associated with charismatic renewal.[7] As well as the major collections of songs, there was also the annual publication of song collections linked to events. These included the songbooks published by Harvest Time linked to The Dales Bible Week and The Spring Harvest Songbooks.

Songbooks were essential for worship leaders and musicians in local churches, since they included not only the musical notation for the songs but they also generally included guitar chords and sometimes directions on how these chords should be played. Songbooks linked to events were particularly important because they tended to be updated every year. So, new songs were introduced and, of course, more royalties are distributed. The range of worship songbooks and their regular updating meant that royalties would be earned on the same song from a variety of different sources. One of the main functions of Christian music publishers soon became the management of the placement of songs in books. It was also their role to encourage artists to record songs and then to collect royalties on both of these activities. A publishing company would generally receive one third of all income gained in this way (but it could be as much as fifty per cent).[8] The multiplication of royalties from individual songs being published represented a significant stream of income for a music publishing company such as Thankyou Music (the publishing arm of Kingsway Music).

It soon became clear that income from royalties was potentially very substantial indeed. Cummings records the case of Karen Lafferty who wrote the song, 'Seek Ye First'. This relatively short, and simple, song was published by the American company, Maranatha Music. As a result, the song was recorded and reproduced in music books many times over. The royalties from this one song, according to

---

[7] News Item, *Buzz*, March 1984, 53.

[8] S. Law and E. Lives, *Keep Music Legal: From the Manuscript to Mass Production*, 8.

Cummings, ran into thousands of dollars.[9] It must be remembered that Lafferty's success was generated out of the American market, rather than the UK. That said, within a few years British artists were also participating in the global charismatic scene and the publishing companies were right at the heart of these developments.

In fact, the diversity of possible royalties to be generated worldwide through the publishing of worship songs is a very complicated business. Nigel Coltman used his specialist knowledge of the Christian worship scene to launch another new initiative. In 1996 he set up CopyCare. This was a new venture that allowed him to use his knowledge of this complex field to manage songs on behalf of publishers.[10] This kind of initiative was necessary because of the range of publishing and other activities generated by the increasingly vigorous and global evangelical culture. A similar initiative was to significantly boost the growth and development of worship music around the world. This was the unique scheme to collect royalties directly from churches for the reproduction of song lyrics and music.

The Christian Copyright Licensing Scheme

In the music business, royalties are generally collected by three main organisations: The Performing Rights Society, the Mechanical Copyright Protection Society and the Phonographic Performance Licensing Company. The Performing Rights Society, founded in 1914, represents the interests of songwriters and music publishers. As such, it collects royalties on behalf of its members for all non-dramatic performing and broadcasting rights of their copyright material.[11] This works on the basis of a simple license fee from all venues of live or recorded performance.

---

[9] T. Cummings, 'Your Church and Copyright', *Buzz* March 1984, 33.
[10] News Item, *Worship Together* November 1996, 18.
[11] Law and Lives, *Keep Music Legal*, 12.

This would include concert venues, clubs, restaurants and pubs that use recorded or live music. The license fee is then distributed to members on the basis of a formula derived mainly from radio airplay.[12] The Mechanical Copyright Protection Society collects royalties whenever songs are recorded. These royalties are generally paid directly to the music publishers.[13] The Phonographic Performance Licensing Company issues licenses for the public performance of recorded works. The Phonographic Performance Licensing Company will deal with the owner of the copyright of each recording; in most cases this will be the record company.[14]

During the early 1980s Christian music publishing companies were beginning to raise the issue of copyright violation in churches and at Christian events. This arose because charismatic worship had created a different approach to the use of songs in churches. A number of factors came together to bring about change. The first was the widespread use of Overhead Projectors (OHP).

OHPs allowed for more freedom and expression in worship. If the song lyrics were displayed on a screen, then worshippers were free to raise their hands in ways that were characteristic of charismatic praise. Before the advent of OHPs this was a little tricky, because hands were required to hold the songbooks. The technology associated with the OHP also speeded up the introduction of new songs within charismatic worship. By writing or photocopying onto an OHP transparency, it was possible for the local church to reproduce new songs extremely quickly and very cheaply. These developments meant that it was possible to introduce new songs without having to wait for them to be published in songbook collections.

Before the advent of the OHP, many churches were making their own songbooks and song sheets. In some

---

[12] Law and Lives, *Keep Music Legal*, 15.
[13] Law and Lives, *Keep Music Legal*, 15.
[14] Lives and Law, *Keep Music Legal*, 15.

churches, photocopiers were being used to reproduce worship songs easily and cheaply on individually designed worship song sheets:

> churches have been making use of some parts of the technological revolution for some years. In many fellowships, song sheets run off on a church member's office photocopier or the church duplicating machine have become a familiar appendage. The hugely popular overhead projector has also made inroads in all but the most conservative sections of the church.[15]

In this new climate, Christian music publishing companies were becoming increasingly concerned with what they saw as a loss of revenue from what were quite common church activities. According to Shearn, the situation could not go on: 'We can't just give an open mandate to any church to do whatever it likes with our copyrights. If we did we might as well close down.'[16]

It is important to note that this kind of copyright problem was quite unique to the Christian music scene. In the secular music business, organisations such as the Performing Rights Society, the Phonographic Performance Licensing Company and Mechanical Copyright Protection Society had been established to allow for royalties to be paid on the conventional activities that shaped their particular market. Each of the organisations was set up to deal with the complex mediations of popular music. The specific activities of charismatics in their distinctive use of song lyrics and the way that they were reproduced using photocopiers and OHPs, was not covered by any of the three main organisations at the time collecting royalties on behalf of artists and music publishers. This meant that common practices within the charismatic subculture were effectively illegal. The copying of songs by any means was,

---

[15] Cummings, 'Your Church and Copyright', *Buzz* March 1984, 30.
[16] G. Shearn quoted in Cummings 'Your Church and Copyright', *Buzz* March 1984, 32.

and is, an infringement of copyright. Even a hand written copy of lyrics made on an OHP slide was an illegal activity.

For churches that wished to remain within the law, the only option was to write to the individual copyright owners of each of the songs they wished to copy. Only when they had been given permission were they legally allowed to copy individual songs. As Cummings points out, this process was extremely difficult: 'Getting copyright permission to reproduce their songs in a song book or on acetate has become for many churches a decidedly irksome task.'[17]

As a first response to this problem, Kingsway Music set up a copyright search service. This was to prove an expensive business: the search service charged a fee of £2 per song. This charge was then added to whatever royalty was demanded by the copyright owner: the cost could be prohibitive. Cummings recounts how when Margaret Pittman, from a church in Mansfield, used this scheme to ask for permission to use songs she found that the sums involved were very high. She initially sent off a list of 100 songs to use in her church and permission was granted, but she was asked to pay a fee of £159.16.[18] Many churches were resistant to paying these kinds of fees. A significant school of thought within the movement said that, 'worship songs were given by the Holy Spirit, and therefore it was wrong to require payment of royalties for their use in worship.'

In 1985, following this line of thought, the restoration-linked music publishing company, Harvestime, announced that they were releasing all of their songs from copyright. This effectively meant that they were giving permission for any group, individual, or church to copy them by any means and as many times as they wanted.[19] The mainstream of worship leaders and publishers, however, were

---

[17] Cummings, 'Your Church and Copyright', *Buzz* March 1984, 30.
[18] Cummings, 'Your Church and Copyright' *Buzz* March 1984, 32.
[19] News Item, *Buzz* May 1985, 17.

unsympathetic. Kendrick was forthright in his views: 'It's a fact of life. If a song gets around and gets into songbooks money is involved. Neither myself, nor my publishers, are money grabbing. The law is there for good reasons – to safeguard people's legitimate interests and rights.'[20]

While he may have been in the right, Kendrick's stance can be contrasted with that of the Performing Rights Society. It was the longstanding convention of the Performing Rights Society that royalties were waived for any music performed during the course of a religious service. This convention, however, did not extend to the copying of music for the use in worship, but it gives a guideline that might have been followed. Of course, such a move would have been problematic for those companies that specialised in worship music. While it would have been possible to waive the copyright for music copied for worship in church, as Harvestime had done, to do so would have been to turn down the possibility of developing a significant source of revenue for songwriters and music publishers. The dilemma was eventually resolved when the publishing companies came together to create a specialised agency to collect royalties from churches and others copying worship songs.

With numbers of churches seeking permission for the use of songs, the Christian Music Publishers Association set up a scheme to simplify the use of copyright material in churches. In 1985 the Christian Copyright Licensing Scheme was launched.[21] Under the scheme, the major Christian music publishing companies joined together to offer a single license which allowed churches, organisations and those running events to reproduce the lyrics of songs specifically for use in worship. The companies involved in setting up the scheme included Thankyou

---

[20] G. Kendrick quoted in *Cross Rhythms* August/September 1991, 31.

[21] Chuck Fromm, of the American publishing company Marantha Music, maintains that such a license was first pioneered by his company. Shearn then introduced the scheme in the UK.

Music, Springtide, Scripture in Song, Word Music, Jubilate
Hymns and Celebration Services.

Licenses for churches were charged according to average
attendance, for example, churches with around fifty
regular worshipers were charged £28.75; those with 100
were charged £143.75.[22] By 1987 the scheme had issued
2000 licenses and a new organisation was launched linked
to the scheme, the Christian Music Association.

The Christian Music Association published its own
magazine, *Worship*, which carried articles on worship
related matters, as well as an update on the publishers
associated with the Christian Copyright Licensing Service.
According to Shearn, who was one of the key players
behind the scheme, the Christian Music Association was a
servant organisation:

> We can serve the church by reducing the pressure of copyright
> administration, we can serve the song-writers, many of whom are
> full-time musicians and pastors by channelling more income to
> them. We've served the publishers by relieving them of a huge
> burden of administration. They, in turn, use additional revenues to
> improve and expand their range of songbooks and recorded music,
> thereby providing the Christian public with a better quality
> service.[23]

The revenue was distributed to the songwriters and
publishers on the basis of detailed forms filled in by each
license holder, indicating which songs they had copied in
the previous year. Licenses could not be renewed without
this completed form being supplied. On the basis of these
returns, a chart of the most popular songs was published in
each issue of *Worship*.[24] By 1990 the scheme was issuing
7,000 licenses annually in the UK, and plans were
developed to extend the scheme to the USA. In 1991 the

---

[22] News Item, *Buzz* September 1985, 15.
[23] Shearn quoted in News Item, *Worship* Spring 1987, 1.
[24] News item, *Worship* Winter 1990, 16.

results of the returns showed the percentage of each denominational group among license holders – Anglican, 29 per cent; Baptist, 21 per cent; Methodist, 9 per cent; Pentecostal, 9 per cent; evangelical, 7 per cent; URC/ Brethren/Presbyterian/Salvation Army/Catholic/other, 17 per cent. It was also found that 90 per cent of Pentecostals and house churches used their own OHP transparencies.[25]

In the 1990s the license was taken over by the now established American company, Christian Copyright Licensing International.[26] According to the publicity material in 1997 there were 27,000 license holders in the UK: these included schools, churches and organisations. Fees ranged from £52, for groups of 0–15, to £543, for those over 1500.[27] In 1997 Christian Copyright Licensing International issued a total of 135,000 licenses in Australia, Canada, Great Britain, Ireland, New Zealand, South Africa and the USA.[28]

Innovations such as the Christian Copyright Licensing International indicate how the worship scene was creatively financed. The scheme created a new source of revenue from song royalties that previously did not exist. The Christian music publishing companies were able to support their claim for these royalties by emphasising the way that many churches were routinely acting in an illegal manner by reproducing song lyrics for use in worship. This source of funding was to be very significant in creating an economically viable market for charismatic worship. The licensing scheme should be seen alongside the other practices which companies developed to use songs in a variety of publications and recordings. These practices not only spread the influence of a particular song or artist, they also maximised revenue from royalties. They demonstrate how a viable market was created and sustained for

---

[25] News item, *Worship* Winter 1990, 16.
[26] This was the successor to the company first started by Chuck Fromm.
[27] Christian Copyright Licensing International, 'Congregational Worship and Copyright' 2.
[28] Christian Copyright Licensing International, 'Reference Manual', 1.

charismatic worship. These economic strategies exploited the market, but at the same time if they had not come about, it is very likely that charismatic worship would not exist, at least in its current form. The economics of worship is therefore essential to its production and also to its consumption.

The Mediation of Worship

The Christian worship scene was not simply about worship leaders, record companies and publishing companies. There were a whole range of other activities which were necessary if Christians were to generate a media-related culture. These included Christians who ran recording studios, tape- and CD-copying services, and the professional hire and sale of sound and lighting equipment. These activities contributed to the shape of the culture and, as such, they are part of the mediation of worship. Contemporary charismatic worship was constructed through a series of mediations. Each contributes to the structure and nature of the worship scene. Mediation is part of the process by which worship leaders perform, songs are recorded, and published, and audiences experience worship. The worship song should perhaps be seen as the 'product' that is produced as a result of these processes.

For businesses and for individuals involved in generating the media of worship there were rewards economically, but there were also rewards and pleasures at the level of creativity. Negus defines mediation in three main ways. First, mediation refers to the concept of coming between or of intermediary action. Secondly, mediation refers to the idea of transmission, as he puts it, 'an agency which comes between reality and social knowledge'.[29] Thirdly, mediation makes reference to the concept that works of art are mediated within social relationships.[30]

---

[29] K. Negus, *Popular Music in Theory: An Introduction*, 66.
[30] Negus, *Popular Music*, 66.

According to Negus, these different meanings of the term 'mediation' are interconnecting and overlap each other. Within the evangelical subculture worship music has come to exist within these kind of mediating structures and relationships.

Contemporary Christian music is generally heard through some sort of amplification. The sound of a guitar, voice, drums, etc., is mediated, or transmitted, through networks of microphones, sound mixers, amplifiers and speakers. From the earliest times of *Buzz*, 'amplification' was one of the topics covered in MGO training conferences. Similar seminars, entitled 'sound reinforcement', were also held during the 1980s by the Christian Music Association.[31] Soon a small number of companies began to emerge from the Christian scene specialising in supplying sound, lighting, and live recording for Christian events.[32] The largest of these specifically Christian sound companies was Wigwam Acoustics. Wigwam stood for 'Without Introduction God Welcomes All'.[33]

The company, which was based in Heywood in Lancashire, was started in 1968 and was closely linked to the Manchester based activities of The Jesus Family. Wigwam was used by both Christian and secular acts. These included: Billy Graham, Reinhard Bonnke, Cliff College, Greenbelt, Jesus Fellowship and Chris Rea.[34] In 1994 their turnover was £2 million pounds. Despite their high profile, they were also keen to do church hall gigs. As the founder of the company Michael Spratt put it, 'we do small things to keep our feet on the ground. Our size gives us the opportunity to support local missions.'[35] Wigwam continues to be a major player in the Christian music scene

---

[31] Advertisement, *Worship* Autumn 1988, 3.
[32] See Advertisement, *Worship* Winter 1988, 14.
[33] Jonathan Bellamy, 'Sound Advice', *Cross Rhythms* December 1994, 49.
[34] Advertisement, *Cross Rhythms* December 1994, 19.
[35] M. Spratt quoted in Jonathan Bellamy 'Sound Advice', *Cross Rhythms* December 1994, 49.

supplying sound and lighting equipment to a number of the largest festivals in Britain.

The demand for sophisticated sound equipment soon transferred from festivals and events to local churches. As a result, a number of Christian companies began to offer advice and sales to churches. One of the more enterprising of these companies was called Big House Audio Company, who advertised their 'Revival Sound Systems' – according to their advertising, 'Faith Comes by Hearing and Hearing Comes by Calling'. Calling, of course, meant getting in touch with Big House Audio and installing a sound system. Big House Audio offered the complete acoustic solution to churches, with free on site consultation, through to design and installation.[36]

The emergence of companies such as Wigwam and Big House Audio indicate the extent to which contemporary worship music required increasingly sophisticated systems to create the right sound. These sound systems are mediators of the music. They transmit the music, but as they do so they affect the way that it is presented and experienced. A sound engineer therefore has a creative role in presenting worship music, be it in a church or at a huge festival. Questions of the right mix and level were essential to the feel of an event. This is why so much energy was put into training for this aspect of the music ministry.

Just as with sound reinforcement a number of recording studios became established by specialising in the Christian market. The most successful of these was International Christian Communications (ICC) Studios in Eastbourne. The company was originally based in Bristol and was run by Don Feltham.[37] In 1970 the studios moved to Eastbourne when Helmut Kaufman took over as the director. Although artists such as Paul McCartney have used the facility, Kaufman was clear about the distinctively Christian basis for the work done at the studio: 'We are not a commercial

---

[36] Advertisement, *Worship Together* July/August 1997, back page.
[37] News Item, *Buzz* July 1976, 23.

studio. We exist only for the ministry involved . . . We are only doing Christian work. We are here to serve the church.'[38]

ICC was legally established as both a charity and a company. Kaufman explains that during the 1970s the studio was being used extensively by Christian record companies. The problem however was that the music that was produced had an emphasis upon quantity rather than quality. Around sixty albums a year were recorded for specifically Christian record labels. In many cases, the studio was using the same group of four or five musicians to perform on many of the albums. The result was lack of respect for the studio:

> There was nothing new. No adventure. We were throwing mud at the wall to see if any of it stuck. Not much did because the records were bad. ICC began to lose credibility, musicians heard these pretty terrible albums which were recorded at ICC and suddenly we had lots of Christian artists going to secular studios rather than to us.[39]

The turning point for ICC came with a major investment in equipment for the studio. The higher standard of the equipment meant that a slow trickle of secular artists started to record at the studio. These included major artists such as Paul McCartney, Aztec Camera and Roger Daltry. When the artists and record companies within the Christian scene became aware of the new status of ICC they slowly returned.[40]

Alongside the activities of the studio in Eastbourne, ICC also led the way in recording seminars and worship at events and conferences such as Spring Harvest and Greenbelt. These seminar tapes were not only available at

---

[38] H. Kaufman quoted in News Item, *Buzz* July 1976, 23.
[39] Kaufman in T. Cummings, 'Tracks of the Apostles', *Cross Rhythms* January 1992, 28.
[40] Cummings, 'Tracks of the Apostles', *Cross Rhythms* January 1992, 28.

the event, but were also sold through the network of Christian bookshops.[41] In 1988 Kaufman invested in the first custom-built cassette duplication machinery. Cummings was clear that this enterprise by ICC was highly successful. In 1992 ICC were handling the cassette duplication for Kingsway, Harvestime, the National Society for the Blind, Spring Harvest and many other groups. The income from this aspect of the business was then used to finance a continual programme of improvement in the studios at ICC.[42]

As well as ICC, there were a number of other recording studios specialising in the Christian market. One of these, Chapel Lane, was started by Rob Andrews. The studio got its name because it was located in a disused chapel. Worship music, as well as contemporary Christian music, formed part of the work of Chapel Lane. Cummings says that the first album recorded at the studio was *Thank Offering*, by Dave Pope and John Daniels.[43]

Another studio, which focused on the Christian scene, was Soundtree Studio, which was based in Bolton. Soundtree was closely associated with the Harvestime group of restoration churches under the leadership of Bryn Jones. The studio, which was run by Brook Trickett, was used frequently by Harvestime's leading praise artist David Hadden. Trickett, however, found the relationship with Harvestime to be limiting:

> For four years I was continually making praise and worship tapes for Harvestime. But it got creatively very depressing. There was a staleness in the music that was coming out. In 1987 our church broke away from Bryn and Co and I was pretty relieved.[44]

---

[41] News Item, *Cross Rhythms* May 1990, 5.

[42] Cummings, 'Tracks of the Apostles', *Cross Rhythms* January 1992, 30.

[43] Cummings, 'Tracks of the Apostles', *Cross Rhythms* January 1992, 28.

[44] B. Trickett quoted in Cummings, 'Tracks of the Apostles', *Cross Rhythms* January 1992, 29.

One of the very first albums to be recorded at Soundtree was Kingsway Music's successful *Songs of Fellowship Volume 1*.[45]

It is clear from the emergence of ICC and from Soundtree that within the Christian worship scene the environment and ethos of a particular studio was very significant. There was a creative relationship between those involved in performing and those involved in recording. This creative relationship existed in a series of mediations represented by the technology of recording. Christian worship music has therefore to some extent evolved by the creative engagement with the technologies of recording. Negus refers to recording engineers, record company executives and record producers as 'intermediaries'.[46] Within the Christian scene the production of worship can be seen to involve a number of intermediaries. It is significant that in the case of ICC and Soundtree Studios the structures and relationships of evangelical ministries are combined with the business and economic realities of running a company. These factors interact and affect one another. Also at play are issues related to artistic and aesthetic value. Within the evangelical subculture the fortunes of a studio are tied to perceptions of taste.

These three factors indicate the extent to which a free-market economy developed within the production of Christian worship music. Studios therefore had to negotiate the complexities of this market and compete for business. Within the evangelical scene the relatively small size of the market decisively affects the activities of studios. A key factor in the quality of Christian record is the budget that Christian record companies make available for recording sessions.

In 1992 record companies would calculate recording costs according to a basic formula £1 to £2 per expected unit sales. Thus for the average UK Christian album the

---

[45] Cummings, 'Tracks of the Apostles', *Cross Rhythms* January 1992, 29.

[46] Negus, *Popular Music*, 64.

recording budget would be around £2,000 to £4,000. These costs should be compared with recording costs for American gospel artists of £10,000 to £20,000 and secular recording budgets of millions.[47]

Until the early 1990s the British Christian music scene was dominated by two major companies, Word UK and Kingsway Music.[48] Word, according to Cummings, through its links to the USA, and its distribution deals into Europe, has been able to sustain a particularly high level of activity. While most of the recording artists on the label were American, Tony Cummings points out that a number of albums featured artists from the UK. These albums, however, were generally financed by release in the USA. The importance of success in the American market to sustain activity in the UK was an important factor in shaping the worship activities of artists in this country.

The activities of record companies and related organisations indicate that a more competitive and dynamic market was developing in the UK. This market allowed for mergers, business takeovers, artists who swap labels in financial deals and for a certain amount of competition for new artists. There are a number of examples of how this new situation began to take hold within the evangelical scene. During the 1990s two record labels, Alliance and ICC, emerged to contend with Word UK and Kingsway Music.

Alliance was born when a number of senior executives left Word UK when it was bought by the American company, Nelson, for $72 million in 1992.[49] Alliance established themselves as one of the main players in the market: in recent years they have released Graham Kendrick's albums. Alliance also signed up the Vineyard churches and, in the youth market, the dance-music based World

---

[47] Cummings, 'Tracks of the Apostles', *Cross Rhythms* January 1992, 30.

[48] T. Cummings, 'Publish and Be Saved', *Cross Rhythms* 1991, 32.

[49] News Item, *Encore* Autumn 1992, 1.

Wide Message Tribe also recorded on their label.

ICC, for their part, slowly expanded their cassette duplication service into what was to become a distinctive record label. The ICC record label tended to concentrate upon live worship albums and children's worship songs. In 1998 their catalogue included six different worship albums all linked to Spring Harvest 1998 – *New Songs 1998, r:age 1998, Praise Mix 1998, Kids Praise 1998, Little Kids Praise 1998* and *Live Worship 1998*.[50]

Economics and Technology: The Worship Scene

The contextualisation of the faith within popular culture inevitably led to the growth in a worship business. The technologies required to produce contemporary music have a logic within them. This logic required the development of record companies, recording studios, and so on. This means that when evangelicals set out on the road to be relevant to culture they were tied to the creation of media related companies. What began as a theological and evangelistic imperative was to result in an economic reality. The worship scene was to be increasingly made up of these various interconnecting media and business relationships.

---

[50] ICC Music catalogue 1998, 4–5.

Six

Merchandising, Mergers and Ministry

The charismatic movement in Britain has been remarkably successful. This has led to the establishment of a number of creative and energetic organisations. Spring Harvest now as an independent organisation has continued to build and diversify. John Wimber's Vineyard church has established itself in many of the towns and cities in Britain. Holy Trinity Brompton has launched Alpha in what has become a worldwide ministry. Almost as remarkable has been the continuing success of the youth festival Soul Survivor. At the same time, the new churches, through initiatives such as the prayer ministry 24/7, have led the way in developing innovative approaches to worship and discipleship.

A crucial aspect of the activities of these groups has been the development of specific resources linked to their ministry. The commodification of ministry through products has been essential to the identity of groups such as Alpha or Soul Survivor. This means that in order to understand the effectiveness of the charismatic movement we need to recognise the way that worship and spirituality is amplified by the ability to extend ministry into people's homes and local churches through these various products. The result has been an explosion in the number and range of worship-related materials that are marketed to Christian people. Groups like Vineyard and Soul Survivor have established strong brand identities for their worship music and worship artists. Through the global connections within the charismatic movement worship leaders such as Matt Redman, Martin Smith, Brenton Brown and Tim Hughes have developed international ministries. Most significantly, British worship music has been enthusiastically embraced by Christians in the USA. Access to the much larger and lucrative American market has transformed the British scene. These developments have been helped considerably by changes in recording technology and in particular by use of the internet to market British worship artists around the world.

Though it would always see itself as led by ministry and the Spirit, the charismatic scene is at the same time sustained by a wide range of companies and businesses. As the market has developed, new organisations emerged, but there have also been those that have fallen by the wayside. Along the path, a number of key alliances and business mergers have characterised the British scene. These activities represent the 'means' to engage in ministry. For a group such as Wesley Owen Bookshops, merchandising is explicitly acknowledged as the way that they are involved in sharing Christ. The connection between selling and faith has a long history but it was to find a particular energy as the charismatic movement took its next turn. Alpha, Soul Survivor, 24/7, Vineyard, they all share a common influence, John Wimber. The British worship scene came to life when Wimber visited this country.

Wimber and the Renewal of Renewal

Wimber made his first visit as a Christian minister to the UK in 1981.[1] Pytches, who at the time was the vicar of St Andrew's, Chorleywood, records that Wimber's visit came about because David Watson was delivering a series of lectures at Fuller Theological Seminary in Pasadena. Watson asked a friend, Eddie Gibbs, to advise him on a

---

[1] D. Pytches, 'A Man Called John', in D. Pytches (ed.), *John Wimber*, 33.

church to visit while he was in California. Gibbs, who at the time was researching church growth at Fuller, recommended that Watson visit Wimber's Vineyard Christian Fellowship in Anaheim. Watson and Wimber very quickly developed a mutual friendship.[2] Gibbs was a parishioner of David Pytches at St Andrew's, Chorleywood. Pytches heard through Gibbs that Wimber was due to visit St Michael le Belfrey in York and he per- suaded him to stop off at Chorleywood on his way north.[3] Wimber's ministry made an immediate impact on both of these churches. Wimber was to visit Britain on many occasions during the early 1980s. On these visits he was to influence a number of key ministers who are presently active. Most notable amongst these were Terry Virgo of the New Frontiers network of churches and Sandy Millar, Vicar of Holy Trinity, Brompton. Wimber's contact with Pytches, Virgo and Millar has had a lasting significance on the shape of contemporary church life.[4]

From 1984 onwards Wimber delivered a significant boost to charismatic Christianity in this country. Walker is clear that:

> From that time, despite, or because of, the inevitable controversy that surrounds miraculous ministries, Wimber became a major force in British Christianity, especially among Anglicans. I do not think that it is exaggerating too much to say that Wimber and the style and methodology of the Vineyard Fellowships has been the greatest influence in mainstream renewal since the ministry of the late David Watson and the hey-day of the Fountain Trust in the 1970s.[5]

Wimber not only affected the vibrancy of mainstream denominational Renewal, he also drew leaders such as

---

[2] Saunders and Sansom, *David Watson*, 203–10.
[3] D. Pytches, 'Fully Anglican, Fully Renewed', in K. Springer (ed.), *Riding the Third Wave: What Comes After Renewal?*, 169.
[4] C. Price, 'The Wonder of Wimber', *Christianity* January 1998, 7; see also Walker, *Restoring the Kingdom*, 334.
[5] Walker, *Restoring the Kingdom*, 311.

Terry Virgo closer to that mainstream. The net effect was that renewal was reinvigorated in the denominations and, at the same time, Walker argues, restorationism was further weakened as a distinctive movement.[6] Bebbington suggests that it was Wimber's emphasis upon the proclamation of the gospel through what he called signs and wonders that made such an impact upon the charismatic movement in this country.[7] This is certainly the case. However, it could be argued that perhaps a more enduring legacy has been left by Wimber's distinctive emphasis upon worship. Pilavachi was certainly influenced by the worship when he attended a conference held in Westminster Central Hall in 1983:

> what stood out most was the worship; it totally unhinged me. I spent a whole part of the week just crying and sniffling my way through songs like 'Isn't he beautiful?' and 'Hold me, Lord in your arms.' Many of the songs were incredibly simple and yet totally intimate. As I worshipped, I found healing for my soul. Intimacy set me free.[8]

Wimber brought a new sense of priority to worship.[9] Worship for Wimber was linked to a desire for intimate encounter with a powerful and transforming God. It was this emphasis which inspired Pilavachi and also Matt Redman. Redman is clear that while the signs and wonders may have been, as he says, 'eye catching', the worship was also of major importance. Wimber's focus upon worship took many in the UK by surprise. According to Redman, Wimber demonstrated an 'uncompromising value of spending quality time in bringing adoration to the Lord'.[10]

---

[6] Walker, *Restoring the Kingdom*, 311.
[7] Bebbington, *Evangelicalism*, 232.
[8] M. Pilavachi and C. Borlase, *For the Audience of One: The Soul Survivor Guide to Worship*, xvii.
[9] M. Redman, 'Worshipper and Musician', in D. Pytches (ed.), *John Wimber*, 64.
[10] Redman, 'Worshipper and Musician', 64.

The style of worship favoured by Wimber, says Redman, was a flow of 'unhindered and uninterrupted worship songs, each taking the congregation one more step along the journey into the depths of God's presence'.[11] Sandy Millar was also deeply affected by the style of worship introduced by Wimber. Millar says that it was the emphasis upon intimacy with Jesus that was probably the most significant aspect of Wimber's teachings.[12] At the time, with the possible exception of Romford Christian Fellowship, there was nowhere in England that followed a similar pattern of worship.[13]

Pytches is clear that Wimber transformed life at St Andrew's, Chorleywood. He quotes one of the parishioners at the church as saying that they had been visited by many preachers and the church had been blessed by their ministries but when they left their ministries went with them. What was different about Wimber was that he left his ministry behind with the people in the church after he had gone.[14] With both Holy Trinity, Brompton and St Andrew's, Chorleywood there is a sense in which they were able to build upon the lessons learned from Wimber and, as they did so, they began to extend their influence and impact beyond their Anglican parochial boundaries. A key factor in the ability of these two churches to effect these changes was their willingness to embrace a worship based on popular culture and the market as a means of promoting charismatic spirituality. Nowhere was this to be more effectively utilised than in the remarkable growth of the Alpha course.

Alpha

At Holy Trinity, Brompton the life associated with the newly invigorated charismatic renewal was to become

[11] Redman, 'Worshipper and Musician', 66.
[12] S. Millar, 'A Friend's Recollections', in Pytches (ed.), *John Wimber*, 271.
[13] Millar, 'A Friend's Recollections', 271.
[14] Pytches, 'A Man Called John', 34.

focused in the development by Nicky Gumbel of the Alpha course. The course spread throughout Britain and the rest of the world. In 1998 Alpha was aware of 7,500 courses running.[15] In 2002 Alpha was reporting that 5 million people had attended a course and the following year there were 27,037 registered courses running worldwide, from Russia to Austria and India to Ireland.[16] Alpha were particularly adept at publicity, displaying their endorsement from the new Archbishop of Canterbury Rowan Williams alongside the latest celebrity Christians. In February 2003 *Alpha News* featured both the winner of Big Brother, Cameron Stout, and disgraced former Tory MP and Cabinet Minister, Jonathan Aitken, as supporters of the course.[17] This kind of celebrity profile was added to a hitherto unprecedented financial investment in advertising. Across the country, advertisements for Alpha could be found on buses, trains and billboards, as well as outside churches. As a result, it should have been expected that Alpha would be widely known in the Great Britain. The impact of such marketing was demonstrated by a MORI poll which found that 20 per cent of British adults could identify the course as Christian.[18]

To run an Alpha course, local churches needed to buy a series of branded products, including books, manuals, videos and worship material. The production and marketing of this material transformed an Anglican parish church into a centre for the production, marketing and promotion of mediated religious culture.[19]

Alpha also developed a line of worship materials to be used alongside the course. The worship songs that accompany Alpha feature worship leaders such as Andy Piercy and Dave Clifton. Piercy, as part of the duo Ishmael and

---

[15] *Alpha News* June 1998, 1.
[16] *Alpha News* February 2003, 2.
[17] *Alpha News* February 2003, 3–5.
[18] *Alpha News* February 2003, 2.
[19] P. Ward, 'Alpha the McDonaldisation of Religion?', in *Anvil* 15.4 (1998), 279.

Andy, was formerly an MGO artist. He then went on to form the successful Christian rock band, After the Fire. Alpha market their recording under their own label. The first of Piercy's tapes was called *Praise God From Whom all Blessings Flow*. Although this recording was only promoted through Holy Trinity, Brompton, it still managed to achieve sales of 7,000. By 2003 Alpha were advertising a series of six worship albums. These were all available as songbooks to enable local worship leaders to use the material locally. Alongside these contemporary recordings were three CDs offering 'Classic' and 'Classical Praise', as well as a recording for youth and two 'Praise Party' recordings for use with younger children.[20]

Alpha is primarily evangelistic but charismatic worship is central to the ethos of the course. This is particularly the case with the importance given to the Holy Spirit weekend. In many ways, this is the emotional heart of Alpha. Through the usual talks and discussions, as well as worship and times of prayer ministry, those on the course are introduced to a charismatic spirituality.[21] In this way, Alpha both reflects and spreads the culture of worship shared by charismatics. For those church leaders attending Alpha Training Courses, or those people in the local church preparing to run Alpha, as well as those who come to the courses, charismatic worship is just part of the package. While the extent of the emphasis on charismatic experience may vary locally from course to course, it is still the assumed culture of the organisation and the materials it produces.

New Wine and Soul Survivor

At St Andrew's, Chorleywood the impact of John Wimber's ministry was to lead to the development of a similarly enterprising work. In the first instance, what

---

[20] *Alpha News*, February 2003, 35.
[21] S. Hunt, *Anyone for Alpha?*, 99ff.

emerged was a ministry to church leaders who wanted to connect with charismatic experience.[22] Conferences for clergy were also held and a number of travelling teams visited churches around the country. As this work grew, a summer festival was started. The aim was to support and to encourage clergy and churchgoers as they explored the charismatic renewal. In 1989 St Andrew's launched the New Wine Festival at the Bath and Wells Showground near Shepton Mallet. The festival was founded on what they described as 'core values' of worship, teaching and ministry in the power of the Holy Spirit.[23] The vision for New Wine was eventually linked to the idea of a network of Christians and, particularly, church leaders who would influence their local churches. In 2004 there were over 1000 members of the network of whom 75 per cent were church leaders.[24]

As well as running the regular summer festivals and a number of other gatherings throughout the year, New Wine has also developed its own lines of resources. These include books, a magazine, online Bible reading materials, as well as a range of worship materials. These include a series of songbooks and CD releases specifically related to the festival, such as live worship albums and worship songs for children and all age worship. Initially started under the leadership of David and Mary Pytches, New Wine was later led by John Coles.[25] The festival and its many related activities has been a focus for the continued influence of charismatic spirituality in Britain. In particular its origins at St Andrew's, and the fact that David Pytches was a bishop, meant that it has had a particular influence on the Anglican Church.

The festival was hugely successful with families and people of all ages, but it soon became apparent that large numbers of young people were coming to what was a

[22] Pytches, 'Fully Anglican, Fully Renewed', 174.
[23] www.new-wine.org, accessed 9.1.04.
[24] www.new-wine.org, accessed 9.1.04.
[25] www.new-wine.org, accessed 9.1.04.

family rather than a youth-orientated event and so in 1993 a similar festival designed for young people was launched. This event, Soul Survivor, ran alongside New Wine on the same site. The first festival attracted 1,800 young people.[26] By the summer of 2003, 19,000 were attending over the two weeks.[27] The event was hosted by Mike Pilavachi and, at first, the worship was mainly led by Matt Redman.

The rapid growth of the festival meant that Soul Survivor was to develop as an organisation and, eventually, New Wine and Soul Survivor were to become independent organisations. This meant that behind the scenes there was a large team of paid workers and voluntary helpers who make Soul Survivor happen.[28]

The success of the event has led to a series of Soul Survivor branded events and products. These have included a magazine for young people, a youth congregation in Watford, a Radio Show on Premier Radio, Celebrations which tour the country, CDs, worship songbooks, as well as books on Christian living and discipleship.

Both Mike Pilavachi and Matt Redman were, at the time, involved with St Andrew's, Chorleywood – Pilavachi was the youth leader and Redman was the worship leader. Redman was a member of the youth group at the church. From a very young age he was made responsible for the music in the evening service.[29] His first album, *Wake Up My Soul*, was released by Kingsway in 1994; his second, *Passion for Your Name*, followed in 1997.[30] Since then, Redman has gone on to release a succession of worship albums with Soul Survivor.

As well as Redman, Soul Survivor brought a number of other worship leaders forward through their festivals, tours, songbooks and regular CD releases. These included

---

[26] www.soulsurvivor.co.uk, accessed 8.1.04.

[27] www.soulsurvivor.co.uk, accessed 8.1.04.

[28] J. Bicknell, 'A Postcard from Soul Survivor', *Youthwork* November 1996, 14.

[29] Pytches, 'A Man Called John', 62.

[30] 'In Sight', *Soul Survivor Magazine* February/March 1997, 24.

Martyn Layzell and Tim Hughes, as well as worship leaders from around the country whose work was featured on their live worship CDs or on compilations of new artists and song writers under the title *The People's Album*.

Although the Soul Survivor worship products carry the Survivor logo and brand they are, in fact, part of Kingsway. The worship songs themselves are signed to Kingsway's Thankyou Music and the label Survivor Records is a subsidiary of Kingsway.

Soul Survivor learned from Wimber that worship was the main priority. This emphasis on worship was been reflected in the kinds of activities and products presented by them. Promoting the events or selling worship CDs is seen as a means to encourage young people in what they term 'lifestyles of worship'.[31] This focus on worship was clearly evident every summer at the youth festivals. From the start, the Soul Survivor festival was worship focused. The timetable at Soul Survivor was very different to that which developed at Greenbelt. Twice a day people gathered together for extended times of worship, teaching and ministry. These worship times might last anything from two to three hours. So the emphasis on worship meant that in total young people could spend up to six hours of each day engaged in worship related activities. Soul Survivor were unapologetic about this: 'First and foremost we're into worship. Everything else flows out from that place. We spend lots of our time in our meetings loving God through music; we're committed to backing up this devotion with our whole lives.'[32]

Worship music is central to this emphasis. This is not simply an attempt to attract young people through the use of contemporary forms of music. Neither is it driven by a feeling that church should be trendy in some way. Soul Survivor believed that when people sing songs together they meet God. This was a theology of encounter with God

---

[31] www.soulsurvivor.co.uk, accessed 8.1.04.
[32] www.soulsurvivor.co.uk, accessed 8.1.04.

through the work of the Holy Spirit in the times of worship. The songs mediate this encounter. This means that the various merchandise of CDs, songbooks, festivals, magazines and the websites were run in the belief that these products and services were 'resources' which helped young people meet with God. The Soul Survivor website was very upfront about the role of the products associated with the organisation:

> Our principle focus is building the kingdom rather than building Soul Survivor. Our events, merchandise, services and this website exist in the hope that we're able to encourage you further into finding out what God has made you for and you living that out in your local churches and communities.[33]

Whilst Soul Survivor has planted some churches, its primary focus has been on supporting Christians in the churches to which they already belong. In particular, New Wine and Soul Survivor have developed strong links with both the Anglican Church and the growing network of Vineyard churches.

Vineyard and the Toronto Blessing

Although Wimber was first known in the UK as an author of books and a speaker on evangelism and healing, he was, first and foremost, a pastor of a church and a church planter. The Vineyard churches grew from John Wimber's global ministry, although the first, Vineyard, was, in fact, founded by Kenn Gulliksen in California during the 1970s.[34] At the time Wimber was pastor of The Calvary Chapel of Yorba Linda. In 1982 this church became a Vineyard Church and Wimber became head of the Vineyard Movement of churches.[35] By 1986 the Vineyard

---

[33] www.soulsurvivor.co.uk, accessed 8.1.04.
[34] www.vineyardusa.org/about/history/timeline.htm, accessed 11.1.04.
[35] www.vineyardusa.org/about/history/timeline.htm, accessed 11.1.04.

had grown to 200 churches. The first Vineyard was started in the UK in 1987 by John and Eleanor Mumford. John was an Anglican priest who had been a curate at St Michael's, Chester Square in central London. Within fifteen years there were seventy Vineyard linked churches in the UK and over 500 in the USA.

Like Soul Survivor the Vineyard churches have always laid considerable emphasis upon worship through song. Perhaps unique in ecclesiastical history, the Vineyard website included the establishing of a record company and music publishing company in 1985 as part of the historic 'timeline' of the church. This commitment to the production of worship resources as part of the activity of the church has continued to grow and develop: 'The part Vineyard Music has to play in the church is to capture the unique expression of worship God has given to the Vineyard, and to give away to the rest of the church.'[36]

Vineyard Music described itself as being 'From the Church, For the Church'. The company was non-profit based and linked directly to the church. Vineyard Music supported worship leaders in local churches by recording their material and making it more widely available. In the UK, Vineyard churches produced a number of influential worship CDs reflecting the creativity and spiritual energy of the congregations. In 1999 Vineyard Music released the *Hungry* CD. This brought together worship leaders from around the UK and Ireland. The project was directly supported by the church with the encouragement of John and Eleanor Mumford. There followed a whole series of CDs and songbooks featuring worship leaders from Vineyard churches in the UK.

In 2003 Vineyard released *Hold on*, which featured the song leaders from the Trent Vineyard in Nottinghamshire, a church planted by John and Debbie Wright, the daughter of David Pytches. These kinds of relational links between the various groups within the charismatic movement in the

---

[36] www.vineyardusa.org/about/history/timeline.htm, accessed 11.1.04.

UK are very common and, perhaps unsurprisingly, the connections between Vineyard and New Wine/Soul Survivor are particularly close. David Pytches has been known to claim that he has trained more Vineyard pastors than anyone else in the world.

These relational connections were to come to the fore in the events that surrounded the Toronto Blessing. Various accounts have already been given of this spiritual movement.[37] The main interest of this episode for *Selling Worship* is that it illustrates how the charismatic popular culture worked to promote a style of spiritual experience.

There are a number of factors at play in the way that the Toronto Blessing was passed around the churches in Britain. The relational links between the Vineyard groups and the Anglican Church facilitated the spread of the blessing. At first, the blessing was located in the rather unlikely setting of a Vineyard Church in Toronto located near to the airport. The experience was first in evidence when Randy Clark, a Vineyard pastor from Missouri, came to preach in Toronto. Clark had, in turn, been influenced by Rodney Howard-Brown.[38] Following Clark's preaching people began to experience what was termed the blessing. Arnott describes the event in vivid terms:

> It hadn't occurred to us that God would throw a massive party where people would laugh, roll, cry and become so empowered that emotional hurts from childhood would just lift off. Some people were so overcome physically by God's power that they had to be carried out.[39]

At this time, the Toronto Vineyard charismatic worship

---

[37] For a brief and accessible survey of this material see J.H.S. Steven, *Worship in the Spirit: Charismatic Worship in the Church of England*, 31ff.

[38] M. Paloma 2003, www.hartfordinstitute.org/research/research-pentecostalsismm-polomart8.html, accessed 11.1.04.

[39] Quoted in Paloma 2003 www.hartfordinstitute.org/research/research-pentecostalsismm-polomart8.html accessed 11.1.04.

services were being held every evening of the week as well as at the weekends. Soon remarkable phenomena were being reported. As well as falling (or being slain) in the Spirit there were uncontrollable shaking, laughing, barking and dancing. Almost immediately she heard about these developments, Eleanor Mumford travelled to the Toronto church where she experienced the blessing. She travelled back to London. At Holy Trinity, Brompton a group of the key leaders gathered together and the phenomena were passed on to them.[40]

Within days the blessing spread around the UK. It was seen at Soul Survivor, in the New Frontier churches and throughout the house church movement as well as in charismatic Anglican churches. From Holy Trinity, Brompton the blessing was in turn re-exported to Pensacola, North America, which was to become the next centre of pilgrimage in the charismatic world after Toronto. In 1995 Steve Hill, an Assemblies of God minister, experienced the blessing at Holy Trinity, Brompton in London. He was involved in the next outpouring of the blessing in Florida.[41] These national and international connections illustrate how the rapid spread of the blessing was facilitated by a combination of locally based centres of worship and global networks of relationships. David Lyon calls this combination glocalisation, i.e. it is both local and global. This means that charismatic culture was enabled by communication and information technologies, as well as by more the softer relational connections which are common within the movement.[42] It is a characteristic of the movement that these connections transcended traditional denominational allegiances. What charismatics held in common was a particular spiritual culture but this was mediated through a number of organisations.

---

[40] Paloma 2003 www.hartfordinstitute.org/research/research-pentecostalsismm-polomart8.html accessed 11.1.04.

[41] www.hartfordinstitute.org/research/research-pentecostalsismm-polomart8.html accessed 11.1.04.

[42] D. Lyon, *Jesus in Disneyland*, 109.

Consolidation and Alliance

As charismatics in Britain came into the twenty-first century, it was clear that the innovation of the last forty years had led to the establishment of a number of mature and confident institutions. Alongside the success of New Wine, Alpha and Soul Survivor, Spring Harvest had continued to evolve. Born out of the creative alliance between Youth for Christ and *Buzz* magazine, Spring Harvest established itself as an independent organisation in 1993.[43] In 1994, 70,000 people attended Spring Harvest at its four main locations – Ayr, Minehead, Pwhelli and Skegness.[44] With a focus on worship and teaching Spring Harvest had been able to maintain its evangelical stance while broadening its appeal into the mainstream of church life in Britain. Central to these developments were the Bishop of Willesdon, Pete Broadbent, and Ian Coffey and Steve Chalke of Oasis. Spring Harvest was to continue to innovate by forming strategic alliances with evangelical organisations. In 1993 they started, with UCCF and the Keswick Convention, Word Alive and in 1996 they launched an initiative with Focus and Holy Trinity, Brompton.[45]

As they set their sights higher, organisations such as Spring Harvest increasingly sought strategic alliances to help them achieve their goals. Key players initiated projects and then arranged that others with similar interests should work with them. In 2004 Alpha, Spring Harvest and Soul Survivor were developing closer links based on particular projects. The re-launch of Youth Alpha was helped by Soul Survivor, with a national conference and seminars at the festival led by the head of Youth for Christ, Roy Crowne. A new initiative aimed at students 'Student Evolution' brought together Soul Survivor, Alpha and Fusion under the leadership of Spring Harvest.

---

[43] www.springharvest.org/information/vi_history.html, accessed 13.1.04.
[44] www.springharvest.org/information/vi_history.html, accessed 13.1.04.
[45] www.springharvest.org/information/vi_history.html, accessed 13.1.04.

Meanwhile, perhaps the most ambitious project launched by Soul Survivor was a mission to London involving a hoped-for 15,000 young people known as Soul in the City, drawing on a range of supporters including Youth Alpha.[46] While Alpha and Soul Survivor may have been similarly influenced by Wimber they have not always been so close historically, for instance it had not been automatic for Soul Survivor church in Watford to run Youth Alpha.[47] The change has perhaps come as Soul Survivor in particular has sought to develop the Soul in the City project. This has led to a more open and symbiotic relationship based on mutual co-operation.

For other organisations, merger and alliance has grown out of necessity. From the mid-1990s the Greenbelt Festival had been limping from one financial crisis to another. Under the leadership of Andy Thornton and Jude Levermore the festival began to rebuild its identity by, in the first instance, seeking alliances with mainstream Christian charitable organisations. A number of major supporters came on board including Christian Aid, the *Church Times* and the Church Mission Society. With a move to Cheltenham Race Course and a renewed emphasis upon itself as an Arts Festival, Greenbelt was able to turn the financial corner in 2002 and look forward in confidence born of increasing numbers and a healthy bank balance. The relocation in the mainstream of denominational groups reinforced the impression that Greenbelt was for those who had rejected or never really been enamoured by charismatic worship. Instead, Greenbelt was a place where a variety of groups could show their wares, including the Iona community and visitors from the world church, and alternative worship groups such as Grace, Vaux and Epicentre.

Mergers and deals were also characteristic of the publishing and recording business. In 2002 the Christian

---

[46] *Alpha News* No. 32 November 2003 – January 2004, 14–15.
[47] *Alpha News* No. 32 November 2003 – January 2004, 14–15.

book distribution company Send the Light bought out Word UK and then later that year Alliance Music. These were brought together under the name Authentic Media. Alliance at the time represented Vineyard Music as well as the Manchester based The Tribe, formerly known as The World Wide Message Tribe. The justification for the merger was expressed in business terms. According to Keith Danby, the chief executive of Send the Light,

> This is an important addition to our media division and we feel privileged to be given the opportunity to represent the labels and artists. Authentic, with the strengthened management team and additional product groups, makes an exciting and formidable business unit. In a short time, Authentic has become an established brand and a leading player in the industry, but I am confident the best is yet to come!'[48]

Send the Light was a publishing company which was started in 1962 by the American youth organisation, Operation Mobilisation. By the end of the 1990s they were able to say that they were the 'largest distributor of Christian product in Western Europe'.[49] Send the Light brought together production, distribution and sales through its chain of Wesley Owen bookshops. The story of Send the Light and Authentic Media is paralleled by very similar developments at *Buzz*.

In the 1970s *Buzz* began to investigate its readership. John Buckeridge explained that the assumption had always been that *Buzz* was read by young Christians in their twenties and early teenage years. When a survey was undertaken, they discovered that *Buzz* was, in fact, read by a much older audience – clergy, youth workers and other interested Christians – who read *Buzz* in order to 'keep up'

---

[48] http://www.alliancemusic.co.uk/html/news/buyout.html accessed 13.1.04

[49] http://www.premieronline.co.uk/authentic/datapage.do? pageid=15 accessed 13.1.04

with the burgeoning Christian youth scene.[50] This led to a rethink for *Buzz*.

Clearly, the readership had grown up with the magazine, but they had not grown out of the youth culture. So *Buzz*, which at the time was owned by Elm House, decided to address the readership directly. In 1988 they launched *21st Century Christian* – which was edited by Hilary Saunders, the biographer of David Watson and daughter of the leading Anglican charismatic, Teddy Saunders – and this was followed by a magazine for clergy, *Leadership Today*. Eventually, the two titles merged to become *Alpha*. This then became *Christianity Magazine* and in 2001 the magazine merged with *Renewal* to become *Christianity and Renewal*.

As the titles changed, so did the ownership. In 1991 Elm House sold the magazine to Malcolm Matson's company, Trinity Square, but they were soon purchased by David Heron's Premier Company, who also owned the London-based Christian radio station.

As these deals took place, a new title aimed at youth leaders was being planned. *Youthwork Magazine* was the brainchild of John Buckeridge and the magazine was eventually launched in 1991. By 2004 the monthly circulation of the magazine had reached 16,000 copies. Things had thus come almost full circle, since Premier Radio was, in the first instance, championed and launched by Pete Meadows.[51]

Making it in America – Delirious?

For British worship music the one escape from the size of our market was the possibility of breaking into the lucrative American scene. For the previous thirty years the tide had flowed only one way from the USA to the UK, but in the mid-1990s this was to change. Leading the way was

---

[50] John Buckeridge, 2004, interview with the author.
[51] Buckeridge, 2004.

the Littlehampton-based band Delirious? Released in 2004, their latest album, *World Service*, has been supported by tour dates ranging across the USA.[52] With sales of over a million and an American-based contemporary Christian music Dove Award to their name, the band has found significant success in America.[53]

Delirious? have defied categories by crossing the boundaries between worship and performance, although their roots – and, arguably, their best material – are to be found in their early worship music. This material was released in the early 1990s as a series of short recordings under the title, *Cutting Edge: Songs by Martin Smith*. Martin and the rest of the band were, at the time, based on the south coast and leading worship for the Arun Community Church, which was linked to the Pioneer network of churches. The privately released tapes were produced by Andy Piercy, endorsed by the leader of the church David Thatcher and carried the logo of the Arun Community Church. 'Having seen how God has used Martin and the band in leading worship, I am excited that this recording will give many the opportunities to taste something of the worship at Cutting Edge for themselves.'[54]

Soon, Martin Smith was to be at the heart of innovative worship in Britain. He appeared at the Soul Survivor festival and was influential in helping Matt Redman begin writing songs. The band appeared at the major festivals bringing a fresh and immediate feel to the worship. Smith's songs were reproduced in all of the major songbook collections including *Songs of Fellowship* and *The Survivor Songbook*. Even with their heart still in the local church in Littlehampton, Delirious? and Martin Smith have been able to promote their songs in America through recording and regular tours. Their success has meant that, alone among UK-based Christian bands, Delirious? have been

---

[52] www.delirious.co.uk/tournews.html, accessed 13.1.04.
[53] *Church Times* 16 January 2004, 50.
[54] Sleeve Notes Original *Cutting Edge* tape.

able to support themselves and their company through the activities of the band and their own record label Furious? Records.

Where Martin Smith was to lead, others were soon to follow. At the turn of the millennium, British worship bands and the songs they had written were to become very successful in the USA. Matt Redman's albums sold in significant numbers and his songs were being used in charismatic churches throughout North America. With the Soul Survivor festival being launched in America, other 'Survivor' label worship artists and their songs were also becoming popular. At the same time, similar developments were happening for the British Vineyard churches. The churches had very natural connections in the USA. For the UK-based worship leaders the network of links in the USA and around the world created the means to circulate songs, CDs and worship artists. Through the Vineyard Music website songs links could be made to the locally based distributors and national artists. This use of the web was taken up by all of the key charismatic groups.

Enter the Web

Evangelicals have always been keen to embrace any new communication possibilities.[55] For the various organisations and individuals promoting worship music in the UK, the web has been a significant advantage. It has meant that groups such as Delirious? have been able to communicate directly with their fan base, effectively bypassing the secular press in the UK and the religious press in the USA, both of whom, for different reasons, tend to ignore British Christian bands. For the record companies, book distributors, festivals and organisations the web has also offered a chance to offer their products to a wider audience.

The network of Christian bookshops has often struggled to keep the range of stock associated with the growing

---

[55] See Sweet (ed.), *Communication*.

number of worship artists. In contrast, on their websites organisations such as Vineyard or Soul Survivor are able to present their whole range. The web, along with new and cheaper recording technologies has led directly to the proliferation of titles and the release of more specialised and targeted CDs. Direct sales through the web are important also because they represent a larger profit for the organisation or company than sales through the traditional bookstores. That said sales associated with an appearance at one of the major festivals such as Soul Survivor remain the most important factor in UK success.

Alongside sales, many groups have sought to use the web as a means of developing their ministry. Soul Survivor transferred *Soul Survivor Magazine*, a youth-oriented publication that seeks to support young Christians in their spiritual lives, to the web in the late 1990s. *Youthwork Magazine* has continued to publish hard copy but it also has developed as a web-based magazine offering articles and materials on youth work to a much wider and more international audience. Spring Harvest and New Wine have used the web to promote their festivals but they also use it to sell their materials and, in recent years, people have been able to book into the festivals on line. The prayer movement 24-7, which was started by Revelation Church in Chichester, uses the internet to connect up groups around the world. The groups sign up to pray every day for a week (or longer).[56] Through the website groups are able to report on their experiences in prayer, communicate with each other as they pray and generate a global perspective in their spirituality. 24-7 was started by Pete Grieg. Pete was the youth pastor at Revelation Church, which was started by Roger Ellis and linked to the Pioneer Group of churches. Revelation has strong links to the nearby Arun Community Church and to Delirious?. With Soul Survivor they run the Cultural Shift conferences which promote a radical form of charismatic worship and

---

[56] www.24-7prayer.com/, accessed 13.1.04.

church planting. Cultural Shift alongside the Manchester-based World Wide Message Tribe, and Ray and Nancy Goudies NGM (previously New Generation Ministries) has popularised the use of dance music and DJs in charismatic worship.

Selling Worship

From its origins in the 1960s, the youth-orientated emphasis of evangelical and charismatic churches has led to the development of a sophisticated media-related worship scene. The business life of the worship scene enables the spirituality of the movement to develop and spread. At the same time, the processes of selling are far from neutral. Questions of influence, cultural assimilation and Christian ethics are clearly there to be explored. Some of these issues will be discussed in Part Three. Before we do that, we need to flesh out the way that worship has changed the theology and practice of the church. To do this, we need look at the lyrics of actual worship songs and examine how they have changed and been changed as the worship scene has evolved.

Part Two

Singing the Story

Seven

Teaching to Worship: *Youth Praise* and *Sound of Living Waters*

Over the last thirty years charismatic worship music has entered the bloodstream of the evangelical churches in Britain. The chief medium for this has been the worship song. Part One has examined how this cultural change has taken place. In Part Two, we turn our attention to the songs themselves. From the early days of *Youth Praise*, though the house church inspired Songs of Fellowship, to the contemporary *The Survivor Songbook* it is clear that worship has undergone a number of changes. The forms of musical expression used in worship have clearly changed. In addition, the technologies of recording and marketing songs have developed. Alongside these innovations there has been a parallel theological evolution. This evolution is evident in the lyrics of the songs themselves.

In this chapter we examine the shift in evangelical worship from the world of the youth group and conservative evangelicalism found in *Youth Praise Book 1*, published by Falcon Books in 1966, to *Sound of Living Waters*, published by Hodder & Stoughton in 1974, which came out of the early days of charismatic renewal. The early charismatic renewal was to have a profound impact on the songs that were sung in youth groups and churches. In the lyrics of the songs we can detect a shift from an emphasis upon teaching doctrine to songs which are meant to be used as a vehicle for a more experiential charismatic worship. Central to this new emphasis was a fresh understanding of the church as a body gathered to receive the Spirit. The water in *Sound of Living Waters* is a reference to the experience of the Spirit filling the church and then flowing out into the needy world around. This experience of the Spirit in worship begins to replace the previous focus on the experience of conversion. Thus the songs turn the gaze from what has happened to believers to what is now happening as the church gathers as a body to worship.

Youth Praise Book One

The Christian story in *Youth Praise* is refracted through the lens of the experience of evangelical conversion. 'If you want joy'[1] sets out the centrality of conversion. The repetitive simple lyrics are given a more insistent feel by the use of three beats rather than the more usual four beats to a bar. According to 'If you want joy', conversion promises a great deal: sins are 'taken away', hearts are 'made over anew', night will turn to day and Jesus will 'come in to stay'. If the believer lets Jesus into their heart, they will also experience 'Joy'. Joy in *Youth Praise* represents a total life-changing event, often expressed as Jesus coming into the life of the believer. 'Life is wonderful'[2] says that nothing will be the same after Jesus has 'come in'. Jesus coming in changes everything and so now life is wonderful.

Both 'If you want joy' and 'Life is wonderful' are seeking to express the profound experience of Christian encounter with Jesus in the present. They do, however, seem to exaggerate the benefits of Christian experience somewhat. The melody of 'Life is wonderful' trips along with optimistic jollity. This rhythmic structure tends to reinforce a superficial impression. The musical style of these songs is in tension with what could be seen as the gravity of

---

[1] YP 72.
[2] YP 46.

encounter with Jesus, the Son of God. This jolly acceptance of conversion is, however, balanced by the presentation of the Christian life as tough and demanding. This is seen clearly in 'When the road is rough'.[3] Here the path may be difficult and the road maybe steep, but the believer is to fix their eyes upon Jesus.[4]

The main image in *Youth Praise* for conversion is 'letting Jesus in'. Jesus is portrayed as 'knocking, patiently waiting, outside your heart's closed door'.[5] The word of God offers this invitation in 'Behold I stand'[6] the indwelling Christ is said to 'sup' with the individual and this is a 'fellowship divine'. When Jesus comes in, personal guilt and sinfulness are taken away.[7] In 'Jesus is the Saviour'[8] individual sinfulness is linked to a more contemporary youth-orientated language. 'Sometimes when you're feeling all alone and blue, Jesus can come in and help you to pull through.'[9] Here the discourse of adolescent anxiety mixes with a theology of redemption. The emphasis upon conversion leads on to a concern for those who have not yet 'let Jesus in'. While *Youth Praise* is a songbook meant for praise and worship, it always does so keeping one eye on those who may not have undergone this experience.

The songs are arranged into sections each with a heading. Three of these headings relate directly to conversion: 'Testimony', 'God's Invitation' and 'Challenge'. 'Make up your mind'[10] delivers a fairly uncompromising challenge to any unconverted within a meeting or a service. 'Which crowd will you follow, the large or the small?' The listener must be sure so that they can make up their mind. Friends may reject the new believer, but Jesus

---

[3] *YP* 96.
[4] *YP* 96.
[5] *YP* 73.
[6] *YP* 68.
[7] *YP* 58.
[8] *YP* 61.
[9] *YP* 61.
[10] *YP* 76.

gives freedom and power. Suddenly, life will find a purpose and Jesus will be the key. But this will only come
when 'you make up your mind'.[11] Here again the Christian
story and the experience of conversion is contextualised
within the world of adolescent peer groups and relationships. In *Youth Praise*, it is an act of will that generates the
promised encounter with Christ, who offers power and
liberty with which it is possible to overcome the crowd.

It is through this emphasis upon encounter with Jesus at
conversion that *Youth Praise* deals with the cross and
resurrection of Jesus. 'Lord of the cross'[12] encourages
reflection upon the passion of Christ. According to the
song, contemplation of the 'cross of shame will set, 'my
cold heart aflame'. The cross takes away sin but it is also an
inspiration to a life of devotion and service. Calvary is a
present reality, a place to be visited for comfort and release.
Jesus is near at Calvary and individual burdens are lifted.[13]
The blood of Christ sets us free in an atoning sacrifice for
sin.[14] In *Youth Praise* the basic rhyme; 'free, me, tree and
Calvary' is a feature of a good many songs. In this way, the
death of Christ is located as an encounter in the present or
in the recent past of the believer. The individual transforming significance of the event is all-pervasive. The
Christian story and the biography of the individual are
welded together: 'There you died for me'.[15]

This contemporary treatment of the events around his
death does not, however, obscure the humanity and
suffering of Jesus. 'I'll be a friend to Jesus' uses the
metaphor of friendship, a further contextualisation within
the lives of young people, to unravel the significance of the
events around the death of Jesus. Here the events of the
passion narrative are recounted with the betrayal of the
disciples and the moral weakness of Pilate given in some

---

[11] *YP* 76.
[12] *YP* 11.
[13] *YP* 104.
[14] *YP* 42, 43.
[15] *YP* 38.

detail. In contrast, the believer offers him- or herself as a friend to Jesus.[16] The sufferings of Christ are also set out at length in 'His hands were pierced'.[17]

Unlike the crucifixion, the resurrection of Jesus is not a major focus of reflection in the songs of *Youth Praise*.[18] Where the resurrection appears it does not seem to carry any particular significance. There is a sense in which it makes it into the song because it is part of the Christian story, rather than a factor of major importance. 'Living Lord' is an example of this, where the events of the gospel events are recited with creedal brevity.[19] The one song where a connection is developed between the resurrection and contemporary life is 'He lives'.[20] Here the resurrection is validated by the believer who can affirm that Christ is alive by saying that he is living in them in the present.

Alongside the crucifixion and resurrection, *Youth Praise* offers several songs which focus on specific Gospel narratives. The events of the life of Christ, for instance, are recorded in some detail.[21] In the 'Jericho road'[22] we meet blind Bartimaeus whose life was so 'empty and flat' until he receives sight from Christ.[23] Brother Williams' song, 'Can it be true',[24] which was arranged by the Venturers, uses a strong melody and powerful lyrics to draw the singer into an extended reflection upon the incarnation and death and resurrection of Jesus as a source of inspiration for the Christian life. The chords G, Em, C, D form a simple but natural riff for the guitar and the final verse, with the rest between the question 'Can it be true?' and the answer 'My Lord, it had to be', has a drama to it that the cheerful sing-a-long tunes of some of the other material sadly lack.

---

[16] *YP* 109.
[17] *YP* 116.
[18] *YP* 114.
[19] *YP* 126.
[20] *YP* 52.
[21] *YP* 89, 80, 10.
[22] *YP* 80.
[23] *YP* 80.
[24] *YP* 36.

Conversion, 'letting Jesus in', leads to a life of 'following Christ'. Christian mission is thus likened to a journey of discipleship. The choice facing the unbeliever is between two different paths. Minds must therefore be made up about which road to be on.[25] 'I want to walk'[26], which, we are told, was written by St Paul's Erith Swiss House Party and is based on a Swiss tune, deals with the journey of faith. Walking with Christ involves giving over complete control of both body and soul to Jesus. Walking with Jesus means yielding to him, because he has 'conquered death' and he is 'King of Kings'. Walking with Jesus is to be a daily reality;[27] the road may well be 'rough and steep' but the answer is to 'fix your eyes upon him'.[28] Jesus is the leader, guiding the believer through the darkness; he is the way.[29] Above all, Jesus is a friend who can be relied upon. He is friend who is 'strong' and 'true' who has changed the life of the believer, 'completely'. Jesus is kinder than every other friend; no one cares like he does.[30]

It is perhaps this emphasis upon Jesus as a friend and as a support in the present that leaves relatively little room for an extended treatment of the Holy Spirit in *Youth Praise*. There are a number of songs, however, which speak of the Holy Spirit.[31] 'Spirit of the living God' is perhaps more of a kind with the later-style renewal songs. The simple slow melody lends itself to a prayerful intimacy. The believer calls for the Spirit to descend and break and mould them. This is a personal prayer where the believer asks the Spirit to 'fill me'.[32]

The journey of discipleship, represented as friendship of Jesus, is generally seen by *Youth Praise* in individualistic

---

[25] *YP* 76.
[26] *YP* 121.
[27] *YP* 101.
[28] *YP* 96.
[29] *YP* 97.
[30] *YP* 58.
[31] *YP* 110, 112, 108.
[32] *YP* 108.

terms. That said, the church makes an occasional appearance, but it is not at all central. The German 'A vessel called the church of God' is an exception, but at times it seems stiff and a little out of place alongside some of the other material in the collection. Mission to the wider world is, however, very much on the agenda. In most cases, this is expressed in terms of witness and evangelism but *Youth Praise* does occasionally connect with the everyday reality of lives. 'Thank you',[33] for instance, includes the line 'thank you for leisure and employment'. 'The Lord who left the highest heaven'[34] connects the events of the birth of Christ with present-day homelessness. (This kind of social and political reference becomes extremely rare in the songbook collections during the next thirty years.)

Sound of Living Waters

The songs in *Sound of Living Waters* are arranged with the amateur guitarist in mind. Many of the songs are set in musical keys and are structured around chord patterns which would be familiar to most folk or rock guitarists, e.g. 'Let us give thanks' (G, C, Am, Em).[35] Where songs are set in a relatively difficult key – e.g. 'The canticle of the gift'[36], which is in B minor – the editors very helpfully supply a further set of simpler chords in A minor with an instruction to place a capo on the second fret. Where songs or hymns are unsuitable for the guitar, *Sound of Living Waters*, unlike *Youth Praise*, refrains from offering a collection of challenging left-hand positions which change on every syllable. In addition to the guitar chords, above each of the songs *Sound of Living Waters* offers some advice on the mood of each song and some basic musical instructions, e.g. 'Morning has broken',[37] for instance, is accompanied by the

---

[33] *YP* 13.
[34] *YP* 89.
[35] *SLW* 8.
[36] *SLW* 2.
[37] *SLW* 9.

rubric 'With an easy swing (1 beat to a bar).'

The accessibility of *Sound of Living Waters* to the amateur guitar player is in marked contrast to *Youth Praise*. *Youth Praise* includes guitar chords, but it is evident that the editors are more familiar with the classical, rather than folk/rock traditions and that they play the piano rather than the guitar. 'Thank you'[38] has a very popular melody that moves at a fair pace. The problem with the song for the guitarist is that it changes chord every other word. The guitar chords are given but they demand considerable, if not professional, expertise. The first two lines read 'Thank You for every new good morning, Thank You for every fresh new day'. The accompanying guitar part is as follows: E, C# minor, F# minor, B13, E, C# minor 7, F# minor 7, B7. If this is not challenging enough, the song ascends through the keys for each successive verse. Thus, starting with the key of E, it finally ends up in the key of A. These musical characteristics would indicate that *Youth Praise* sits somewhere in between the genre of spiritual songs and more traditional hymns.

Youth Praise is musically quite challenging, if a little trite at times. In contrast, *Sound of Living Waters* is presented in an accessible and easy to use manner which connects with the folk-art values of some elements within the renewal movement. These basic values are very much in evidence in the way that *Sound of Living Waters* presents the Christian story. Accessibility is seen in the lyrics of songs that have been reduced and greatly simplified. 'Alleluia'[39] a song which is to be sung, according to the instructions, with 'quiet adoration', has a first verse which consists of the word 'Alleluia' repeated eight times. 'Jesus'[40] has a verse where the name 'Jesus' is repeated five times. Again, the advice is that this song should be sung 'Slowly and reverently'. The radical simplification of lyrics allows for a

---

[38] *YP* 13.
[39] *SLW* 25.
[40] *SLW* 57.

variety of usage associated with charismatic renewal. If there is no need to recall a lyric, or if the cue can be taken from the music group or worship leader, then this frees the worshipper to kneel in prayer, raise their arms or even close their eyes while they are singing.

Sound of Living Waters is primarily concerned with worship rather than teaching. This is reflected in the way that songs are gathered into a number of sections. These include titles such as: 'Hallelujah! . . . Songs of praise and Thanksgiving', 'Kneel and Adore . . . Songs of Hope and Vision'. The emphasis upon praise and worship is closely related to the community of the church. While *Youth Praise* generally speaks of encounter with Christ as an individual and perhaps one-off event, *Sound of Living Waters* is mainly concerned with an encounter with Christ within the community life and the praise of the church. This is the dominant theme in the songbook. 'God himself is with us'[41] speaks of the church adoring a God who is within the group. God is here and the believers appear before him in awe.[42] There is still the sense of God being 'in' but this time the concept is presented corporately. A similar community encounter is found in 'We see the Lord'.[43] The song is presented in *Sound of Living Waters* with the Bible passage that refers to Isaiah's vision in the temple.[44] It is interesting that the passage from Isaiah recalls the experience of an individual set apart by the experience for his prophetic ministry. 'We see the Lord' takes this distinctive and uncharacteristic Old Testament experience and widens it to a more communal and everyday event. Praise and worship, therefore, for *Sound of Living Waters* represents a moment of potential encounter with God.

Throughout the songbook this encounter with God is presented in relation to the work of the Holy Spirit. 'Holy, holy',[45] which is taken from the Jimmy and Carol Owens'

---

[41] *SLW* 22.
[42] *SLW* 22.
[43] *SLW* 23.
[44] Isaiah 6:1.
[45] *SLW* 19.

musical, *Come Together*, expresses these ideas very clearly. As believers 'lift their voices' the Holy Spirit comes and fills the heart again in a new way. The corporate singing is an expression of love to God a 'love token' and in response the Spirit is poured out.[46] *Sound of Living Waters* emphasises the continual filling with the Holy Spirit. Being filled, however, is located in the corporate communal life of the church.

The fifth section in the book is given the title 'Songs of the kingdom . . . the body of Christ'. This close association between the kingdom of God and the church characterises the songbook. The gospel story is arranged around this central connection between experience of God and the church as the kingdom. 'The body song'[47] sets out the vision for interdependence in terms of the Pauline image of the body of Christ. One person on their own is not a body, says the song; there are many members in the body.[48] The play on the words of the passage from 1 Corinthians 12:14–26 is deliberate; the reference is included in the title.

A further metaphor for the church in *Sound of Living Waters* is 'God's house'. According to 'God is building a House'[49] each individual is part of the plan and the house will 'stand'. Christ is head of the house and he 'abideth in its praise'.[50] Personal fulfilment and spiritual encounter are seen as being dependent on community life. In particular, the songbook places emphasis on the need for Christians to 'Love one another'.[51] When the community comes together the kingdom of God is manifested. So the song can say that 'The kingdom of God is neither lo here nor lo there', because the kingdom of God is among us.[52]

Sound of Living Waters, like *Youth Praise*, places significant

---

[46] *SLW* 19.
[47] *SLW* 111.
[48] *SLW* 111.
[49] *SLW* 60.
[50] *SLW* 60.
[51] *SLW* 66, 70.
[52] *SLW* 61.

emphasis upon the historical life of Christ. Through songs such as the 'The canticle of the gift'[53], which deals with the Incarnation, and 'Calypso carol',[54] with its extended reflection on the birth of Jesus, the songbook interacts with the Christological heart of the Christian story. As a result, the humanity of Christ and several aspects of his earthly ministry are used as the basis for songs. Much of this material, while still being firmly rooted in the narrative of the Gospels, is intended to locate encounter with Christ in the present. A good example of this is, 'Here comes Jesus'.[55] Here the believer is located in the narrative of the Gospel. The believer sees Jesus walking on the water, but the same Jesus, says the song, will, 'make you whole'.[56] In a similar way, 'The foot washing song', recalls the Gospel story where Jesus washes his disciples' feet and the song encourages the followers of Jesus to act in a similar fashion.[57]

This emphasis upon the humanity of Jesus is also reflected in the way that *Sound of Living Waters* treats the suffering and death of Christ. 'The canticle of the gift' recounts the Christian story as a cause for wonder and celebration. From being born of Mary, through to the Last Supper, the suffering of the Father and the Son at the crucifixion, his victory over death in the resurrection, to his reigning at God's right hand. 'The canticle of the gift' offers a sophisticated and comprehensive theological content.

While the centrality of Jesus to the Christian story is well reflected in *Sound of Living Waters*, the work of the Holy Spirit is also regularly featured. 'Holy, holy'[58] follows an orthodox trinitarian pattern. Creation is reflected in the relationship between the Father and his children; Jesus is presented as the redeemer; and, the Holy Spirit is

---

[53] *SLW* 2.
[54] *SLW* 118.
[55] *SLW* 49.
[56] *SLW* 49.
[57] *SLW* 125.
[58] *SLW* 19.

represented as being active in continually meeting believers in the present. The believer calls upon the Spirit, 'Come and fill our hearts anew, Holy Spirit'.[59] It is the Holy Spirit that will fall upon us 'afresh', imparting gracious powers.[60] 'Fear not, rejoice and be glad'[61] encourages believers that God has 'poured out his Spirit'. According to the song, something exciting is clearly happening in the present. The trees are coming into bud, vines are in fruit, and the wheatfields are golden. Now is the time to thrust in the sickle because the Lord has given rain.[62] When the Spirit comes there is teaching,[63] healing[64] and repentance. 'Spirit of the Living God', which appears in *Youth Praise*, is also included in *Sound of Living Waters*.[65] This is, perhaps, evidence of its continued popularity and use within the renewal movement.

In *Sound of Living Waters* the dominant image for the blessings associated with the Holy Spirit is water. 'The Holy Ghost medley'[66] talks of living water that satisfies. The believer is to drink in the 'living water'.[67] The song goes on to speak of this water as 'springing up' within the believer and 'flowing out'. The water has the power to effect miraculous changes. The lame walk, the blind see and the prisoners are set free. Thus, the mission of the church, and of individuals, is connected to the dominant motif within the songbook – an encounter with God, in the praise and worship of the Christian community. The believer encounters God, and is filled with living water, through the power of the Holy Spirit, and then this blessing is seen as flowing out to effect a missiological change. Betty Pulkingham's song, 'Ho! everyone that

---

[59] *SLW* 19.
[60] *SLW* 33.
[61] *SLW* 59.
[62] *SLW* 59.
[63] *SLW* 41.
[64] *SLW* 50.
[65] *SLW* 29.
[66] *SLW* 77.
[67] *SLW* 77.

thirsteth'[68] is based upon Isaiah 55:1–2, and it offers an invitation to those outside, and also those inside the community, to come and drink from the waters. Here the world around the community is a desert into which the peace of God will flow. The reception of the Holy Spirit therefore inevitably delivers a missiological imperative. Based on Luke 4:16–30 'God's Spirit is in my heart' presents a missionary call growing from the indwelling Spirit. The believer is to 'go' and 'tell everyone'.[69]

The dominant metaphors within *Sound of Living Waters* are of the body of Christ and the living water of the Spirit. However, throughout the book there are a number of songs which touch upon what could be called prophetic and apocalyptic themes. Jesus is referred to as the Lamb[70] and also as the one who mounts in triumph riding on the clouds.[71] The believers are a royal priesthood who meet with God.[72] There are also the references to 'my Father's House'.[73] While *Sound of Living Waters* uses apocalyptic imagery only fleetingly, in *Songs of Fellowship* it will become the dominant theme.

---

[68] *SLW* 88.
[69] *SLW* 93.
[70] *SLW* 34.
[71] *SLW* 34.
[72] *SLW* 95.
[73] *SLW* 87.

Eight

Marching to Intimacy: *Songs of Fellowship*, Graham Kendrick and *Songs of the Vineyard*

The symbolic world of *Songs of Fellowship Book One* represents another shift in charismatic spirituality. Here, in the songs of the house churches, we engage in a restored Old Testament vision of the temple and the people praising the enthroned Christ.[1] Around the temple there are 'the nations' who are to be won and conquered by the praises of God's people.

It is this restorationist vision which also forms the backdrop to Graham Kendrick's Make Way material found in *The Graham Kendrick Songbook Volume 2*. Here the witness of the church is invoked through the public expression of faith in marching. Yet, even as the marching was at its height, a new and more personal style of worship was to start to gain strength. This was linked to John Wimber.

Through Wimber's ministry a new emphasis upon worship was to become common in many churches and it was characterised by a further shift in way that God was encountered in worship. This can be summed up by the phrase intimacy. Wimber focused on the way that praise and worship grew towards intimate moments in the presence of God. These were expressed in metaphors drawn from the private worlds of romance and sexual encounter.

---

[1] For more on restorationism see Walker, *Restoring the Kingdom*.

Songs of Fellowship Volume 1

Strange as it may seem, the first volume of *Songs of Fellowship* contains hardly any references to the earthly life of Jesus. There is little or no reference to the incarnation of Christ, no song that deals with the ministry of Jesus, nor are there any which deal with his teaching, or which speak about his healing ministry. Incredibly, events of the passion are also barely recorded.

One quite remarkable song seems to suggest that the historical Christ is something of a distraction from spiritual experience in the present. 'Jesus, come closer to me'[2] speaks about an encounter with Jesus in the present moment. To emphasise the immediacy of the experience, the song says that Jesus will no longer be just a historical or factual figure, because they can only be known in the present.[3] The humanity and life of Jesus is thus bypassed. Instead, a vision of the risen and ascended Lord who reigns on high is favoured. This vision is the basis for the dominant themes within the song collection. 'He is Lord' speaks of the risen Christ to whom all people will bow and confess that 'Jesus Christ is Lord'.[4]

In 'The name of Jesus is higher than any other' the writer recounts the names of Jesus – 'Lord', 'Counsellor', 'Prince of Peace', 'Wonderful', 'Mighty God'.[5] These names again emphasise the transcendent powerful nature of God. In this sense, Jesus and 'God' become somewhat interchangeable as each carry the connotation of majesty and enthroned power; thus, Christ the Lord is referred to as 'our King'.[6] Worship is an expression of joy and love for the one who is both Lord and King.[7] The worship of the believer is to be a 'sweet sweet sound' in 'the ear' for Jesus.[8]

---

[2] *SF* 67.
[3] *SF* 67.
[4] *SF* 36.
[5] *SF* 37.
[6] *SF* 17.
[7] *SF* 49.
[8] *SF* 49.

Praise is something to be sung, 'with feeling' according to the rubric of 'I love you, Lord'.[9] The worship of the people, however, is also said to, 'build a throne' for Jesus the King. 'Jesus we enthrone you' speaks of the praises of the people raising Christ onto a throne built from the worship of the people. Worship in this sense builds a throne for Christ.'[10] Jesus on the throne is 'clothed in his righteousness' and the worshipper is to give him 'glory and honour' and bow before him.[11] That Jesus reigns is to be seen as a reason for rejoicing and the believer is encouraged to 'give all the glory to him'.[12]

While Jesus is seen as enthroned as King and Lord of all, this does not mean that *Songs of Fellowship* presents him as entirely distant from Christians. Jesus lives in the believer. This identification is such that, 'It is no longer I that liveth, but Christ who lives in me'.[13]

There is also an almost sickly sweet sentimentality in the way that many of the songs speak of Jesus. He is 'lovely', 'pure' and 'kind'.[14] According to 'My Lord, you are so good to me'[15] Jesus is, 'sweet as honey', and 'more lovely than the lilies'. The portrayal of Jesus in these terms, perhaps, replaces the affection often found in the way that the humanity of Christ is dealt with in the previous songbooks. 'Jesus how lovely' does, however, record in passing the fact that Jesus died and rose again. Such references are nearly always somewhat fleeting and almost without fail they are treated in relation to the benefits of the cross for the individual. An example of this is David Mansell's 'Jesus is Lord'.[16] This song manages to cover the basic elements of the Christian story, but it does so, in common with much of the

---

[9] *SF* 49.
[10] *SF* 86.
[11] *SF* 26.
[12] *SF* 30.
[13] *SF* 56.
[14] *SF* 68.
[15] *SF* 94.
[16] *SF* 71.

material in *Songs of Fellowship*, almost in caricature. The pain of the cross is given a mention, as is the incarnation, but the passion of the crucifixion lies somewhat hidden in the rhymes and phrases, which in many ways echo those found in *Youth Praise*. The benefits of the death of Christ, in contrast, are to be celebrated. Forgiveness, according to 'I get so excited, Lord', is a matter for exuberant dancing, hand-raising and singing.[17] Jesus as friend features with some frequency in *Songs of Fellowship*; however, it is the constant love of Jesus, and his presence with the believer, which is a matter for thanksgiving rather than *Youth Praise*'s vision of a companion on a rough and tough walk of faith.[18]

The King Jesus enthroned on his people's praises seems to inspire songs which, even though they were all written in Britain during the 1980s, express themselves in a curious Old Testament imagery. The use of Old Testament metaphor is compounded by a style of lyric that is reminiscent of the King James Version of the Bible. Words such as 'magnify', 'acclaim' and 'ascribe' appear regularly. This self-conscious archaic use of expression is linked to a particular vision of the people of God. The people of God are those who 'enter his gates' and 'enter his courts'. This is a vision based upon the Jerusalem Temple.[19] To be in the 'House of the Lord' is to be purified, refined like gold.[20] The people of God are pictured in worship as being in this spiritual temple. The servants of God stand and serve at night in the temple. Here, in the House of the Lord, they lift up their hands in the holy place and bless the Lord.[21] There is a mystical encounter with God in the temple, for here it is that the 'royal priesthood' worship and it is 'within the veil' where they can look upon the face of God.[22] Here, again, they are portrayed as lifting holy hands and blessing

---

[17] *SF* 44.
[18] *SF* 117, 102.
[19] *SF* 62.
[20] *SF* 70.
[21] *SF* 15.
[22] *SF* 155.

the Lord.[23] The royal priesthood is also described as a 'holy nation'.[24]

Alongside the imagery of the temple, and closely associated with it, there is the metaphor of Zion, the city of God. Believers are encouraged to take time out and walk around the walls of the city of God. Setting down their tools, they can contemplate what God is doing and give the glory to Jesus the King.[25] Elsewhere, the labourers are described as the stones in the wall of the city.[26] The city is enclosed by fire and built out of living stones.[27] The close identification of those singing the songs and the work of God is expressed in the song, 'I want to sing about Jesus'.[28] This song, again, bypasses the earthly life of Christ almost entirely. Singing about Jesus, according to this song, means describing what he is doing today in his kingdom, and his kingdom are the people of God. The blessing that is abroad is identified with the kingdom and it is seen in those who are holy, washed and free.[29]

In *Songs of Fellowship*, the Christian story is arranged around this central vision of the people of God gathered in the temple. Jesus is the Lord enthroned on high on his people's praises. It is a continuing theme that believers find safety and security within this temple environment.[30] The city and temple imagery are associated with escape from a threatening outside world. Dwelling in the courts of the Lord offers the worshipper finds refuge. Outside, many may fall to the right and to the left, but God is our shelter. So good is it in 'Thy House' that a believer may desire permanent residence. Sheltering under the wings, it is possible to imagine living in the temple 'forever'.[31]

---

[23] *SF* 16.
[24] *SF* 14.
[25] *SF* 17.
[26] *SF* 17.
[27] *SF* 98.
[28] *SF* 17.
[29] *SF* 60.
[30] *SF* 145.
[31] *SF* 33.

Closely connected with the interest in safety and security is the treatment of the Fatherhood of God. 'Abba, Father'[32] asks that God will let the believer be 'yours and yours alone', that his or her heart may never, 'grow cold'. 'Father' represents a dependable relationship into whose hands family, friends, our past and our future may be placed.[33] In the family of the church, God is Father and, as 'We shall be as one' says, we are all 'sons'.

The use of the masculine sons without the feminine daughters is typical of the treatment of gender in many of the songs. Indeed, *Songs of Fellowship* presents as a fiercely masculine book, at times choosing lines such as, 'we are all your sons', where 'sons and daughters' would scan just as easily.

Outside of this secure relationship with the Father, outside of the temple and outside of the city, the royal priesthood are ringed by fire and 'the nations'. It is primarily in these terms that *Songs of Fellowship* deals with missiology and the wider non-Christian world. The nations will eventually come to Mount Zion and offer their praise to God.[34] The nations are in need of healing[35] and they are thirsty.[36]

Closely related to the nations is the use of the metaphor 'the land'. The people of power will 'move through this land by my Spirit'.[37] In the land, the church will be built by God, and it will be strong and ready. Eventually, the church will 'march upon the land'. God's own army are the children of God's Son. This army, when it moves as a body, will be able to claim the land which God's mighty hand has set before it.[38] The Promised Land is right at the feet of the church, and they are to take it, and build a New Jerusalem

---

[32] *SF* 1.
[33] *SF* 21.
[34] *SF* 91.
[35] *SF* 48.
[36] *SF* 13.
[37] *SF* 25.
[38] *SF* 142.

upon it, according to 'The promised land'.[39] This conquering metaphor is taken further in, 'I hear the sound of rustling'.[40] This song portrays the present time as one where the church, which was once asleep, is now starting to awake. The watchmen on the towers are ready to answer the call. The climax is an apocalyptic encounter. Where the church is likened to a body of soldiers prepared for war. With the lead of the spirit believers will be commanded to rise as a mighty army and the devils will 'see and hear for their time is at hand'.[41]

The Graham Kendrick Songbook Volume 2

The Graham Kendrick Songbook Volume 2 shares a number of themes with *Songs of Fellowship* but these are located within a more considered emphasis on the church. In these songs, it is the church which forms the starting point for the treatment of the Christian story. 'All heaven waits'[42] speaks of the need for the church to wake up and pray. If the church would pray, victories would be won. The Spirit will fill the mouth of the church when it wakes up and starts to pray and then the church may place its feet on 'Satan's ground'.[43]

The waking church is putting off the old things, because God is doing a new thing.[44] A highway is being made in the wilderness, rivers flood the desert and, from these, 'My chosen people can drink'.[45] The songs locate the church as being central to the activity of God. The people are 'chosen' and provided for, and, when they start to 'wake up', exciting things will happen.

There is a direct challenge to the people of God in

---

[39] *SF* 126.
[40] *SF* 48.
[41] *SF* 48.
[42] *GK* 9.
[43] *GK* 9.
[44] *GK* 12.
[45] *GK* 12.

particular to 'pray'. The healing of our land depends on the prayer of the church. So believers must humble themselves and seek God; it is through repentance that healing will come.[46] These lyrics, which are based on 2 Chronicles 7:14, imply that the spiritual and, perhaps, moral and political well-being of society lies in the hands of the people of God.

The church, however, is prone to failure. 'O Lord, the clouds are gathering',[47] is a dark vision of storm clouds with the fire of judgement being imminent. God is appalled at floated laws and broken lives. In the face of this, the church seems weakened and in need of reviving.

All around there is sin and wickedness. The streets are full of sin and dark powers are 'poised to flood' these streets. Yet, the love of the Lord will 'reclaim lives' and 'sweep away sin'. When this happens, the kingdom will have come.[48] Again, the church is challenged to wake up, and to allow God to 'reclaim' lives. 'Tell me, why do you weep?'[49] is a vision of eschatological hope. The King will come, the feast is ready and the end of the age is coming. The church has a profound role to play in the end times, and this should change what happens in the present. Believers are invited to view themselves as 'the Lord's invited'. They are chosen and God delights in them.[50]

This realisation of an eschatological hope is a motivation for faithful, and risky, Christian living in the present. The hope of the coming of Christ must transform the sleeping church and draw it on to action. Of course, one suggestion is, March for Jesus.

The march material written by Kendrick offers a particular understanding of God's interaction with the world. 'Make Way'[51] speaks of Jesus the King, who arrives in splendour. The gates should be flung wide and Christ welcomed into

---

[46] *GK* 16.
[47] *GK* 25.
[48] *GK* 25.
[49] *GK* 28.
[50] *GK* 28.
[51] *GK* 1.

our lives. This is a call for all to worship the King. 'Let God arise'[52] has a more combative theme. God will arise and 'his enemies will be scattered'. The enemies flee, but the righteous are glad. These songs see the parading of worship as a sign of God's activity in the world, generally portrayed as the breaking in of the kingdom of God. The song 'We declare that the kingdom of God is here'[53] makes these claims explicit. The kingdom of God is 'among you', miracles can be seen – the blind see, the deaf hear and all sickness is banished. All of this is evidence that Jesus is King.[54]

There is a close association, if not a causal connection, between these declarations and the marching of Christian people. Marching enacts, in a prophetic way, the advent of God. It is in this context that the sovereignty of God the creator is to be asserted. In the song, 'The Earth is the Lords (and everything in it)',[55] God is portrayed as the maker of all things, and everything belongs to him. According to the song, the proper response is for 'rebels to bow down'. 'We believe'[56] and 'Jesus put this song into our hearts'[57] offer an explanation of the creedal belief-structure and the fellowship of those marching. 'The Lord is Marching Out',[58] however, describes the church as an army marching out 'with dancing'. With this martial metaphor Kendrick uses language similar to some of that found in *Songs of Fellowship*. Rebellion brings 'the sword'.[59] The church is seen as 'royal diadem' and 'The nations will see your righteousness, and all kings will see your glory'.[60] The church, however, may also experience suffering, but this will serve to display 'the glories of her Christ'.

Kendrick's treatment of the Jesus of the Christian story is

---

[52] *GK* 3.
[53] *GK* 2.
[54] *GK* 2.
[55] *GK* 4.
[56] *GK* 5.
[57] *GK* 6.
[58] *GK* 7.
[59] *GK* 11.
[60] *GK* 13.

related to his concern for the church. 'Lord, the light of Your Love'[61] presents Jesus as a light shining in the darkness. Better known as 'Shine, Jesus, Shine' the song invokes Jesus as the Light of the World to shine in the land, bringing in the Father's glory. The Spirit is called upon to 'blaze', to set hearts on fire and make the rivers to flow. All of this will bring grace and mercy to the nations.[62] The presence of Jesus is seen as 'awesome', a 'radiance' and a 'brightness'. The light of Jesus consumes our darkness.

'May the fragrance' offers similar abstract notions of Jesus.[63] Here Jesus is described as a 'lovely fragrance' that fills 'this place'. The glory of Jesus fills his church, and the beauty of Jesus fills 'my life'.

The cross of Jesus is rarely referred in this collection of songs. 'Jesus is King'[64] presents a vision of Jesus enthroned on high as 'King of kings and Lord of lords'. The 'hosts of darkness are under His Feet' because of his death on the cross.

The only song in the collection that deals at length with the humanity of Christ comes in the short section of children's songs.[65]

The basic pattern of the people of God meeting with their conquering King, Jesus, and declaring his Lordship amongst the nations predominates in this collection. Mission is primarily presented in these triumphalistic terms.

This emphasis is balanced somewhat by references to justice and social concern. An example of this is 'Come now, let us reason together'.[66] The Lord calls his people to account concerning their sins. They may be 'as scarlet' but they can be made 'white as snow'. The challenge is straightforward. The believer must wash him- or herself

---

[61] *GK* 20.
[62] *GK* 20.
[63] *GK* 22.
[64] *GK* 17.
[65] *GK* 30.
[66] *GK* 11.

now and do away with evil deeds. In place of evil, they should do what is right, defending the 'helpless and the poor' and restoring justice.[67]

Songs of the Vineyard Volume 1

The Christian story is interpreted in *Songs of the Vineyard* through the metaphor of an intimate relationship with God. Intimacy is the main characteristic of charismatic worship in these songs. According to Wimber, 'These are not songs about Jesus, they are songs to Jesus: intimate and personal.'[68]

Songs offered to Jesus mean that the most frequently used term is 'You'. All three persons of the Trinity – Father, Son and Holy Spirit – are all called by the intimate term 'You'.[69] The sentiments expressed are close to those used in popular music for the romantic relationship between a man and a woman. Jesus is spoken of as someone to love. Echoing popular song the believer speaks of loving Jesus, 'most of all because you are you'.[70]

Romantic metaphors are found in a number of other songs. The believer wants to be 'closer to thee'[71] and he or she can feel they are being drawn closer. The Lord is calling and they are coming closer. There is no one in the world like the Lord. The sentimental and sweet references to Jesus found in *Songs of Fellowship* are repeated in *Songs of the Vineyard*. Jesus is lovely, but this is someone who we can 'come home to'.[72] Here it is evident that the songwriters are using the kind of language more usually used in romantic pop songs to speak of the relationship with Jesus – wanting to be closer, wanting to come home to a person. These are

---

[67] *GK* 11.
[68] Wimber quoted in *Songs of the Vineyard,* back page.
[69] *SV* 1, 6, 16, 17, 20, 21, 22, 23, 28, 27, 29, 31, 33, 36, 38, 40, 41, 42, 45, 47, 48, 49, 50.
[70] *SV* 21.
[71] *SV* 35.
[72] *SV* 38.

the kind of sentiments commonly associated with being in love or newly married. This aspect of the lyrical content of *Songs of the Vineyard* is seen clearly in 'Thank you for being'[73] where the worshipper expresses him or herself by singing 'Thank you for being just who you are'.[74]

The imagery, while generally remaining of a more idealistic nature, occasionally strays towards what could be interpreted as the more sexually explicit end of the spectrum. 'Lord, I'll seek after you'[75] speaks of the Lord as 'the only one that satisfies', as 'I draw near to you', I, 'Turn to kiss your face'. Kissing is fairly tame. The implications of being 'cover'd in your love', are a little more sexually ambiguous.[76]

Percy argues that the sexual imagery in Wimber's music connects to an ideology that is based on a sublimated eroticism.[77] 'You' in Wimber's songs, he argues, functions as a key metaphor of this ideology.[78] 'You', says Percy, first connotes a receptive lover. This relates to the paradox where God as 'you' may be aware of what the worshipper has to say before it is uttered. At the same time, 'You' fixes God, says Percy, as intimate and personal:[79] 'You is effective because it binds the community of feeling together, harmonises its desires, and permits little in the way of contradiction or paradox.'[80]

The intimacy of worship is the arena where the relationship between the believer and Jesus is celebrated and enacted. Jesus is 'always near, when we call'.[81] Praise is a sacrificial gift which involves offering ourselves in love to

---

[73] *SV* 45.
[74] *SV* 45.
[75] *SV* 34.
[76] *SV* 33.
[77] M. Percy 'Sweet Rapture: Subliminal Eroticism in Contemporary Charismatic Worship', *Theology and Sexuality* 6 (1997), 71.
[78] M. Percy, *Words, Wonders and Power: Understanding Contemporary Christian Fundamentalism and Revivalism*, 71.
[79] Percy, *Words*, 74.
[80] Percy, *Words*, 74.
[81] *SV* 16.

God and falling down upon our knees before him. In turn, the worshipper meets with God in the intimate space. The Spirit 'moves upon' the believer. With hand lifted to the throne, God meets the deepest need.[82] In worship, the encounter with the Spirit brings healing and the meeting of needs. The believer can speak of Gods power being 'on me now'.[83] 'I receive you' is a song about the moment of worship. God's touch is felt 'right now'. It is at the very moment of worship that encounter and personal transformation take place. This is a power encounter as well as the enactment of a loving relationship. The believer is invited to sing that God is touching them at that very moment and they can feel God's touch. The touch of God comes with a revelation of power.[84] The effects of this encounter are expressed in a number of different ways – as healing,[85] as a breaking of chains,[86] as knowing love,[87] as satisfaction,[88] as a calling,[89] as filling,[90] as a touch.[91] The act of worship is a time where problems and pain can be offered to God. Lifting hands to God and surrendering to him we can give him all our 'years of pain'.[92] The Lord mends broken hearts[93] by touching the worshipper from inside. The heart is also likened to clay that can be moulded by God.[94]

Percy identifies 'Lord' as the second key metaphor in Wimber's worship music. 'Lord' connotes power and omnipotence and is a semantic problem-solving device.[95] Percy argues that 'Lord' linked with 'You' creates an ideology

---

[82] *SV* 18.
[83] *SV* 20.
[84] *SV* 20.
[85] *SV* 20.
[86] *SV* 18.
[87] *SV* 31.
[88] *SV* 34.
[89] *SV* 35.
[90] *SV* 37.
[91] *SV* 36.
[92] *SV* 39.
[93] *SV* 36.
[94] *SV* 3.
[95] Percy, *Words*, 75.

which connects love and power in Wimber's music.[96]

Love, however, is also expected of the worshipper. This can be illustrated in the way that the image of 'the heart' is very closely linked to the idea of offering love to God.[97] 'Hold me, Lord'[98] asks the Lord to 'Hold me in your arms' and 'touch my heart'. The love that the worshipper offers is welcome to the God who visits in power.[99]

In *Songs of the Vineyard* the worshipper and God are linked by this drama of a loving intimacy and exchange. This songbook places the enactment of the gospel within the arena of intimate worship. The one exception to this is, 'You are the King who reigns',[100] where a more objective treatment of the Christian story is presented.

That said, the events of the life of Jesus are generally outside of the dominant paradigm in *Songs of the Vineyard*. More usually, Jesus is presented in abstract terms. Jesus is the one who 'enfolds us in his arms' like a 'sweet perfume'.[101] He is the one who is able to offer healing through his 'mighty touch'.[102] He is to be worshipped as 'the Lamb'.[103] He is worthy of praise and love.[104] He will fill his lambs[105] and he is the King who reigns.[106]

Outside of an encounter with God in worship there seems little, if any, imperative towards mission. 'I'm yours'[107] does imply that discipleship might involve some kind of action. This action is presented as a sacrifice. There is no attempt to develop what this offering might be outside of the encounter in worship. The Spirit is invoked

---

[96] Percy, *Words*, 76.
[97] *SV* 6.
[98] *SV* 10.
[99] *SV* 31.
[100] *SV* 48.
[101] *SV* 5.
[102] *SV* 7.
[103] *SV* 24.
[104] *SV* 29, 30.
[105] *SV* 39.
[106] *SV* 24, 22.
[107] *SV* 22.

to guide the church in 'Come, Holy Spirit',[108] but, again, where the Spirit might lead, and which way the believer should walk, remains outside the scope of the song collection. 'I am a wounded soldier'[109] speaks of the wounds that come from being involved in 'the fight'. Once again, what exactly this struggle might entail appears to be subsumed by the desire to receive healing and binding of the wounds.

---

[108] *SV* 4.
[109] *SV* 15.

Nine

The Heart of Worship:
The Survivor Songbook

The Survivor Songbook[1] is part of a series of songbooks published in relation to the Soul Survivor Festival. The songbooks focus almost exclusively on songs written by the artists appearing at the festivals. This means that, unlike *Youth Praise* or *Songs of Fellowship*, they do not collect material from a wide range of sources. The first collection of songs linked to the festival was published in 1996 under the title, *The Way of the Cross*.[2] *The Survivor Songbook* incorporates much of the material from this collection and subsequent songbooks. So while *The Way of the Cross* contained just forty-four songs, the 2001 songbook had 200 songs. The songbook was compiled by Les Moir[3] and it featured material from all of the key worship leaders who had appeared at the Soul Survivor festivals over the previous ten years.

The songbook marks a significant departure in format in that it does not print musical notation. Instead, the music is supplied on a CD-Rom that comes with the book. The CD-Rom also contains lyrics that can be used to create OHP acetates and to download onto computers for use with a video projector. This means that as they are printed in the

---

[1] Survivor/Kingsway 2001.
[2] There were songbooks published earlier but these carried the New Wine rather than the Soul Survivor label.
[3] Thanks to Matt Redman for putting me right on this point.

book the songs appear simply as lyrics with guitar chords only. The chords are given in a tablature form at the top of the page. In addition, each song is referenced to the relevant recording. In this way, the worship leader can listen to the song on the worship CD and, using the chords, it is a simple matter to work out how to reproduce the music. This method of communication bypasses the need to read musical notation.

The Survivor Songbook has a distinctive voice. In part, this has come from the focus on a small number of songwriters. The link to the one festival is also significant because a number of key metaphors and images which recur in the songs are shared between songwriters. It would be possible to discuss the distinctive contribution of Martyn Layzel, Matt Redman, Tim Hughes or Paul Oakley to *The Survivor Songbook*, but here I focus on the themes that tie these writers together.

Heart

A key metaphor in *The Survivor Songbook* is the idea of heart. There is a heart to worship. This is what happens when the music fades and the believer comes to God.[4] This heart is located in acknowledging that worship is all about Jesus. Heart here relates to the essence or the deepest truth of worship. It is possible to drift from this 'heart' to be distracted even by worship itself. We can make worship something that it should not be but this is a mistake because the pure, essential nature of worship relates to Jesus. This is its heart.[5]

At the same time, Jesus also has a heart. The heart of the Lord is something that we should search for.[6] Knowing God's heart will help us to steer our lives. Heart in this sense relates to the feeling, sensing and willing nature of

---

[4] *SS* 181.
[5] *SS* 181.
[6] *SS* 104.

God. To approach God's heart is to experience the grace of God who gives and gives.[7] This is the heart of the Father, the merciful graciousness of the Lord. God's heart has a centre and it is this heart that we must continually seek.[8] The language of the heart is thus the language of an embodied feeling. The God who 'has our heart' receives the emotional centre of the believer.[9] Searching for God's heart is the response of one lover to another. God holds our heart in his hands and we are committed to seeking after him. To this end, our heart is fixed after his emotional and gracious 'heart'. The believer focuses the eyes of their heart towards the object of their love.[10]

The heart of the believer can be described as full and burdened. 'Here I am once again' says that no matter what 'state' the believer's heart may be in, through the encounter of worship they will approach God. The heart is then said to be 'poured out' in love to God. Pouring out the heart as well as speaking of the 'love' of the believer also expresses that they need God and they are thankful to God.[11] Pouring out the heart to God is not just offloading problems; it is also an act of praise. We pour out our heart to God when we say that he is wonderful.[12] This heart of worship sings with praise; as the believer offers all of themselves they offer their heart.[13] The Vineyard Song 'Hungry: Falling on my knees'[14] describes the believer as broken, empty and hungry. Acknowledging this need, the believer 'runs' towards a God whose arms are open in welcome. The believer may be weary but God's love does not run dry. With an attitude of waiting, the believer falls to his or her knees. Here the believer offers him- or herself. Here in the

---

[7] *SS* 25.
[8] *SS* 25.
[9] *SS* 104.
[10] *SS* 17.
[11] *SS* 31.
[12] *SS* 31.
[13] *SS* 52.
[14] *SS* 37.

moment of encounter, honesty and intimacy the confession is made. Jesus is all the believer's 'heart is living for'.[15]

The heart of the believer not only has eyes, it also has music. The heart reveals itself through the singing of songs. 'Lord, hear the music of my heart' speaks of the Lord as the ruler of the believer's heart and the lover of the soul. Pouring out the heart in worship comes through the confession of the closeness of the Lord. At the same time, the worship of the believer is a demonstration of love for Jesus. Such worship itself may be said to bless the heart of Jesus.[16] Worship is the secret place where Jesus and the believer share their intimate connection. By drawing close to God in this way, the heart can be said to 'burn' with a fire. This is a fire that can burn for all eternity.[17] God also is said to be a fire that consumes. The fire of God can search our hearts and see if they are pure.[18] This pure heart is God's heart, which is given to us according to 'Search me, O God'.[19] Here, again, the heart of God is linked to God's grace and mercy. So, to share God's heart is to be connected to God's mercy and compassion.[20]

In 'I'm giving you my heart'[21] the believer surrenders themselves to God. In singing the songs they 'give up their heart'. Here the heart is connected with everything that is within. Giving up the heart is perhaps painful; certainly it lacks security because here the believer is in God's hands. Giving themselves up in this way is risky, precisely because they do not know what such a gift of the heart may entail. This is an unconditional gift for the believer. Giving up the heart means that they abandon a pride in their life and there is some suggestion that what may come may be a sharing in Christ's pain.[22] Here the heart of worship is

---

[15] *SS* 37.
[16] *SS* 97.
[17] *SS* 116.
[18] *SS* 139.
[19] *SS* 139.
[20] *SS* 139.
[21] *SS* 56.

located in a notion of the sacrificial giving of praise to God. This is another of the key themes in *The Survivor Songbook*.

Giving Praise as a Sacrifice of Love

Singing praise is often seen as a gift offered to God. 'My Jesus, my saviour'[23] speaks of praise as something to which the believer will give all their days. This praise should never cease, it should be for all of our days and it should take every breath that we have. In particular, singing of the work of God's hands is identified as the focus for this praise.[24]

Giving honour to God in praise and worship is a hard task. How can we offer God anything? In 'O sacred King'[25] this idea is explored further. It is a mystery deep within the universe that this holy God should welcome a soul 'like me'.[26] The believer who draws near may have little more than 'broken love'. So, as they come close through singing a song of love they must bow their head while they cry out with thirst.[27]

'My Jesus, my saviour'[28] also speaks of the Lord who is incomparable. There is no one like Jesus. The 'mighty love' of God becomes, for the believer, a tower and a refuge. In Jesus, the believer finds their strength. At the sight of this, it is not just believers who will bow down in praise; nature is also enlisted in God's praise. Mountains and seas will join in the act of worship. Singing praise to God in this way connects to the wider of creation.[29]

Singing to God is not just an individual thing. To sing from the heart is an act of glory and this is echoed by

---

[22] *SS* 56.
[23] *SS* 113.
[24] *SS* 113.
[25] *SS* 121.
[26] *SS* 121.
[27] *SS* 106.
[28] *SS* 113.
[29] *SS* 113.

heaven and earth. 'Sing to the Lord: Awaken the dawn'[30] encourages singing as the means to give God what he is due. Singing comes from the soul and from the mind; the believer also sings with all of their strength. Giving all of ourselves in this way in worship brings a connection to the very core of creation. The songs of believers 'awaken the dawn'.[31]

Giving all to God in praise links directly to lives lived in praise to God.[32] This link is made explicit in 'Many are the words we speak: Now we live the life'.[33] There are a great many songs sung, and many words spoken. Now there is a challenge, we must be prepared to live the life. Living the life brings something that is 'real' and 'true'.[34] To live the life is to go the extra mile, to turn the other cheek. It may even mean sharing in Christ's suffering.

Living the life comes about through the sacrifice of the heart. 'When the music fades: The heart of worship'[35] makes this clear. It is not just songs that are brought to God. With the song, the believer brings their heart. Coming to God, the believer may be searched and examined. Indeed, the Lord looks into the believer's heart. In this moment of intimacy, Jesus is told that though the believer is weak and poor, everything they have is God's.[36]

'I lift you high, you must increase'.[37] Lifting Jesus high is related to bowing down. The believer asks how high Jesus can go and how low they should bow. Taking the words John the Baptist spoke about Jesus,[38] this song speaks of the believer bowing down and of adoration as the decrease of the self in relation to the glorification of Christ. Sacrifice in praise relates directly to the treatment of the cross in the songs.

---

[30] *SS* 144.
[31] *SS* 141.
[32] *SS* 141.
[33] *SS* 105.
[34] *SS* 105.
[35] *SS*181.
[36] *SS* 181.
[37] *SS* 51.
[38] John 3:30.

The Way of the Cross

Singing songs of praise, the worshipper is blessed by the blood that was shed on the cross. In 'Thank you for the blood'[39] the experience of blessing is linked to Christ's sacrifice and his blood. The songs of freedom find their origin in the battle that Jesus has won on the cross. This is why these are songs of victory. The blood of Christ brings liberty. In 'The cross has said it all'[40] the celebration of Christ's victory is linked to the love of God expressed in the suffering of Jesus. The cross speaks to the believer of God's love. Turning to the cross, there is an assurance of God's love for the worshipper.

At the cross, Christ is seen as paying the price for human sin. There is a great 'cost' to be paid. In 'I will love you for the Cross'[41] this transaction is spoken of as an over-whelming mystery. Jesus was broken and beaten, wounded and rejected. Yet his punishment means that the believer 'goes free'.[42] The cross inspires love for Jesus. His death brings life and his blood brings us 'home'.[43] The sacrifice forms the focus of intimate worship. In 'Jesus Christ: Once again'[44] the sacrifice of Christ is expressed as a 'pouring out'. This is a gift of life that inspires the worshipper to wonder.[45] So worship is seen as a moment where, once again, we look upon this sacrificial gift of God. To look in this way upon the cross makes us in turn 'broken inside'.[46]

Brokenness in worship is often spoken of as coming to the foot of the cross. Christ's pouring out inspires a response of sacrifice so once again we pour out our lives. 'I'm giving you my heart: Surrender'[47] connects waiting at the cross to

---

[39] *SS* 147.
[40] *SS* 148.
[41] *SS* 78.
[42] *SS* 78.
[43] *SS* 78.
[44] *SS* 83.
[45] *SS* 83.
[46] *SS* 83.
[47] *SS* 56.

surrender and self-giving. Jesus is the King and the believer is to lay down their life and give all that is within them to the Lord.[48] Waiting at the cross is a moment of self-examination and exposure, surrendering all. It is the realisation of the inadequacy of the believer that makes for the brokenness at the cross. The sacrifice of Christ leads to an understanding of the weight and extent of human sin. Sin in *The Survivor Songbook* is often expressed in related to the metaphor of shame.

In 'Praises: At the foot of the cross'[49] the death of Christ takes away shame and the believer is given clothes of white.[50] The death of Christ is a scorning of shame to rescue the believer.[51] 'Here I am, a sinner free'[52] speaks of the pardon and freedom that comes when Christ makes the believer's heart his own. As this acceptance comes, the believer feels like a leper who has been set free. 'Lost and dirty' the believer has been found. Though 'stained by sin' they are cleansed by the Holy God who is upon the throne. 'I will offer up my life'[53] speaks of worship as the pouring out of the oil of life. Surrendering every part the Lord receives the sacrifice of the believer's broken heart.[54] The picture is of someone who is emotionally or physically wounded. It is this person who offers his or her very hurt to God. The tension posed by the song is that the worshipper is really unable to 'bring' anything to Jesus. Even singing does not bring what is required.[55] The thankful worshipper can bring nothing, because Jesus has given him or her everything. Jesus died and 'paid the great cost' of 'death on the cross' and, as a result, 'You took all my shame away, there defeated my sin'.[56] The offering in worship is a response to the love of Jesus and in particular

---

[48] *SS* 56.
[49] *SS* 135.
[50] *SS* 135.
[51] *SS* 45.
[52] *SS* 29.
[53] *SS* 80.
[54] *SS* 80.
[55] *SS* 80.
[56] *SS* 80.

to his death on the cross. 'Jesus Christ: Once again'[57] describes the act of worship as a meditation on the sacrifice of Christ. The worshipper has wondered many times about the 'gift of love' and says, 'I'm in that place once again'. The idea of place links directly to the idea of intimacy in the songs.

Intimacy, Place, Coming Before and Now

Intimacy relates to encounter with God in the present. In 'I come to you: Here with me now'[58] the believer approaches the 'Lord of all hope'. He is the giver of life, the Prince of peace. The believer is to draw near and to feel the presence of God. Although it is acknowledged that God is always present there is a desire to know that this is so 'here and now'.[59] Reference to the present moment locates this intimacy within the act of singing. In this sense, the 'now' connects to the experience of those currently singing the song. Today those singing the song are coming to God.[60] This is immediate and made present by those who use the song in worship. Salvation itself is given a similar kind of immediacy. 'I Love you, Lord: Joy'[61] speaks of the Lord who saves the believer's life 'today'.[62]

The immediacy of today connects with the idea of 'place'. 'Oh, lead me'[63] is a prayer that God will lead the believer to the place where God may be found. This is the cross where the first meeting took place. Brought to their knees, the believer can feel the presence of God. Indeed, the experience is so vivid that they can feel the breath of God.[64] This intimacy is also expressed as gazing on the face of

---

[57] *SS* 83.
[58] *SS* 41.
[59] *SS* 41.
[60] *SS* 42.
[61] *SS* 54.
[62] *SS* 54.
[63] *SS* 125.
[64] *SS* 125.

God. Here the idea of being within the veil, in the holy, intimate space where God may be seen and adored is used. For 'One thing I ask'[65] the place within the veil is characterised by purity. Here we can 'search behind the eyes of love' and the light will pour over us and in the light we are changed. 'Lord, you have my heart'[66] speaks of God revealing his face in a show of glory. This is all said to happen 'here'. The act of singing is directly related to the glimpse of God's glory.

The place of worship is a wonderful sight. The worshipper longs to see this inner place of intimacy. This is none other than the dwelling place of God. In 'How lovely is your dwelling place: Better is one day',[67] one day in the house of God is said to be better than a thousand days 'elsewhere'. Here the believer is asking to see the place where God dwells in his beauty. This is the place where the glory of God dwells.[68]

The place of worship is often spoken of as the throne of God. Here, before this throne, the believer is to bow down.[69] The confession that we belong to the Lord on the throne is an act of humble adoration. In 'We bow down at your throne, O Lord'[70] before the throne the believer gives themselves so that they may be 'yours and yours alone'.[71] In worship, the believer can be said to be at the feet of Jesus.[72] It is at these feet that the worshipper should lay their crown,[73] humbly coming to God on bended knee. In 'We bow our hearts'[74] the approach to God on the knees precedes the casting down of 'our idols'.[75] Coming to God

---

[65] *SS* 128.
[66] *SS* 104.
[67] *SS* 36.
[68] *SS* 36.
[69] *SS* 164.
[70] *SS* 164.
[71] *SS* 164.
[72] *SS* 167.
[73] *SS* 167.
[74] *SS* 165.
[75] *SS* 165.

on our knees indicates our need. We are hungry for God.[76]

Coming to God is about approaching the moment of intimacy in worship. The believer comes to God, 'just to be with you' and to hear your voice.[77] This is a moment of love and communication. In 'I have come to love you, Lord'[78] the believer sees the expression of love for God located in the singing of praise. God is worthy of praise and the believer longs to 'worship you'.[79] In return, God is said to have 'come' to heal a broken heart. In this mutual communication, the worshipper is said to 'cling to you'.[80] This intimacy is the one thing 'my heart is set upon',[81] every day to look upon God's beauty, to see God's glory and his heart.[82]

The experience of God's presence is also expressed as 'coming'.[83] Here the experience of falling on the floor is described as the coming of God. In this place, God came closer and closer, even closer than the air which the believer is breathing.[84] Here, in this place of intimacy, the believer experienced God call their name.[85] The presence of God is like a fire and a flame. It is like a river which can raise us off our feet and sweep us away.[86] Walking along the street, or in the quiet of our room, we can experience this place. Here we feel God's love, we sense his touch.[87]

Jesus Christ, Lover of the Soul

In 'What a friend I've found: Jesus friend for ever',[88] Jesus is a friend who is said to be 'closer than a brother' and more

---

[76] *SS* 37.
[77] *SS* 46.
[78] *SS* 46.
[79] *SS* 46.
[80] *SS* 46.
[81] *SS* 129.
[82] *SS* 65.
[83] *SS* 65.
[84] *SS* 65.
[85] *SS* 65.
[86] *SS* 137.
[87] *SS* 142.
[88] *SS* 175.

'intimate than lovers'. This is a friend whose touch can be felt and who is more faithful to the believer than a mother.[89] The love of Jesus can be felt not just for the believer, but also on behalf of those who have not found faith. 'Sometimes when I feel your love: I love your love'[90] speaks of the love of Jesus being so strong that the worshipper may 'burst'. Yet, this is a strong yearning which itself is an object of love. So the believer can sing 'I love your love'.[91]

The love of Jesus is overwhelming. To know that Jesus is near is a treasure. Worship is like being lost in the gaze of Jesus and it is at this time that the believer's 'heart sings with praise'.[92] In 'I love you'[93] these moments are linked by a Jesus who is saviour, lover and king. Worship is all about Jesus. In 'Jesus, lover of my soul: It's all about you'[94] the love of God is likened to a consuming fire. This fire comes from the gaze of Jesus who is the 'lover' of the believer's soul.[95] This is the Jesus who is desired by the worshipper. To be in the shining light of his eyes the believer can be said to be safe in his arms.[96]

The Spirit of Christ participates in these intimate moments. In 'I have come to love you, Lord'[97] it is the Spirit who will touch the believer and fill them with power and love'. 'I come running: Only you'[98] links Father, Son and Holy Spirit in the secret place of love. Thus, the thirsty and hungry worshipper may appeal to any person of the Trinity.[99] A similar trinitarian pattern is used in 'Moving with the Father: Joy'. Here the flowing power of love is recognised as the movement of Father, Son and Holy Spirit. As songs addressed to an intimate lover, they most often speak of God as 'you'.[100]

---

[89] *SS* 175.
[90] *SS* 142.
[91] *SS* 142.
[92] *SS* 52.
[93] *SS* 52.
[94] *SS* 86.
[95] *SS* 86.
[96] *SS* 87.
[97] *SS* 46.
[98] *SS* 40.
[99] *SS* 40.
[100] *SS* 1, 2, 5, 17, 45, 98.

Part Three

Worship: A Critical Appreciation

Ten

Worship and Culture

The worship story shows how the church changed its style of worship through the use of popular music. The energy behind these changes came from the desire to communicate an evangelical faith in the new youth culture of the 1960s and 1970s. What took place was a gradual 'contextualisation' of evangelical and charismatic expression in a new cultural form. It was this expression in a particular kind of music and through the use of contemporary forms of communication that enabled the charismatic movement to have such an impact upon the worship of the church in this country. Through the festivals, record companies, worship artists and, above all, the worship songs, we have been able to share in this new worship culture. All of this indicates the extent to which the expression of faith and worship in this popular cultural form has successfully helped the charismatic movement to spread.

If faith is to communicate it must be expressed in culture. Culture, however, is never neutral. As we express the faith, there are problems and contradictions that inevitably arise. We should never be surprised by this; it simply goes with the territory. As we explore new expressions of faith, new theological issues come to the surface. From a theological perspective, culture is best seen as a mixture of good and bad, useful and unhelpful. This means that as we use culture to express faith, aspects of the culture will fit well with what we are doing while some other characteristics of the culture will be problematic. To fail to acknowledge that there are weaknesses as well as strengths in any culture is to risk going down the road of syncretism. If we uncritically baptize a culture, we inevitably incorporate elements of cultural expression that are less than helpful to the true expression of the gospel.

The difficulty here is that the helpful and the not so helpful come as part of the same package. We may feel very positive about the charismatic worship scene. It is easy to get caught up in the exciting and ever changing culture of worship events, new songs and CD releases and fail to be critical or analytical in the way we use these new forms of expression The songs we sing may be a source of encouragement and even a way to encounter God. At the same time, however, the worship scene brings with it issues and problems. This becomes particularly significant if we reflect on the extent to which the songs we sing may be subtly changing the way we think about and experience the Christian faith. In Chapter Eleven we will look at the way that charismatic worship has been changed through the use of communication technology and the conventions of popular music culture. Chapter Twelve picks up on the theological significance of changes in song lyrics. In this chapter the more general question of contextualisation will be discussed in relation to contemporary forms of charismatic worship.

Faithful and Relevant

Christian worship, according to Graham Cray, should be 'in Spirit and in truth'.[1] Worship, therefore, he argues, must be in a process of continual revision and change, or

---

[1] G. Cray, 'Justice, Rock and the Renewal of Worship', in Robert Sheldon (ed.), *In Spirit and in Truth: Exploring Directions in Music in Worship Today*, 3.

renewal, inspired by the Holy Spirit. Cray develops his argument by discussing John 4:23–24: 'But the hour is coming, and is now here, when the true worshippers will worship the Father in spirit and truth, for the Father seeks such as these to worship him. God is spirit and those who worship him must worship in spirit and truth.'

He interprets the reference to 'truth' in this passage as meaning 'integrity'. Worship, Cray says, must have integrity to the whole message of Scripture and to the mission of the church. At the same time, it must strive to have integrity in relation to contemporary culture. Cray sees this as being, 'worship that is true and appropriate to the time, context and culture in which the gospel is being lived and proclaimed'.[2] It is the search for a style or styles of Christian expression that enables a connection to contemporary culture, both in terms of evangelism and worship, which has been the key motivation and value behind the rise of a mediated religious culture.

This idea can be seen to be at work in the 'gospel beat' groups as they developed *Buzz* magazine and MGO.[3] These developments were predicated on the need to use popular music as a means to attract young people to the church. *Youth Praise* also was conceived out of a desire to make available new songs which were closer to the youth culture of the 1960s so that they could be used in youth fellowships up and down the country. During the early 1970s, the style and music of the American Jesus Movement was originally adopted because it was seen as being evangelistically effective. The evangelistic imperative was the legitimating theological principle upon which these new developments were seen as desirable and possibly necessary. An example of this is the way that established Christian leaders began to support the Christian subculture. 1971 Billy Graham endorsed the new youth orientated 'Jesus Revolution': 'I have become convinced that the 'Jesus Revolution' is

---

[2] Cray, 'Justice', 3.
[3] See Chapter 4 for more on this

making a profound impact on the youth of America and shows all signs of spreading to other countries. One thing is certain Jesus can no longer be ignored . . .'[4]

In the UK Michael Green, who was then the Principal of St John's College, Nottingham, also backed these developments. Green recognised in the Jesus People the life and vitality of what he regarded as 'true' Christian believing. He contrasted the enthusiasm and commitment of the Jesus People to the domesticated comfortable religion found in many churches.[5] According to Green, 'The movement is spreading widely, in the States particularly. It may well be that the revival for which Christians have been praying has come outside the churches.'[6]

It was the desire to see faith as 'relevant', especially to young people, which gave legitimacy to the contextualisation of popular culture within evangelicalism. This incorporation of popular culture, however, was to bring about significant changes within worship.

Changing the Content and Form of Worship

The changes in worship that have characterised the charismatic movement have also been generated out of a search for relevance to contemporary culture. Carl Tuttle, one of the worship leaders linked to Wimber's Vineyard Fellowship, argued that, since the early days of renewal in the 1960s, charismatics have been seeking to change both the form and the content of Christian worship. These developments have come about, he says, 'not for the sake of change, but because of their desire to express their love for God in new and relevant ways'. It is this desire for new expressions of worship that has led to the increase in the numbers of songs being written and used all around the world.[7]

---

[4] Graham, *Jesus Generation*, 11.
[5] M. Green in Palms, *Jesus Kids*, 7.
[6] Green in Palms, *Jesus Kids*, 7.
[7] C. Tuttle, 'Foundations of Praise and Worship' in Sheldon (ed.), *In Spirit and in Truth*, 161.

Relevance is also a factor in what Steven calls 'accessibility'. Accessibility, he argued, is a key characteristic of the worship music growing out of the restoration movement. According to Steven, the music could be termed 'middle-of-the-road' or as having a 'Radio 2 feel'.[8] This was seen as being a virtue, by both Steven and by many within the movement, because middle-of-the-road locates this worship within a mass market. This meant that a greater number of people were likely to recognise their own cultural taste in the style of music used in charismatic worship. Writing in the 1980s, the restoration-linked worship leader, Dave Fellingham, also saw this aspect of contemporary charismatic worship as being of importance: 'The new songs have had a simple non-controversial "middle of the road" musical style. Their effectiveness has been demonstrated by the ease with which they are learned. Congregations are increasingly singing songs whose musical style identifies with their culture.'[9]

It is a mistake to focus exclusively on the introduction of particular forms of music into church life. Tuttle identified how it was not just the form of worship that was changed by the charismatic movement. As the form has changed, so has the content and meaning of worship itself. Contextualisation has been a welcome development but there have been problems along the way. Those within the charismatic movement have been very aware of some of these problems and they have sought to address them as they arise.

The Contradictions of Culture

The contextualisation of popular music into evangelical and charismatic religious life has not been without its problems. The sense of authenticity, or the truth, or the

---

[8] J. Steven, *Worship in the Restoration Movement*, 19.
[9] D. Fellingham, 'The Focus and Direction of Contemporary Worship', in Sheldon (ed.), *In Spirit and in Truth*.

genuineness, of both the production and the consumption of worship, has been placed under stress by the process of contextualisation. While advocating the adoption of new forms of music and ways of worship, many within charismatic evangelicalism express concerns that the movement may, at times, be in danger of losing integrity in worship. Authenticity is perceived as being threatened by the process of contextualisation. As a result of the assimilation of popular culture into the subculture of charismatic worship, some elements of this culture are experienced as contradictions. Contradictions may arise from behaviours, economic processes, advertising, representation, modes of expression, or technologies. A common feature, however, is that an element within popular culture which is natural and comfortable begins to be experienced as unnatural and uncomfortable when it is incorporated into Christian worship.

A major area of tension is related to the rate of change that the use of popular culture in worship has introduced into evangelical life. Pilavachi identifies an increasing number of 'trends' within worship: 'Recently, we in the church have had our fair share of chart toppers, ranging from 1995's fancy tribal worship (remember the sticks?), to the predicted revival that was due to land sometime in May 1997.'[10]

Pilavachi's tone indicates his reserve about such developments. From an earlier period Gunstone also expresses certain unease by talking about being, 'invaded by an astonishing upsurge in newly-created forms of music'.[11] Elsewhere, he describes how songs have a rapid turnover within the movement. So quickly do songs come into fashion and out again that worship groups and congregations have a repertoire which changes every year.[12] Songs in the 'hundreds and thousands appear and

---

[10] Pilavachi and Borlase, *Audience of One*, 16.
[11] J. Gunstone, *Pentecostal Anglicans*, 20.
[12] J. Gunstone, *A People for His Praise*, 37.

disappear within a few years'.[13] 'Christian songs, like so much else in the modern world, have become disposable.'[14] Other writers have also expressed an awareness of the problem of trying to keep up with the numbers of songs that emerge and are then disposed of. The restoration-linked worship leader, Chris Bowater, observed that, 'There is a real pressure to keep up to date with the latest songs.'[15]

A media generated and transmitted religious culture is one that is affected by the pace of change and communication, which is characteristic of contemporary culture. While there are more songs from which to choose, and many of these songs may be seen as being relevant, there is also a tendency for a rapidly changing consumer-based worship culture to itself appear less than genuine. The more involved and engaging the mediated cultural environment within which worship is constructed, the greater the possibility of a perceived threat to authenticity. An example of this is the experience of the Soul Survivor congregation, which is based in Watford.

In 1997 the community began to experience problems. To an outside observer the congregational worship would have probably been regarded as exemplary, says Pilavachi. There is little doubt that the worship would have been recognised as conforming to all of the latest trends in charismatic worship culture. The problem, as expressed by Pilavachi, was that 'people weren't relaxed'.[16] He continues by explaining that instead of focusing upon God, the leaders and the congregation had become intent on the external arrangements associated with worship. The congregation and the leaders had become, 'connoisseurs of worship instead of participants in it'. The quality of the worship was seen as being related to particular performers or individual songs. Those leading worship were being

[13] Gunstone, *Pentecostal Anglicans*, 211.
[14] Gunstone, *Pentecostal Anglicans*, 211.
[15] C. Bowater, *The Believer's Guide to Worship*, 61.
[16] Pilavachi and Borlase, *Audience of One*, 134.

judged on the quality of their performance.[17] Eventually, these attitudes became problematic and the whole congregation began to question the manner of their involvement in worship. As a result of this questioning, a policy of return to root values and key theological perspectives began to emerge. Clearly, notions of authenticity were seen as being under threat and to maintain the integrity of the congregational life a re-examination was called for:

> We were challenged to ask ourselves individually, 'When I come through the door of the church, what am I bringing as my contribution to worship?' Then the truth came to us: worship is not a spectator sport, it is not a product moulded by the taste of the consumers. It is not about what we get out of it. It is all about God.[18]

As a result of these conclusions, the congregation agreed to 'ban the band'. Worship was conducted for a number of weeks with very few of the trappings associated with popular music. Meetings were simplified and space allowed for individuals to contribute songs or prayers. If no one participated in what Pilavachi terms 'the sacrifice of praise' there would just be silence.[19] Over a period of time, the congregation began to learn how to praise God without relying on the music. The meetings became structured around the varied contributions of those present – be it in prayer, bible reading, unaccompanied singing, or in prophecy. The excitement of worship began to return, 'We were once again meeting with God', said Pilavachi.[20]

Through their worship songs, festivals, magazine and other products, Soul Survivor have played a considerable part in developing a culture of production and consumption within English evangelicalism. The experience related by Pilavachi draws attention to the way that the enculturation of a mediated religious culture into worship

---

[17] Pilavachi and Borlase, *Audience of One*, 134.
[18] Pilavachi and Borlase, *Audience of One*, 134.
[19] Pilavachi and Borlase, *Audience of One*, 134.
[20] Pilavachi and Borlase, *Audience of One*, 134.

is not entirely smooth. The Soul Survivor congregation experienced tensions or contradictions between the cultural logic of production and consumption, and the perceived integrity of their charismatic spirituality and theology. Banning the band was an attempt to return to core or authentic values of charismatic renewal based on individual participation in worship. At the same time, there was a reassertion of the foundational nature of charismatic experience, expressed as 'meeting with God' as the key theological value in worship. The perceived effect of these policies within the Soul Survivor congregation was a return to integrity in their worship times.

Much like Pilavachi, Graham Kendrick also expresses the problem of contradictions between the cultural forms adopted by charismatic worship and the need for theological integrity:

> To adopt new forms of expression – new music, dance, drama, and so on in worship – is by no means to guarantee the reality of its acceptability to God, and in many places we are in serious danger of mistaking these actual developments for true worship in the sight of God.[21]

The emphasis upon new forms of creativity, that characterises charismatic worship, may lead to an inappropriate search for 'experiences', says Kendrick.[22] Worship is in danger of becoming 'an end in itself'. It is possible 'to become so caught up in the pursuit of better, freer, richer and more creative worship that we have no time or energy left for the world outside'.[23] Worship therefore needs to be placed within a wider theological context, argues Kendrick. To do this, he argues for a theology based upon the idea of the 'kingdom of God'. He interprets the kingdom as a community that is based on relationships of justice and equality.[24] Worship is not just to be seen as an

---

[21] G. Kendrick, *Worship*, 31.
[22] Kendrick, *Worship*, 32.
[23] Kendrick, *Worship*, 55.
[24] Kendrick, *Worship*, 42.

individual experience, primarily located in religious meetings; it should also have social, economic and political implications.[25] Community should be expressed by a sense of togetherness. He is therefore critical of worship that involves people just sitting in rows, unable to see each other, as if they were attending a performance, or a show.[26] Integrity in worship, according to Kendrick, is linked to the 'spirit of unity' within the worshipping group. There should be evidence of reconciliation and acceptance of one another. God is searching out individual and group motivation, 'and is not fooled when we try to substitute beautiful music for beautiful relationships'.[27] Kendrick's writing is again evidence of contradictions within the subculture of charismatic worship and it serves as a further example of the way that integrity is reasserted as a corrective to the more uncomfortable aspects which emerge from the enculturation of popular culture into charismatic worship.

Bowater supports the general approach taken by Kendrick and Pilavachi. He identifies a tendency within the subculture that he calls, 'worshipping worship'. This is a situation where people are absorbed in the latest songs but are not 'taken up with God'.[28] He also sees the possibility that the experience or the atmosphere of a worship service may become the sole reason for participation. He gives an example of someone who said to him, 'I love it when I come here . . . I always have a good cry.'[29] Bowater is critical of these sentiments and he is concerned to locate true worship in a search for God rather than in a mood or in an experience. Authenticity for Bowater is also primarily located in charismatic encounter with God.[30]

Fellingham similarly deals with questions of authenticity in relation to new developments in charismatic worship.

---

[25] Kendrick, *Worship*, 32.
[26] Kendrick, *Worship*, 44.
[27] Kendrick, *Worship*, 52.
[28] Bowater, *Believer's Guide*, 12.
[29] Bowater, *Believer's Guide*, 16.
[30] Bowater, *Believer's Guide*, 20.

He prioritises worship that is rooted in a trinitarian theology over any particular style of music. A church which is worshipping is one which consists of people who 'bring glory to Jesus as they worship the Father in the power of the Holy Spirit'. This kind of worship relates more to 'holiness of life and obedience' than to the style of songs that we sing.[31]

These examples drawn from discussions of worship within the charismatic movement illustrate some of the contradictions in the enculturation of popular music into worship. This process appears to take charismatic spirituality in directions in which it seems, at times, unwilling to go. As a result, what can be seen to be taking place is a continual process of correction and reorientation. The use of popular culture in worship leads to continual adaptation.

Adapting the Culture

The contextualisation of worship both adopts and adapts the cultural forms in popular culture. There is an element of negotiation between the culture and the theological commitments of charismatics. Evidence of this process of tension and realignment can be illustrated by the way in which congregations and worship leaders interact.

Pilavachi identifies the way that worship leaders have a tendency to 'perform' rather than to 'lead worship'.[32] An example of this is the way that song leaders have a propensity towards the repetition of parts of songs. According to Pilavachi, repetition can be a good thing, but it can also be detrimental to congregational participation. Musicians are, however, inclined towards repetition, very often for musical reasons. The rhythmic pleasures of playing move them in this direction, they 'sit in "the groove"' of the music, says Pilavachi.[33] The problem is that

---

[31] Fellingham, 'Focus and Direction', 53.
[32] Pilavachi and Borlase, *Audience of One*, 120.
[33] Pilavachi and Borlase, *Audience of One*, 116.

what brings musical satisfaction can lead to audience 'stupefication', Pilavachi observes. Musicians will often explain their choice of repetition by talking of the Spirit leading them. Pilavachi acknowledges that this may be so, but he says that it is not always the case: 'The musicians' enjoyment of a certain moment can be an indication of its anointing, but it can also be their downfall as leaders and their flock drift apart. The magic comes when the band on stage manage to take the people with them.'[34]

Two authenticities are in conflict in this example from Pilavachi – the authenticity of musical expression and the authenticity of congregational participation. Pilavachi is clear that the needs of the congregation must be paramount. Leading worship, he argues, should be about the group. Priority should be given to a consideration of the way that God has been leading the group, and the thoughts and concerns of those present. The worship should be constructed in a way that reflects these dynamics.[35] According to Kendrick, the role of the leader in worship should be as servant to the needs of the group. A servant approach would mean that leaders would avoid self-aggrandisement or any temptation to 'wield power'.[36] Integrity in leading worship, argues Tuttle, is also located in a spiritual self-awareness. This self-awareness comes from a basic honesty in answering the question, 'What is the Lord leading me to do?'[37]

For the worship leader to maintain integrity, two disciplines are necessary. In the first instance, the worship leader must avoid the temptation to become a performer. Pilavachi recognises that worship leaders are 'creative types'.[38] This is essential because they must be able to create music. At the same time, acting against their inclinations and their nature, they need to avoid the temptation of

[34] Pilavachi and Borlase, *Audience of One*, 116.
[35] Pilavachi and Borlase, *Audience of One*, 108.
[36] Kendrick, *Worship*, 154.
[37] Tuttle, 'Foundations', 140.
[38] Pilavachi and Borlase, *Audience of One*, 120.

performance. Pilavachi is very clear that performance is a problem in worship: 'A performing worship leader will distract attention from God and should be reminded that their role is to draw the congregation into worship.'[39] At the same time, he admits that performance is part of the instinct and the role of the worship leader. The best worship leaders, he says, are visible and strong enough in their leading that people are enabled to follow their lead, but they must do this in such a way that they themselves do not become the focus of the event.[40]

Again, what is illustrated here is the way that aspects of behaviour and convention within the culture of popular music sit uncomfortably within charismatic worship. They therefore need to be renegotiated or reinterpreted to make them fit more readily; this is a basic tension within the process of contextualisation. In this, it is the 'normal' dynamic between performer and audience which gives rise to tensions. When it appears within charismatic worship, this dynamic becomes a problem and is experienced as a contradiction between the key values of participation and the worship of God and the cultural form which is being used to achieve this end.

Pilavachi's resolution of this contradiction is to assert the need for leaders to be continually mindful of their role in helping those in the congregation to worship and to be active. Worship, unlike attending a rock concert, is not a spectator sport. His treatment of this subject is perhaps an indication of how widespread these problems have become. Pilavachi appeals to the integrity of the worship leader to combat the cultural 'pull' which results from enculturation. He therefore argues that key role of the worship leader is to always remain a worshipper of God and their second function is to lead others in worship.[41] These values are used to correct the tendency towards performance.

[39] Pilavachi and Borlase, *Audience of One*, 120.
[40] Pilavachi and Borlase, *Audience of One*, 122.
[41] Pilavachi and Borlase, *Audience of One*, 122.

Performance in worship is also discussed by Bowater. In his treatment of the role of the worship leader he identifies two kinds of integrity that are required for this role. In the first instance, there is a need to be close to the leading of the Spirit. Bowater expresses this in terms of anointing and what he calls a 'prophetic gift'. At the same time, the worship leader is exhorted to 'direct people's attention to God's greatness and goodness'. These elements are to work together to 'create an atmosphere which is charged with inspiration and illumination'.[42]

The contradictions that result from the enculturation of popular music into worship stem not only from the role of the worship leader, but also from the technology of contemporary music, the behaviour of the congregation and the atmosphere which is created. Bowater makes the point that in the early days of renewal many Christians reacted negatively to the use of guitars and electronic instruments in worship. For some, these new developments appeared 'worldly'. Guitarists were perceived as being inappropriately 'sensuous', says Bowater, because they 'swayed in time to the music'.[43] This example is interesting because it demonstrates how there was some resistance to the enculturation of popular music into the mainstream of the church. This resistance appears to have become focused on the iconic significance of the guitar and the guitarist that is commonplace within popular music, especially rock music. Just as there has been some problem with the acceptance of the instruments associated with popular music there have also been some tensions around behaviour within the subcultural world of charismatic worship.

Bowater discusses the problems experienced by worship leaders when the congregation breaks out into applause at the end of a worship song. This is a situation which is 'hard to handle', says Bowater, and many worship leaders find

---

[42] Bowater, *Believer's Guide*, 64.
[43] Bowater, *Believer's Guide*, 101.

themselves confused by the experience.[44] Again, this situation can be seen in the light of the enculturation of popular music into charismatic worship. Applause is a common and acceptable behaviour within popular music and, in the right place, it is encouraged by performers. The contradictions experienced by the worship leader arise from the way that the charismatic congregation has incorporated a convention associated with popular music into worship. This aspect of popular culture is experienced as a tension by many worship leaders. Bowater's response is to advise the worship leader to 'receive it as though gathering praise offerings to the Lord. Deflect applause that is offered to you as a thank offering to God.'[45] The integrity of worship is thus ensured by asserting the value that worship should be directed towards God. This move means that authenticity is restored.

Selling Out to the Culture

Popular culture has a logic of production and consumption within it. This cultural logic has at times affected the worship of the church adversely. Some of these problems have been identified by those within the charismatic scene, but some of them unfortunately have not. Most have been aware of the problem of 'hype' and emotional manipulation. The incorporation of popular music into worship has also led to problems related to the mood or atmosphere that this kind of music creates. Carol Wimber describes how in the early days of the Vineyard church, in the USA, singing songs was very often the starting point for their worship: 'occasionally we sang a song personally and intimately addressed to Jesus, with lyrics like, "Jesus, I love you"; it was during songs like these that people began to experience God deeply.'[46]

---

[44] Bowater, *Believer's Guide*, 144.
[45] Bowater, *Believer's Guide*, 144.
[46] Carol Wimber quoted in Redman, 'Worshipper and Musician', 64.

Very soon with Wimber and those associated with him, says Redman, the singing of songs moved beyond an attempt to 'get in the mood', it became the 'main event'.[47] The use of the word 'event' is interesting because of its connotations of concert, entertainment and performance, which arise from popular culture. The problem is that the atmosphere that is associated with an 'event' may be seen as a falsification of true worship.

Nigel Scotland uses another word, derived from the discourse of popular music and advertising, to identify this tendency within charismatic worship: 'hype'.[48] Hype, says Scotland, was characteristic of the early period of the restorationist churches which saw the introduction of 'The Dales two-step' and stampeding raucous 'warfare' songs.[49] Scotland, however, defends the simple repetitious nature of charismatic worship from the accusation of hype. Repetition, he says, enables the worshipper to eventually move beyond the words and the act of singing. He likens it to learning to dance without thinking of the individual steps.[50] Again, participation and encounter with God are used to legitimate the authenticity of a style of music within charismatic worship.

Largely unacknowledged are the problems that have arisen from the economic and business side of the worship scene. Thus the roles of record companies, music publishers and festival organisations have not really been examined in any detail. In particular, the weaknesses and failings of individuals, organisations and companies, whilst evident to many, are very often glossed over by the need to appear successful, or Christian, or morally correct. Part of the problem here is that the various mechanisms of the culture and the market are generally regarded as being used by God. What God is doing is often expressed in sales

---

[47] Redman, 'Worshipper and Musician', 64.
[48] N. Scotland, *Charismatics and the Next Millennium: Do they have a Future?*, 51.
[49] Scotland, *Charismatics*, 51.
[50] Scotland, *Charismatics*, 51

figures, or the numbers attending a festival, or indeed a local church. The anointing of a worship leader may be linked to how many people come forward for ministry at an event. This raises difficulties, for whilst I would be happy to say that God was often at work in the business side of worship. I would be wary of too close an identification between sales and the Spirit.

This issue is not new to the church. There has always been a tension between the church as divine institution that has been inaugurated by God and filled with the Spirit and the social organisation of denominations and churches. People and organisations are sinful and they often act in ways that are outside of the will of God. Yet these are the very same structures that are used by God to bless and to bring people to salvation. The church lives in this tension. In fact, the acknowledgement of the tension is very important. When the balance tips towards the divine institution, ministers and clergy are above criticism. If the human failing of institutions are over-emphasised, we very soon drift into a cynical bureaucracy. The tension between human institution and movement of the Spirit goes to the heart of what the church is about.

These kinds of insights need to be used as we assess the impact of charismatic worship on the church. In particular, we need to acknowledge the ambiguity of organisations, even when they are as successful as Soul Survivor or Spring Harvest. In particular, we should treat as suspect the way that some Christian organisations have embraced the marketplace uncritically. Graham Cray's concern for a connection to culture, but also a concern for theological integrity, is extremely important. This balance is essential to the future health of the church. Many of those involved in the worship scene are faithful and conscientious Christians. At the same time, it is evident that the commercial pressures experienced by the impetus of the various worship-related businesses and organisations should be examined much more critically in the future if our church is to remain healthy and continue to grow.

Eleven

Participation: From Folk to Fan

It was the discovery of every member ministry that brought renewal to life in churches across the country. Suddenly, there was a sense that everyone could bring something to worship and to the life of the church. In 1 Corinthians many of these early charismatics found a vivid account of the work of the Spirit. As they searched for a theology of the experience of baptism in the Spirit and the charismatic gifts, they found these to be embedded in a description of church that valued a range of participation and involvement. 'The body song',[1] in *Sound of Living Waters* deals, with these themes from 1 Corinthians 12. The parts of the body depend upon each other, says the song. On their own, an 'I' cannot be a body; God has decided that we are members of one another. The idea of communal participation and every member ministry were to find a resonance in the wider culture of the day.

In the 1970s Britain was enjoying a folk revival. For many young people, this meant the rediscovery of community and creativity, as well as an unlikely interest in Morris Dancing and bands like Steeleye Span and Fairport Convention. These cultural trends seemed to merge in the charismatic renewal with the Pauline theology of every member ministry. What developed was an open space

---

[1] *SLW* 111.

where particular forms of expression could be explored. This 'folk' feel informed and shaped charismatic church life in such a way that it was a key characteristic of the movement. By the mid-1990s, however, the communal folk nature of the charismatic renewal had given way to a more consumer based, commercial and media-related worship scene.

The contemporary charismatic church has moved a long way from the home-grown folk art of the early days of renewal. The current scene is delivered through a series of media and consumer related activities. Worship music and worship artists are packaged, promoted and sold in much the same way as their secular pop counterparts. The implications of this shift in cultural emphasis are very significant. Not least because of the widespread fears over the influence that the current media-related worship scene may exercise. It is not uncommon for clergy and parents, for instance, to express concern over the manipulation of young people at large worship events. My own feeling is that while we may have gained a great deal through the contextualisation of worship in a pop or rock culture, there is every possibility that we may have lost something of the original fire and creativity of the early days of renewal. The key issue here is the nature of participation in worship and church life. This chapter explores this issue.

Participation and Renewal: Folk Art

In many ways, David Watson's ministry at St Michael le Belfrey led the way for renewal in the UK. Andrew Maries, the director of music at the church, was clear that there was a link between the growing experience of renewal in the church in York and the high level of participation. Worship is not to be regarded as a 'spectator sport'.[2] Worship, he says, 'is not a presentation or a performance from the front.

---

[2] A. Maries, *One Heart One Voice: The Rich and Varied Resource of Music in Worship*, 77.

For the body to function properly it requires that every member give themselves to worship whether down the front or up in the gallery.'[3] 'The body' and 'members' are a reference to the ecclesiology of 1 Corinthians 12:12–30 where Paul speaks of the Christian community as the 'body of Christ'. Maries goes on to link the theology of the body with two other concepts. The first is the family and the second is the idea of 'folk art'. The love and acceptance within the body of Christ leads to what he calls an 'intimate family experience'.[4] The church is to be seen as being like a family consisting of all ages, tastes and interests. Worship, he says, opens us up to God and to one another, and in so doing it 'begins to embody the warmth and tenderness of a family occasion'.[5] The new creativity and styles of music facilitate 'participation'; they are therefore welcomed into the life of the community.

The use of term 'folk art' is closely related to a theology of the church as a family or the body of Christ. Within charismatic renewal reference was made to a new flowering of creativity and expression. 'Folk art' was a commonly used term to describe these developments. It was a desire to communicate with believers and those outside the church that drove the new movement, says Maries.[6] The use of the term 'folk art' meant both 'folk' expression – i.e. creativity which arises from within the community – and it also relates to notions of communal ownership of what is produced. Participation, or folk art, signifies a particular way in which groups operate creatively. Maries describes how the church in following notions of folk art becomes a cultural producer:

> We are always looking for ways in which to draw people in and give
> them the opportunity to offer themselves and their gifts in worship.
> Many people write their own songs, make banners, and create new

---

[3] Maries, *One Heart*, 77.
[4] Maries, *One Heart*, 59.
[5] Maries, *One Heart*, 60.
[6] Maries, *One Heart*, 62.

dances, for example. In this way they interpret the present activity of the Spirit among us and provide avenues of communication between God and one another.[7]

Renewal let loose a creative energy in many congregations; Gunstone argues that some of these changes were already underway before the advent of charismatic renewal. He gives as an example the introduction of *Youth Praise* and *Psalm Praise*. He says 'it is the sharing of praise which has been the distinctive impact of Pentecostal renewal in Anglican worship'.[8] 'Sharing in praise' is a reference to the high degree of involvement that characterises the charismatic movement. Gunstone also makes use of the term folk art to refer to these aspects of charismatic worship. He describes how those involved in Renewal within the Anglican Church, have tried to bring together Pentecostal praise and their traditional liturgies. Pentecostal praise Gunstone regards as being a folk element in worship. He argues that such folk elements have, in fact, 'always been present in Anglican Worship'. It has been the development of a professionalised clergy and the choral tradition which, according to Gunstone, have combined to suppress the folk element. Folk arts for Gunstone expresses an ideal of participation by as many people as possible, whatever their expertise.[9]

It is this emphasis upon participation and community creativity that has been the significant contribution of the charismatic movement to the contemporary church, says Wilson-Dickson. Whereas, in terms of musical expression, the songs of charismatic renewal may appear to be very similar to the populist hymns and songs of the 1950s, what is distinctive is the way that the new songs have emerged from those who are involved in the movement.[10] This is obviously still the case: worship leaders and the songs they

---

[7] Maries, *One Heart*, 63.
[8] Gunstone, *Pentecostal Anglicans*, 211.
[9] Gunstone, *Pentecostal Anglicans*, 211.
[10] A. Wilson-Dickson, *A Brief History of Christian Music*, 415.

write emerge from the movement. At the same time, it is clear that the folk element of creativity has been substantially altered as the kinds of media and communication technologies adopted by charismatic Christians have become more complex. This has meant that the nature of participation has been altered. Instead of a folk culture, where songs and worship emerge from the group gathered in the local place, contemporary charismatic worship locates the worshipper as consumer of a more sophisticated media-generated and sustained culture. This is still a kind of participation, but it is involvement which is different than that which was characteristic of the more communal 'folk' values of the early days of renewal in this country.

Participation in a Media-generated Worship Culture

The worship scene has developed for one very simple reason: Christian people have bought the products. This means, in effect, that the participation of the fan and the consumer has replaced the more communal and folk aspects of renewal. Participation has come to be seen more in terms of the accessibility and cultural relevance of the style of music used in worship. Fellingham expresses this as 'identification', i.e. in the close affiliation between musical style and the cultural tastes of the audience. Scotland is convinced that charismatic worship is a 'burgeoning success'.[11] He suggests that one of the reasons for this is that charismatic worship is, in his words, 'in touch with the culture and ethos of the late twentieth century'.[12] Previous styles of worship, he says, reflected a hierarchical and authoritarian ecclesiology. In contrast to these traditional patterns of church life, the charismatic movement is more democratic in spirit, allowing worshippers free participation in the worship: 'In very general terms the music, the culture, and the buildings are much

---

[11] Scotland, *Charismatics*, 65.
[12] Scotland, *Charismatics*, 65.

closer to the level at which ordinary people live their daily lives.'[13] This has an evangelistic effect, according to Scotland, because those who are not connected to the church, or to use his term, 'unbelievers', find it much easier to walk into the schools and community centres used by charismatic congregations. Their sense of a cultural 'fit' is reinforced by the informal dress of the clergy and leaders, as well as by the warm acceptance and love which, Scotland says, characterises charismatic worship.[14]

Steven uses the term 'appropriate cultural expression' to describe the character of charismatic worship. As an example, he discusses the custom of clapping within worship. 'Giving God a clap' may be read by Anglicans as a shallow form of worship, but Steven argues that in contemporary culture clapping is accepted a social code for approval and praise. To use clapping as a form of praise for God is therefore to incorporate this social custom into Christian worship.[15] The goal of this kind of cultural accessibility in charismatic worship is the participation of the individual in the act of worship.[16] This discussion of applause is particularly telling because it signals the extent to which contemporary worship has mirrored the practices of popular culture. In this more media-related environment, participation has been relocated from the creation of songs, art, dance, and other aspects of worship, to behaviours normally associated with the rock audience or the fan.

Carl Tuttle deals directly with some of these issues, but interestingly he also relocates participation in the accessibility of the songs and styles of music, rather than in the creation of the worship itself. Participation is a core value within charismatic worship, argues Tuttle: 'it is undoubtedly true that the whole approach to worship, coming out of the renewal movement, has been towards

---

[13] Scotland, *Charismatics*, 66.
[14] Scotland, *Charismatics*, 66–7.
[15] Steven, *Worship*, 22.
[16] Steven, *Worship*, 23.

everyone being fully involved and giving out rather than sitting back and receiving.'[17]

The songs that have emerged from charismatic renewal, says Tuttle, may be criticised as being light on doctrine or somewhat 'trite' musically. They are this way, however, in order that the maximum number of people may be able to very easily learn them and use them as a means to express their feelings to God.[18] The incorporation of new styles of music and expression into church life is therefore justified by Tuttle on the basis that it allows people to participate in worship. Here participation is seen as a kind of consumption rather than as an active role in composing songs or the creation of worship. Here, again, the worshipper is more of a fan than a productive agent in worship.

Being a Fan: Investment in Worship

While the 'folk' feel of renewal may have passed, there are aspects of participation in worship that have remained unchanged. The true worshipper, within charismatic discourse, is seen as being the one who is willing to give him- or herself to God in worship. This represents a significant personal investment in worship. Participation in this sense is a total involvement. To worship God is to 'give God his worth', says Maries.[19] Kendrick sees worship as involving a commitment to living sacrifice; this is a whole body reality.[20] Pilavachi speaks of worship as 'our highest priority':[21]

> Whatever way you look at it, you cannot alter our highest priority. Try as hard as you like, but you'll never twist the definition of our purpose on earth to read 'I am here to shop' or 'I exist to make money'. Sure, shopping and making a living are part of the fabric of

---

[17] Tuttle, 'Foundations', 162.
[18] Tuttle, 'Foundations', 162.
[19] Maries, *One Heart*, 46.
[20] Kendrick, *Worship*, 24.
[21] Pilavachi and Borlase, *Audience of One*, 1.

our lives, but they can never be the main reason that we are here. That place is reserved for something special: worship.[22]

Investment in worship operates at a number of different levels. At the first, and most basic, level within charismatic spirituality there is a high commitment to the act of worship itself. Redman expresses this in terms of an active love for God. The worshipper is to place a priority on worship and devotion to God. Right living then emerges as a consequence of devotion to worship. As Redman says, 'When we get our priorities right and put the worship of God first, then everything else falls into place.'[23] Charismatic spirituality therefore prioritises worship as a site of significant investment. It does not replace ethics, or mission, or theological education as such; rather, worship is seen as the starting point for all of these.

Investment in worship is also seen in the key value of participation by charismatics. As Bax puts it, 'The lay person in Renewal is entering into the life, work and ministry of the church among all members.'[24] She later observes that within renewal there is an element of people 'shopping around' for churches. The criteria by which churches are judged is less the style of worship, or the kind of preaching, or the liturgical pattern on offer, and more the desire is for what she calls 'a quality of commitment'.[25]

An example of investment can be seen in Kendrick's account of creativity in the local groups that organise Marches for Jesus. Kendrick points out that people find a variety of different ways to be active in preparing for a local march. This may be in rehearsing songs, practising as musicians, sewing banners, or in developing choreography to be used on the march.[26] This kind of investment is also

---

[22] Pilavachi and Borlase, *Audience of One*, 1.
[23] M. Redman quoted in Pilavachi and Borlase, *Audience of One*, 4.
[24] J. Bax, *The Good Wine: Spiritual Renewal in the Church of England*, 5.
[25] Bax, *Good Wine*, 184.
[26] G. Kendrick, *Shine Jesus Shine*, 45.

illustrated by the variety of ways that worshippers are active during worship as participants, or worship leaders, or as song writers.

The various products developed by March for Jesus and Graham Kendrick's Make Way organisation enabled the global and local action of Christians who were then able to go out on to the streets and perform their act of praise and witness. The commercial aspects of the movement can therefore be seen as a way to empower participation. This reading of the worship scene needs to be balanced by a more critical analysis of the role of businesses and organisations in the spread of worship.

Participation and Production in Contemporary Worship

The charismatic movement has given rise to a number of powerful organisations such as Spring Harvest, Alpha and Kingsway. The way that these organisations act to promote and defend their particular franchise and business interests has led many to feel uneasy about the commercial nature of the worship scene. The widespread unease among Christian people with television and the film industry has been to some extent reflected in the way that some see charismatic worship as manipulative and commercially led.

On the whole, I am unsympathetic with this analysis of wider charismatic scene. There seems to be some truth in the way that Christian organisations act in a similar manner to commercial companies being driven by the desire to promote their own products. These may be sold as 'resources' but they are nevertheless sold. This means that at a festival such as Soul Survivor, worship artists linked to the 'brand' are generally featured and the songs in the songbook, the CDs in the record store, and the other books and merchandise necessarily reflect this fact. Where organisations develop significant alliances, the openness to those outside the 'cartel' has sometimes been even more limited. Partly this comes from the need for every stakeholder to feature their own speaker or worship band or latest initiative. The effect of this on the wider church, however, is that it tends to cut out the independent or grass-roots initiative.

The size of the British scene naturally lends itself to monopolies. Because the market is so small, any significant success in the UK will almost inevitably create a large fish in what is really a very small pond. Over the last thirty years organisations such as Spring Harvest, *Buzz*, Authentic Media, Kingsway and others, through their own success and the acquisition and merger of companies, have, at times, threatened to establish a near monopoly in their fields. In the wider secular scene, business practices are regulated through government intervention and through the regular scrutiny of the media. When the Christian media are owned by the media companies, or when they begin to promote events and their own resources, clearly problems may emerge. This makes it imperative that we develop an appreciative but also critical culture among the worshippers in the churches.

To be critical, however, does not mean that we should not be aware of the immense value in the activities of Christian organisations and businesses. It is simplistic, in my view, to dismiss all commercial or business activity as some form of manipulation. As I have argued throughout this piece, the adoption of particular forms of communication simply represents the means to contextualise the faith. In developing a critique of the worship culture of the church, we should not focus solely on the activities of the 'producers'. We also need to examine the way that people consume the product and make something of it in their own spiritual lives. Here we return again to the idea of the worshipper as a fan and worship as an investment.

The Worship Apparatus

Investment in charismatic worship is enabled by the existence of a complex network that could be termed the 'worship apparatus'. The worship apparatus includes songwriters, recording studios, record companies, local church worship bands, festivals, OHPs, styles of singing, book publishers, worship leaders, magazines, youth groups, and so on. Investment takes place and is structured by this apparatus. An example of this is the way that advances in technology meant music publishing could mass produce songbooks relatively cheaply. Wilson-Dickson was clear that this was one of the significant developments associated with evangelical worship:

> Around Britain the speed and ease of modern music publishing has released an avalanche of spiral-bound books, Mission Praise (1983) and Songs of Fellowship (1985) being in wide circulation. The simplicity of their contents implies that the creation of Christian music is not longer only the province of the expert, but that it can be for all.[27]

Wilson-Dickson identified how contemporary advances in the printing and distribution of music led to an increase in the number of books. These technological advances are, at the same time, linked to locally based creativity and mass circulation. Worship can be seen to exist in the creative interaction between and within this complex network of published music, local songwriters and the wider consumer base.

The March for Jesus also illustrates how the apparatus of worship produces spaces where individuals may invest. As such, it can be read as a worship apparatus. The origins of the March for Jesus are complex, but they are expressed by those within the organisation as a coming together of a number of factors. These include the early Marches led by Ichthus Fellowship, Graham Kendrick's song writing and music publishing, the organisational abilities and commitments of Youth With A Mission and the spreading influence of the Pioneer Trust.[28] At the same time, the

---

[27] Wilson-Dickson, *Christian Music*, 415.
[28] Kendrick et al., *March For Jesus*, 8.

creation of the March for Jesus was represented as the combined vision of a group of friends: Graham Kendrick, Gerald Coates, Roger Forster and Lynn Green:

> March for Jesus did not start in a committee room with church leaders trying to find a new way to mobilise the church. It started spontaneously as four friends were prompted to lead believers out onto the streets.[29]

At the same time, the remarkable response of individuals and groups to the 'vision' is emphasised. Kendrick, in particular, is at pains to describe the way that local owner-ship and involvement in the March for Jesus is at the heart of its success. In fact, he expresses surprise at the numbers of people who have wanted to run their own marches.[30] The March for Jesus was therefore presented as both the initiative of leaders and a localised grass-roots organisa-tion.

A similar pattern can be seen in the way that Kendrick discusses his Make Way materials that are used on the Marches. On the one hand, he says that the resources are produced to 'encourage the churches onto the streets'.[31] This would imply that production of resources happened before local marching iniatives. Yet elsewhere, Kendrick says that it was the existence of localised marches which gave birth to what he calls the 'service industry'. By this he means Make Way Music and the March for Jesus UK Office.[32] The various accounts of the origins of the March for Jesus are an indication of the complexity of the worship apparatus.

Rather than argue that the power of the Christian businesses and organisations leads to the manipulation of the worshipper and of the market, I would suggest that what is happening here is an interaction between various

---

[29] Kendrick et al., *March For Jesus*, 7.
[30] Kendrick et al., *March For Jesus*, 25.
[31] Kendrick et al., *March For Jesus*, 25.
[32] Kendrick, *Shine*, 64.

aspects of the charismatic subcultural world. This can lead to a recognition that the interpretation of worship (and its critical appreciation) lies in a reading of the spaces between text and audience, consumption and production, agency and authority. The apparatus structures investment and makes investment possible. This view also focuses attention upon the centrality of communal and individual investment in charismatic worship. Somehow, we need to ensure that we understand what worship means to those involved. A clue to this, of course, lies in the various ways that people make the culture of the charismatic movement part of the spiritual lives. At the heart of this 'investment' lies the widespread acknowledgement that charismatic worship is primarily to be understood as divine encounter, or intimacy. This forms the subject of the final chapter.

Twelve

Songs as Narratives of Encounter

Worship songs carry the culture of the charismatic movement. As the style of music has changed, so have the technologies required to reproduce the songs. In much the same way as previous styles of church music encouraged the building of pipe organs and the training of large choirs, charismatic worship songs have led the way in the gradual evolution of the worship scene with its record labels, web sites, festivals and worship artists. These developments have come about not simply because a new generation wanted to see guitars and amplified music in church. At the heart of charismatic worship lies a very important theological innovation.

In the past, the singing of hymns and songs functioned in worship in a number of ways. Hymns were used to create a group feeling and bond a congregation together. This is why preachers and evangelists have often been keen advocates of hymn singing. The way that hymns work to create a feeling of community means that it is easier to preach following a rousing or emotionally stirring hymn. At other moments in worship the hymn may act as means of response in the liturgy. After a sermon or as the service comes to an end, the right hymn pulls the worship together and helps to develop a sense of 'moving on' with God or journeying forward from worship into service and mission. Hymns are also important in worship because they signal

points of transition. The procession of communion elements to the altar or the movement of the minister to the
pulpit are generally conducted during the singing of a
hymn, Hymns therefore act as kind of glue joining the
different parts of worship together. This is how we get the
idea of the hymn sandwich. This could mean that we see
the service as layers in a sandwich. The prayers and
sermon, and other elements of the worship, are the filling
and the hymns are the bread. In this pattern, the hymns do
not just mark the start or end of services. The hymn
sandwich is more of a multi-layered creation with five or
six hymns commonly being used in the average service. As
well as having a liturgical function, hymns have also been
seen as important in the theological education of the
worshipper. *The Methodist Hymn Book*, for instance, was
always regarded as a means to teach doctrine. The
Methodist leaders, John and Charles Wesley, realised that
people learned their faith not just from sermons but also
from songs. They accepted that theology is made much
more accessible when it is set to music. So, worship songs
and hymns have generally been valued for their doctrinal
content as well as for the way they function in a worship
service.

Charismatic worship songs function in worship in an
altogether different manner to hymns or the older style of
spiritual song. The charismatic worship song is not
primarily a means to teach doctrine. Neither is it a way to
create a flow or to punctuate worship. While singing in
charismatic worship may generate a feeling of togetherness, the songs are not primarily meant as a means to
generate this feeling. The contemporary worship song
occupies a particular space in charismatic spirituality: it is
the means to a personal encounter with God.

Songs in Charismatic Worship

For the contemporary charismatic, worship equals singing
worship songs. When they gather charismatics will often

speak of entering into 'a time of worship'. This phrase invariably denotes a thirty- or forty-minute period where several songs are sung one after another. This is what the Vineyard churches refer to as the 'worship set', i.e. a block of songs. This style of singing is seen as worship because it is through the songs that intimacy between worshipper and God is expressed. It is through singing that praise, adoration, devotion and love are given to God. In turn, through the work of the Holy Spirit, God's presence is experienced by the worshipper. Intimacy is therefore both expressive and experiential.

The songs are therefore central to the theology and practice of charismatic worship. One way to express the importance of singing is to compare charismatic worship to other traditions in the Christian church. For the Roman Catholic, the sacraments and, particularly, the Mass is the central act of worship. The sacraments are a means of grace. In Catholic theology God meets the worshipper in the bread and the wine of the communion service. In charismatic worship the songs function in a very similar way as the means of encounter with God. For the churches of the Reformation the ministry of word has replaced the centrality of the Catholic Mass. Here God comes to the worshipper through the reading of Scripture and through the preaching of the gospel. These churches of 'the word' locate the presence of God in these acts of witness and proclamation. For the charismatic worshipper, though many still value the sermon and, indeed, the act of communion, encounter with God is located primarily in the singing of songs and in the intimate times of prayer and ministry which are often the climax of a time of worship. This means that as the Mass is for Catholics and the sermon is for Protestants, so the singing of songs for charismatics. This emphasis upon the singing of songs and worship as encounter with God came with the spreading influence of the charismatic movement.

Charismatic Renewal and Encounter with God

The *Youth Praise* era, according to Kendrick, seemed to regard worship as a kind of 'sing-song'. Freedom, at that time he says, got little further than individuals in the youth fellowship shouting out their favourite songs to be sung. Kendrick describes how, although he was performing as a musician at this time, both he, and those around him, knew 'almost nothing about praise and worship'.[1] It was his encounter with the charismatic movement and the experience of being filled (or baptised) in the Holy Spirit that first introduced him to the new forms of worship.

In *Youth Praise* the songs tend to be focused on the moment of conversion. While 'Life may be wonderful' in the present and there may be frequent references to joy and peace, the reference point remains the encounter with God in the past at conversion. So, 'Life is wonderful' emphasises how Jesus 'came in' and changed everything.[2] 'I'm singing for you Lord'[3] tells how the worshipper is singing about Jesus everywhere that they go. Here, again, the focus is upon what God has done in the past when they first came to faith or what was achieved by Jesus by his death on the cross. The charismatic experience moved evangelical Christians into a more immediate and experiential understanding of worship. David Watson describes how his initial experience of the Holy Spirit led him on towards a new appreciation of worship:

> I had seen, almost as if it were for the first time, the rich variety of worship mentioned in the psalms. I had realised, too, how strait-jacketed we had become with our stilted formal services, or with our hearty evangelical hymns. How little we understood about adoration in worship! How stiff we were in bodily expression! . . . how inhibited we were when it came to clapping, raising hands, or dancing.[4]

---

[1] Kendrick, *Worship*, 86.
[2] YP 46.
[3] YP 7.
[4] Watson, *You Are My God*, 105.

Watson's characterisation of evangelical hymn singing as 'hearty' echo's Kendrick's description of 'sing-song' worship in the youth fellowship.

Watson soon began to use worship in his evangelistic campaigns. At first, like other evangelists, he would use worship and music as a preparation to the evangelistic message. However, Poulton argues that Watson increasingly saw the presence of the Holy Spirit in worship as itself an act of proclamation. His experience in the church in York and his experience of charismatic worship generally had shifted Watson away from a more exclusive evangelical reverence for the preaching of the word.[5] Coming from outside of the evangelical tradition, the Anglo-Catholic John Gunstone was also impacted by the experiential and expressive nature of the renewal movement. He speaks of his first visit to a prayer meeting as being extremely embarrassing:

> I had never been to anything like it before. Speakers referred to the Lord as if they were on intimate terms with him. Hands were lifted in the air. One chorus followed another in an interminable procession, and participants appeared to be carried away by praise in a manner that was totally foreign to what I had been used to in the Church of England. Worst of all, I felt miserably conspicuous because of my inability to join in.[6]

Within a short period of time, Gunstone found that he was able to participate by raising his hands and lifting his head during prayers. He explains this as the work of the Holy Spirit dealing with his prejudices and inhibitions.[7] Gunstone is describing his identification with styles of expression within worship which was held in common within this prayer meeting (and many others at the time). He expresses a discomfort because, although he had

---

[5] J. Poulton, 'St. Michael-le-Belfrey', in E. England (ed.), *David Watson: A Portrait by His Friends*, 131.

[6] Gunstone, *Pentecostal Anglicans*, 34.

[7] Gunstone, *Pentecostal Anglicans*, 34.

previously experienced baptism in the Spirit and he was in the habit of speaking in tongues, he had, until this time, been outside of the subcultural circulation of symbolic representation that characterised the discourse of the movement. His participation in raising his hands in worship and lifting his head during prayer can be read as a marker of identity within the subculture. He goes on, however, to explain how his new found freedom in worship left him feeling a measure of discomfort in his role as an Anglican priest. He says that he was left feeling that he was living something of a double life, 'behaving in one way during prayer meetings and another way during church services'.[8]

Through the ministry of pioneers like David Watson in York, Tom Walker in Birmingham and Michael Green in Oxford the distinctive spirituality of the renewal movement gradually became part of the every day life of the parish church. For the Soul Survivor generation baptism in the Spirit had been largely replaced by the idea of intimacy with God in worship. The effect of this was that encounter with God as a past event at conversion, or even with a baptism in the Spirit had been replaced by a more regular and continual communion with God. The life of the disciple was expressed in terms of coming regularly to God in worship. 'I just want to love'[9] makes this clear. The intimacy means coming before God. This is where a life is lived out 'before God'. At the heart of this lies a particular expression of being loved and of loving God. This love is expressed through singing songs of love.

Narratives of Encounter

The songs of the charismatic movement have been written not simply to express or speak about an encounter with God through worship. The songs are rather themselves

---

[8] Gunstone, *Pentecostal Anglicans*, 34.
[9] SS 49.

individual narratives of encounter. The various metaphors and images used in the songs connect to the idea of coming before God and singing songs of love to him and sharing in his blessing and presence. A song such as 'I love You, Lord'[10] speaks of the worshipper coming to God singing of their love. The soul is said to rejoice and God should 'take joy' in what God hears. Here the lyrics of the song speak of an intimate love encounter in worship. The song is not about God. Instead, it is meant to be sung to God. This makes the song very personal. It is hard for the worshipper to sing this kind of song with integrity, especially if they have not been on the emotional journey that the lyrics speak of. 'Lord, you have my heart'[11] is another example of way that the charismatic worship song operates as story or narrative of encounter. The song speaks of the Lord having the worshipper's heart and in turn the worshipper searching for God's heart. The worshippers 'heartfelt' search for God is expressed as a sacrifice. In the chorus of the song, the praise of the worshipper is explained in terms of the glory of God that is revealed in the place of worship. Here we see God's face.[12]

The emphasis upon a relational encounter with God is a key distinctive of charismatic worship. The conviction is that intimacy in worship is normal and a regular part of Christian spirituality. Whereas in the past such experiences were seen as being initiatory or an occasional mountain top moment, for the charismatic, this is what worship is meant to be. There are, of course, problems with such an emphasis.

Charismatic worship songs are very explicit. The images used in many of the songs come from the edge or the limits of emotional and spiritual experience. The language of being 'desperate for God' or 'loving God always' or 'giving our whole heart to God' is in a sense problematic. The worshipper may be in tune and ready for this kind of intensity, especially in the context of large festival or a

---

[10] *SF* 49.
[11] *SS* 104.
[12] *SS* 104.

significant event or occasion. With four or five people gathered in a house group singing along to a CD, or even on at Sunday morning service, it may be difficult to inhabit these kinds of sentiments with honesty or integrity. The explicit nature of the song lyrics can leave the spiritually numb, or troubled, or asleep, with very little place in which to hide. It might be said that this is a good thing; we all need to be encouraged into worship. There is, however, a pastoral issue here in that in contrast to the traditional hymn or more liturgical worship with its extensive use of the psalms, charismatic worship has no reflex which may accommodate those who are grieving or in the darker corners of spiritual experience. As a result, some the songs and the worship become a problem for some charismatics. Some speak of the tone and the language of the worship songs as a cause of spiritual harm in their lives and some drop out of charismatic churches because they feel that their spiritual journey is more complex and ambiguous than what seems to be allowed in the regular worship of the church.

This is a problem which songwriters and charismatic leaders will need to address in the future. Matt Redman's song 'Blessed be the name' was written in response to just these kinds of observations. The song takes the biblical theme of praise for God in the middle of suffering and loss. The chorus echoes the funeral service speaking of God both giving and taking away. Praise in the context of grief and mourning is clearly a Christian response to suffering, but this tone may be pastorally disastrous. We all need times in which we rage against life and God. The Psalms give ample witness that wrestling with God and expressing loss and lament are perfectly possible in the context of faith. Anger – even anger with God – may be, at times, not just sane but even appropriate. The feeling of being abandoned or left by God is a part of spiritual experience and growth. We should not forget that, admittedly in extremis, Jesus uttered the words 'My God, my God, why have you forsaken me?'[13]

---

[13] Matthew 27:46.

Mission and Encounter

The emphasis upon a particular style of worship and the experience of encounter with God has caused other significant issues for charismatic Christians, not least in relation to mission and evangelism. *Youth Praise* is very clear about the relationship between the singing of songs and the witness of the faith. This reflected a wider emphasis upon evangelism through youth work and the local church that characterised evangelicalism of the 1960s and early 1970s. This is also seen in the coffee-bar outreach of the early days of MGO. Charismatic renewal did not diminish evangelical theological commitments to evangelism, but it did impact these areas in significant ways.

In *Sound of Living Waters* and in *The Graham Kendrick Songbook Volume 1* a clear pattern emerges of the relationship between worship and mission. Mission will flow out from the right worship of the church. In *Sound of Living Waters* songs like 'Peace is flowing'[14] are clear that mission emerges from worship. When the church gathers together before God, the Spirit will begin to flow and fill the worshippers. From the abundance the water will flow out into all the land.

In Graham Kendrick's Make Way songs the faithful prayer and worship of the people of God leads to the healing of ills in society. Here praise becomes the instrument of mission. The proclamation of the reign of God is affected through public praise.

For the Soul Survivor generation worship has become the 'main event'. Perhaps in contrast to other charismatic groups, Soul Survivor through their regular teaching and at events such as Soul in the City emphasise that mission and social justice are part of the call of God.

In this way, Soul Survivor are addressing a long-term issue within the charismatic movement. This has been

---

[14] *SLW* 91.

caused by an overt emphasis upon encounter with God through a particular expression of worship – singing songs. The issue here is that if God is met in worship what of the rest of life? How do we encounter God through service and mission? Perhaps even more pressing, how is God present in the everyday lived realities of life? This is what lies behind the problems associated with the language of worship. If we cannot see God in the everyday, how much more will we find it to be a challenge to identify the work of God in times of suffering?

It is important to identify from where this problem emerges. It comes from the vividness of worship. God is so real – we see the face of God and feel his touch in worship. In contrast, a faithful life of service, or the challenges of parenthood, or a regular job, can seem to be rather mundane or unrelated to the God we worship. What emerges is a kind of dualism. In worship we are in God's presence, when we are outside worship, we can feel that we are like batteries running down. Like a laptop computer or mobile phone, we need regular top-ups and charges. Such a view will not fuel the kind of mission advocated at events like Soul in the City. The challenge for charismatic Christians remains the same. The question is how we can value the regular everyday life of service as worship given to God without devaluing worship as the main event. My own feeling is that the charismatic movement has been guilty of a lack of theological sophistication and balance in the way it connects worship and mission. This is an area that needs to be addressed with much more vigour in the future.

Singing about Singing; From Objective to Reflexive Worship

The hymnologist, Lionel Adey, divides hymns into three categories: objective, subjective and reflexive.[15] Objective hymns are those which simply give an account of a

---

[15] Adey, *Hymns and the Christian Myth*.

theological theme or biblical event. Subjective hymns focus on theological or biblical content, but they also include some reference to the implications of this for the worshipper. The reflexive hymn focuses on the act of worship itself. Analysing individual hymns can be problematic because more than one of these forms may be present at the same time. A lengthy song may switch from objective to reflexive modes as the hymn reaches its climax. In the much less complex and shorter songs of renewal it is possible to locate the main emphasis of a song as either objective, subjective or reflexive. By analysing a number of songs, it is possible to build up an impression of the tendencies within that group of songs. In this way, we can see that *Youth Praise* has a very different feel to *The Survivor Songbook*. These changes indicate that there has been a distinct shift away from the objective and the subjective songs and towards more reflexive songs.

The emphasis upon encounter with God in the present has lead to songs that focus upon the worshipper and what is happening in the present moment. The 'now' of the worship song indicates the extent to which attention is directed to the present intimacy between the worshipper and their Lord. In the earlier songbooks, there was a more traditional emphasis upon the events of the life of Christ and the Gospel narratives as the focus for our worship and adoration. With contemporary songs, the desire to sing songs to God rather than about God has tended towards a lack of interest in the traditional theological content of hymnology or, indeed, the Psalms. In some cases, the songs have very little specifically gospel content. Instead, they speak about what is happening between the worshipper and God at that moment.

The reflexive form of hymn has always been a part of worship. In its right place it gives a sense of urgency and significance to a worship service. That said I feel uneasy when these songs form the main diet of worshipping life. There are clearly issues here. The most obvious is that the reflexive song substitutes gospel content for metaphors related to the intimacy of worship. It is worth contrasting two recently written worship songs. Kathryn Scott's 'Hungry: Falling on my knees'[16] and 'Light of the world: Here I am',[17] which was written by Tim Hughes. Before I do this I want to say that I like both of these songs. I have used them regularly when I have led worship and they have helped me many times to journey into the presence of God.

'Hungry' can be seen to fall clearly within the reflexive category of hymns. The song gives an account of the worshipper coming before God. They come hungry, thirsty and empty. God, in turn, is seen as welcoming with open arms. As the worshippers falls on their knees they receive the touch of God who restores their life and in return they offer themselves to Jesus. (*SS* 37) The song has deep theological roots. The welcome of Father is there in the story of the prodigal Son and the idea that Jesus is the food of the believer forms a strong eucharistic and spiritual tradition which is common to Catholic and Reformed traditions. The metaphors have a power because they connect to significant elements of the Christian experience. At the same time, the theological content of 'Hungry' is limited. If the chorus did not use the word Jesus it would be hard to identify any specifically Christian content in the song. In fact, the theological content relies upon the worshipper filling in the gaps.

There is an important theological issue at stake here. We know about God because he is revealed in Jesus Christ. The dynamic of the gospel as God's welcome rests on the life, death and resurrection of the historical Jesus. The theology of God who is revealed to us in Christ is not just a higher mathematics of 'theology', which only a few need to know while the rest of us live it in practice. It is in Jesus that we know and are known by God's grace. God's goodness does not just rely on these events. We experience God's goodness as we see God revealed in Jesus. In other words,

---

[16] *SS* 37.
[17] *SS* 95.

we cannot simply take the experience and disconnect it from Jesus who is the revelation of God.

Charismatic worship has tended to focus on the work of the Spirit or on the ascended Lord. In the reflexive hymn, we are generally singing about a disembodied 'you'. In focusing on singing songs to God there is a danger that we leave open the question, 'To which God we are singing?' It is for this reason that I am convinced that we need to look for a balance in the content of the songs we sing. It is not good enough to relegate the historical Christ to a theological hidden knowledge, i.e. something with which practical people need not be concerned with as long as the thing 'works'. If we are to continue to be 'Christian' then our experience of worship must be explicitly related to the revelation of God in the life of Christ.

'Light of the world'[18] addresses some of these concerns. This is still to a large extent a reflexive song, particularly in the chorus where the worshipper speaks of being 'here' to worship and bowing down before God. The verses, however, give some content to the God that we are worshipping. Jesus is not named, but both verses locate the object of worship as the 'Light of the world' and the 'King of all days' who in humility 'self-emptied' himself by stepping into the dark world. The reference to the incarnation does not just give specific content to the song; it also serves as a point for mediation and praise. By dwelling on the incarnation we see God as he has revealed himself and thus we come to worship.

Matt Redman is clear in 'When the music fades'[19] that the heart of worship is 'all about you Jesus.' This is a crucial insight but it could be observed that very few of the songs are really all about Jesus. In fact, many of the songs including 'When the music fades' are not really all about Jesus at all; rather, they are all about the worshipper and their experiences in worship. In other words, the songs lay

---

[18] *SS* 95.
[19] *SS* 181

themselves open to the criticism that they have replaced the content of the Christian gospel with human experience. Instead of worshipping Jesus, they give the impression that we are worshipping worship. In other words, it could be said that this trend in contemporary worship is in danger of being accused of a kind of idolatry.

My own view is that these songs are not idolatrous in themselves. The problem comes in the overall diet, not just of worship songs but also of teaching and learning within the charismatic churches. Things could be improved by encouraging songs writers to begin to focus on the historical Jesus. These kinds of songs should not just deal with the ascended Lord, but also with the events of his life and how in Jesus we see the glory of God revealed. 'The light of the world' shows how a song with explicit theological content can lead to intimacy in worship and balance the reflexive with the objective in lyrical content.

Bibliography

Adey, L., *Class and Idol in the English Hymn* (Vancouver: University of British Colombia Press, 1988)

—, *Hymns and the Christian Myth* (Vancouver: University of British Colombia Press, 1988)

Adorno, T.W., 'On Popular Music', in John Storey (ed.), *Cultural Theory and Popular Culture: A Reader* (Hemel Hempstead: Harvester Wheatsheaf, 1994), 199–201

—, *The Culture Industry* (London: Routledge, 1991)

Albrecht, D.E., *Rites in the Spirit: A Ritual Approach to Pentecostal/Charismatic Spirituality* (Sheffield: Sheffield Academic Press, 1999)

Allan, J., 'From Elvis Presley to Quentin Tarantino: Has Film Become the New Rock and Roll', in B. Borgman and C. Cook, *Agenda for Youth Ministry* (London: SPCK, 1998), 151–70

Archbishops' Commission on Church Music, *In Tune With Heaven* (London: Church House Publications, 1992)

Arnold, M., (1994) 'Culture and Anarchy', in John Storey (ed.), *Cultural Theory and Popular Culture: A Reader* (Hemel Hempstead: Harvester Wheatsheaf), 6–12

Barclay, O., *Evangelicalism in Britain 1935–1995: A Personal Sketch* (Leicester: Inter-Varsity Press, 1997)

Barthes, R., *Mythologies* (English trans.; London: Paladin, 1972 [1957])

Baudrillard, J., *Selected Writings* (ed. Mark Prosser; Cambridge: Polity, 1988)

Bauman, Z., *Life In Fragments: Essays in Postmodern Morality* (Oxford: Blackwell, 1995)

—, *Postmodernism and its Discontents* (Cambridge: Polity, 1997)

Bax, J., *The Good Wine: Spiritual Renewal in the Church of England* (London: Church House Publishing, 1986)

Bebbington, D.W., *Evangelicalism in Modern Britain: A History from 1730s to the 1980s* (London: Unwin, 1989)

—, 'Evangelicalism in its Settings: The British and American Movements since 1940', in M. Noll, D.W. Bebbington, G.A. Rawlyk, *Evangelicalism: Comparative Studies of Popular Protestantism in North America, the British Isles and Beyond* (Oxford: Oxford University Press, 1994), 365–88

Becker, H., 'The Culture of a Deviant Group: The Jazz Musician', in K. Gelder and S. Thornton (eds.), *The Subcultures Reader* (London: Routledge, 1997), 55–64

Begbie, J., 'The Spirituality of Renewal Music', *Anvil* 8.3 (1991), 227–39

Bicknell, J., 'A Postcard from Soul Survivor', *Youthwork* November 1996, 14

Binfield, C., *George Williams and the Y.M.C.A.* (London: Heinemann, 1973)

Borgman, B. and C. Cook (eds.), *Agenda for Youth Ministry* (London: SPCK, 1998)

Bourdieu, P., *Distinction: A Social Critique of the Judgement of Taste* (trans. Richard Nice; London: Routledge, 1984)

Bowater, C., *The Believer's Guide to Worship* (Eastbourne: Kingsway, 1986)

Butler, J., *Awash on a Sea of Faith: Christianizing the American People* (Cambridge, MA.: Harvard University Press, 1990)

Carey, G., *The Church in the Marketplace* (Eastbourne: Kingsway, 1984)

Carpenter, J.A., *Revive Us Again: The Reawakening of American Fundamentalism* (Oxford: Oxford University Press, 1997)

Castle, B., *Sing a New Song: The Power and Potential of Hymns* (London: Darton, Longman & Todd, 1994)

Cavicchi, D., *Tramps Like Us: Music and Meaning Among Springsteen Fans* (Oxford: Oxford University Press, 1998)

de Certeau, M., *The Practice of Everyday Life* (trans. Steven Rendall; Berkley: University of California, 1984)

Clarke, G., *Defending Ski-Jumpers: A Critique of Theories of Youth Subcultures* (Occasional Papers; Birmingham: Centre for Contemporary Cultural Studies, 1982)

Coates, G., *An Intelligent Fire* (Eastbourne: Kingsway, 1991)

Cohen, A.K., 'A General Theory of Subcultures', in K. Gelder and S. Thornton (eds.), *The Subcultures Reader* (London: Routledge, 1997), 44–54

Cohen, S., *Rock Culture in Liverpool: Popular Music in the Making* (Oxford: Oxford University Press, 1991)

—, 'Symbols of Trouble', in K. Gelder and S. Thornton (eds.), *The Subcultures Reader* (London: Routledge, 1997), 149–62

Cotton, I., *The Hallelujah Revolution: The Rise of the New Churches* (London: Little Brown, 1995)

Coutts, F., *The Weapons of Good Will: The History of the Salvation Army 1946–1977* (London: Hodder & Stoughton, 1986)

Cox, H., *Fire From Heaven: The Rise of Pentecostal Spirituality and the Reshaping of Religion in the Twenty-First Century* (London: Cassell, 1996)

Cray, G., 'Justice, Rock and the Renewal of Worship', in R. Sheldon (ed.), *In Spirit and in Truth: Exploring Directions in Music in Worship Today* (London: Hodder & Stoughton, 1989), 1–28

Davies, I., *Cultural Studies and Beyond Fragments of Empire* (London: Routledge, 1995)

Dorsett, L.W., *Billy Sunday and the Redemption of America* (Grand Rapids: Eerdmans, 1991)

Dorsett, L.W., *A Passion for Souls: The Life of D.L. Moody* (Chicago: Moody Press, 1997)

Dudley-Smith, T., *John Stott: The Making of a Leader* (Leicester: Inter-Varsity Press, 1999)

Dunstan, A., 'Hymnody in Christian Worship', in C., Jones, G. Wainwright and E. Yarnold (eds.), *The Study of Liturgy* (London: SPCK, 1978)

Eddison, J. (ed.), *Bash: A Study in Spiritual Power* (Basingstoke: Marshalls, 1982)

England, E. (ed.), *David Watson: A Portrait by His Friends* (Crowborough: Highland Books, 1985)

Enroth, R.M., E.E. Ericson and C.B. Peters, *The Story of the Jesus People: A Factual Survey* (Exeter: Paternoster Press, 1972)

Everett, P., *You'll Never be 16 Again: An Illustrated History of the British Teenager* (London: BBC Publications, 1986)

Fellingham, D., 'The Focus and Direction of Contemporary Worship', in R. Sheldon (ed.), *In Spirit and in Truth: Exploring Directions in Music in Worship Today* (London: Hodder and Stoughton, 1989), 49–68

Finney, C.G., *Lectures on Revival* (Minneapolis: Bethany House, 1988 [1935])

Fiske, J., *Understanding Popular Culture* (London: Routledge, 1989)

Ford, C., *Jesus and the Street People: A First-hand Report from Berkley* (Lutterworth: Lutterworth Press, 1972)

Foucault, M., *The History of Sexuality Volume One: An Introduction* (trans. Robert Hurley; Harmonsworth: Penguin, 1978)

Fowler, B., *Pierre Bourdieu and Cultural Theory: Critical Investigations* (London: Sage, 1997)

France, R.T. and A.E. McGrath (eds.), *Evangelical Anglicans: Their Influence in the Church Today* (London: SPCK, 1993)

Frith, S., *Sound Effects: Youth, Leisure, and the Politics of Rock and Roll* (London: Constable, 1983)

—, *Music for Pleasure* (Cambridge: Polity, 1988)

—, *Performing Rites* (Oxford: Oxford University Press, 1996)

Frith, S. and C. Gillett (eds.), *The Beat Goes On: The Rock File Reader* (London: Pluto, 1996)

Frith, S. and A. Goodwin (eds.), *On Record Rock: Pop and the Written Word* (London: Routledge, 1990)

Frith, S and J. Savage, 'Pearls and Swine: Intellectuals and the Mass Media', in S. Redhead (ed.), *The Clubcultures Reader* (Oxford: Blackwell, 1997), 7–17

du Gay, P. (ed.) *Production of Culture/Cultures of Production* (London: Sage, 1997)

Gelder, K. and S. Thornton (eds.), *The Subcultures Reader* (London: Routledge, 1997)

General Synod of the Church of England, *The Charismatic Movement and the Church of England* (London: Church House Publishing, 1981)

Gordon, M.M., 'The Concept of the Subculture and its Application', in K. Gelder and S. Thornton (eds.), *The Subcultures Reader* (London: Routledge 1997), 40–3

Graham, B., *The Jesus Generation* (London: Hodder & Stoughton, 1971)

Grossberg, L., 'On postmodernism and articulation: An interview with Stuart Hall', in D. Morley and K.-H. Chen (eds.), *Stuart Hall: Critical Dialogues in Cultural Studies* (London: Routledge, 1996), 131–50

—, 'History, politics and postmodernism: Stuart Hall and cultural studies', in D. Morley and K.-H. Chen (eds.), *Stuart Hall: Critical Dialogues in Cultural Studies* (London: Routledge, 1996), 131–51

—, 'Another Boring Day in Paradise: Rock and Roll and the Empowerment of Everyday Life', in K. Gelder and S. Thornton (eds.), *The Subcultures Reader* (London: Routledge 1997), 477–93

—, 'Cultural studies, modern logics and theories of globalisation', in A. McRobbie (ed.), *Back To Reality?: Social Experience and Cultural Studies* (Manchester: Manchester University Press, 1997), 7–35

Gunstone, J., *Pentecostal Anglicans* (London: Hodder & Stoughton, 1982)

—, *A People for His Praise* (rev'd edn.; London: Hodder & Stoughton, 1984 [1978])

Hall, S., 'On Postmodernism and Articulation: An interview with Stuart Hall', in D. Morley and K.-H. Chen (eds.), *Stuart Hall: Critical Dialogues in Cultural Studies* (London: Routledge, 1996), 131–50

—, 'The Meaning of New Times', in D. Morley and K.-H. Chen (eds.), *Stuart Hall: Critical Dialogues in Cultural Studies* (London: Routledge, 1996), 223–37

—, 'The Problem of Ideology: Marxism without guarantees',

in D. Morley and K.-H. Chen (eds.), *Stuart Hall: Critical Dialogues in Cultural Studies* (London: Routledge, 1996), 47–70

Hall, S. and T. Jefferson (eds.), *Resistance Through Rituals: Youth Subcultures in Post-war Britain* (London: Hutchinson, 1975)

Hambrick-Stowe, C.E., *Charles G. Finney and the Spirit of American Evangelicalism* (Grand Rapids: Eerdmans, 1996)

Harvey, D., *The Condition of Post-modernity* (Oxford: Blackwell, 1989)

Hastings, A., *A History of English Christianity 1920–1990* (3rd edn.; London: SCM, 1991)

Hatch, N.O., *The Democratization of American Christianity* (New Haven: Yale University Press, 1989)

Hebdige, D., *Subculture: The Meaning of Style* (London: Methuen, 1979)

—, *Hiding in the Light* (London: Routledge, 1988)

Henderson, S., *Since the Beginning Greenbelt* (London: Greenbelt, 1984)

Hoggart, R., *The Uses of Literacy* (London: Penguin, 1958)

Hollenweger, W.J., *The Pentecostals* (English translation; London: SCM Press, 1972)

Hunt, S., *Anyone for Alpha?* (London: Darton, Longman & Todd, 2001)

Hunt, S., M. Hamilton and T. Walter (eds.), *Charismatic: Christianity Sociological Perspectives* (Basingstoke: Macmillan, 1997)

Hylson-Smith, K., *Evangelicals in the Church of England 1734–1984* (Edinburgh: T&T Clark, 1988)

Irwin, J., 'Notes on the Status of the Concept of Subculture', in K. Gelder and S. Thornton (eds.), *The Subcultures Reader* (London: Routledge 1997), 83–9

Jaspers, T., *Jesus and the Christian in a Pop Culture* (London: Robert Royce, 1984)

Johnson, D., *Contending for The Faith: A History of the Evangelical Movement in the Universities and Colleges* (Leicester: Inter-Varsity Press, 1979)

Jones, C., G. Wainwright and S.J. Yarnold (eds.), *The Study of Liturgy* (London: SPCK, 1978)

Kendrick, G., *Worship* (Eastbourne: Kingsway, 1984)

—, *Shine Jesus Shine* (Milton Keynes: Word, 1992)

Kendrick, G., G. Coates, R. Forster and L. Green, *March For Jesus* (Eastbourne: Kingsway, 1992)

Krims, A., *Rap Music and the Poetics of Identity* (Cambridge: Cambridge University Press, 2000)

Laing, D., 'Rock Anxieties and New Musical Networks', in A. McRobbie (ed.), *Back To Reality?: Social Experience and Cultural Studies* (Manchester: Manchester University Press, 1997), 116–32

Law, S. and E. Lives, *Keep Music Legal: From the Manuscript to Mass Production* (London: Sea Dream Music, 1982)

Lawson-Johnston, P., 'Power in Praise-Worship, Cloud and the Bible', in R. Sheldon *In Spirit and in Truth: Exploring Directions in Music in Worship Today* (London: Hodder & Stoughton, 1989), 151–76

Leach, J., *Hymns and Spiritual Songs: The Use of Traditional and Modern in Music* (Nottingham: Grove Books, 1995)

Leaver, R., *A Hymn Book Survey 1962–80* (Nottingham: Grove Books, 1980)

Leavis, F.R., 'Mass Civilisation and Minority Culture', in J. Storey (ed.), *Cultural Theory and Popular Culture: A Reader* (Hemel Hempstead: Harvester Wheatsheaf, 1994), 12–21

Leech, K., *Youthquake Spirituality and the Growth of a Counter-Culture* (London: Abacus, 1976)

Longhurst, B., *Popular Music and Society* (Cambridge: Polity, 1995)

Lyon, D., *Jesus in Disneyland* (Cambridge: Polity, 2000)

Lyotard, J., *The Postmodern Condition: A Report on Knowledge* (trans. Geoff Bennington and Brian Massumi; Manchester: Manchester University Press, 1979)

Macan, E., *Rocking the Classics: English Progressive Rock and the Counterculture* (Oxford: Oxford University, 1997)

Maries, A., *One Heart One Voice: The Rich and Varied Resource of Music in Worship* (London: Hodder & Stoughton, 1986)

Marsden, G.M., *Fundamentalism and American Culture: The Shaping of Twentieth-Century Evangelicalism 1870–1925* (Oxford: Oxford University Press, 1980)

—, *Reforming Fundamentalism: Fuller Seminary and the New Evangelicalism* (Grand Rapids: Eerdmans, 1987)

Martin, William, *The Billy Graham Story: A Prophet with Honour* (London: Hutchinson, 1991)

Marty, M., *Pilgrims in their Own Land: 500 Years of Religion in America* (USA edn.; New York: Penguin, 1986)

McClary, S. and R. Walser, '"Start Making Sense!": Musicology Wrestles with Rock', in S. Frith and A. Goodwin, *On Record Rock: Pop and the Written Word* (London: Routledge, 1990), 277–92

McDannell, C., *Material Christianity* (New Haven: Yale University Press, 1995)

McGrath, A., *Evangelicalism and the Future of Christianity* (London: Hodder & Stoughton, 1994)

McGuigan, J., *Cultural Populism* (London: Routledge, 1992)

McRobbie, A., *Postmodernism and Popular Culture* (London: Routledge, 1994)

— (ed.), *Back To Reality?: Social Experience and Cultural Studies* (Manchester: Manchester University Press, 1997)

McRobbie, A and J. Garben, (1975) 'Girls and Subcultures: An exploration', in S. Hall and T. Jefferson, *Resistance Through Rituals: Youth Subcultures in Post-war Britain* (London: Hutchinson, 1975), 209–22

Middleton, R., *Studying Popular Music* (Milton Keynes: Open University, 1990)

Millar, S., 'A Friend's Recollections' in David Pytches (ed.), *1998 John Wimber* (Guildford: Eagle, 1998), 269–87

Moger, P., *Music and Worship: Principles to Practice* (Cambridge: Grove Books, 1994)

Moore, R.L., *Selling God: American Religion in the Marketplace of Culture* (Oxford: Oxford University Press, 1994)

Morley, D. and K.-H. Chen (eds.), *Stuart Hall: Critical Dialogues in Cultural Studies* (London: Routledge, 1996)

Murray, I. H., *D. Martyn Lloyd-Jones: The Fight of Faith 1939–1981* (Edinburgh: Banner of Truth, 1990)

Nava, M., *Changing Cultures: Feminism, Youth and Consumerism* (London: Sage, 1992)

Negus, K., *Popular Music in Theory: an Introduction* (Cambridge: Polity, 1996)

Nehring, N., *Popular Music, Gender and Postmodernism Anger is an Energy* (London: Sage, 1997)

Noll, M., *A History of Christianity in the United States and Canada* (London: SPCK, 1992)

Noll, M., D.W. Bebbington and G.A. Rawlyk, *Evangelicalism: Comparative Studies of Popular Protestantism in North America, the British Isles and Beyond* (Oxford: Oxford University Press, 1994)

O'Sullivan, T., 'Audience', in T. O'Sullivan, J. Hartley, D. Saunders, M. Montgomery, J. Fiske, *Key Concepts in Communication and Cultural Studies* (London Routledge, 1994), 119–20

O'Sullivan, T., J. Hartley, D. Saunders, M. Montgomery, J. Fiske, *Key Concepts in Communication and Cultural Studies* (London Routledge, 1994)

Palms, R.C., *The Jesus Kids* (London: SCM Press, 1972)

Park, R.E., 'The City: Suggestions for the investigation of human behaviour', in K. Gelder and S. Thornton (eds.), *The Subcultures Reader* (London: Routledge 1997), 16–27

Percy, M., *Words, Wonders and Power: Understanding Contemporary Christian Fundamentalism and Revivalism* (London: SPCK, 1996)

—, 'Sweet Rapture: Subliminal Eroticism in Contemporary Charismatic Worship', *Theology and Sexuality* 6 (1997), 71–106

Pilavachi, M. and C. Borlase, *Live the Life* (London: Hodder & Stoughton, 1998)

—, *For the Audience of One: The Soul Survivor Guide to Worship* (London: Hodder & Stoughton, 1999)

Plowman, E.E., *The Jesus Movement* (English edn.; London: Hodder & Stoughton, 1972)

Pollock, J.C., *The Good Seed: The Story of the Children's Special Service Mission and the Scripture Union* (London: Hodder & Stoughton, 1959)

Poulton, J., 'St. Michael-le-Belfrey', in E. England (ed.), *David Watson: A Portrait by His Friends* (Crowborough: Highland Books, 1985), 119–36

Price, C., 'The Wonder of Wimber', *Christianity* January 1998, 7

Pulkingham, G.W., *Gathered for Power* (London: Hodder & Stoughton, 1972)

—, *They Left Their Nets* (London: Hodder & Stoughton, 1974)

Pytches, D., 'Fully Anglican, Fully Renewed', in K. Springer (ed.), *Riding the Third Wave: What Comes After Renewal?* (Basingstoke: Marshal Pickering, 1987), 164–76

—, 'A Man Called John', in D. Pytches (ed.), *John Wimber* (Guildford: Eagle, 1998), 9–39

— (ed.), *John Wimber* (Guildford: Eagle, 1998)

Redhead, S. (ed.), *The Clubcultures Reader* (Oxford: Blackwell, 1997)

Redman, M., 'Worshipper and Musician' in D. Pytches (ed.), *John Wimber* (Guildford: Eagle, 1998), 62–70

Rowe, D., *Popular Cultures: Rock Music, Sport and the Politics of Pleasure* (London: Sage, 1995)

Saunders, T. and H. Sansom, *David Watson: A Biography* (London: Hodder & Stoughton, 1992)

Saward, M., *Evangelicals on the Move* (Oxford: Mowbray, 1987)

Schultze, Q.J., R.M. Anker, J.D. Bratt, W.D. Romanowski, J.W. Worst and L. Zuidervaart, *Dancing in the Dark* (Grand Rapids: Eerdmans, 1991)

Scotland, N., *Charismatics and the Next Millennium: Do they have a Future?* (London: Hodder & Stoughton, 1995)

Shedd, C.P., *History of the World's Alliance of Young Men's Christian Associations* (London: SPCK, 1955)

Sheldon, R. (ed.), *In Spirit and in Truth: Exploring Directions in Music in Worship Today* (London: Hodder & Stoughton, 1989)

Shepherd, J. and P. Wicke, *Music and Cultural Theory* (Cambridge: Polity, 1997)

Shuker, R., *Understanding Popular Music* (London: Routledge, 1994)

—, *Key Concepts in Popular Music* (London: Routledge, 1998)

Sizer, S., *Gospel Hymns and Social Religion* (Philadelphia: Temple University Press, 1978)

Slack, J.D., 'The theory and method of articulation in cultural studies', in D. Morley and K.-H. Chen (eds.), *Stuart Hall: Critical Dialogues in Cultural Studies* (London: Routledge, 1996), 112–30

Small, C., *Music of the Common Tongue* (London: Calder Riverrun, 1987)

Sparks, C., 'Stuart Hall, cultural studies and Marxism', in D. Morley and K.-H. Chen (eds.), *Stuart Hall: Critical Dialogues in Cultural Studies* (London: Routledge, 1996), 71–101

Springer, K., *Riding the Third Wave: What Comes After Renewal?* (Basingstoke: Marshal Pickering, 1987)

Steven, J., *Worship in the Restoration Movement* (Bramcote: Grove Books, 1989)

Steven, J.H.S., *Worship in the Spirit: Charismatic Worship in the Church of England* (Carlisle: Paternoster, 2002)

Storey, J. (ed.), *Cultural Theory and Popular Culture: A Reader* (Hemel Hempstead: Harvester Wheatsheaf, 1994)

Stout, H., *The Divine Dramatist: George Whitefield and the Rise of Modern Evangelicalism* (Grand Rapids: Eerdmans, 1991)

—, 'Religion, Communications and the Career of George Whitefield', in L.I. Sweet (ed.) *Communication and Change in American Religious History* (Grand Rapids: Eerdmans, 1993), 108–25

Straw, W., 'Characterizing Rock Culture: The Case of Heavy Metal', in S. Frith and A. Goodwin (eds.), *On Record Rock: Pop and the Written Word* (London: Routledge, 1990), 97–110

Sweet, L.I. (ed.), *Communication and Change in American Religious History* (Grand Rapids: Eerdmans, 1993)

Sylvester, N., *God's Word in a Young World: The Story of Scripture Union* (London: Scripture Union, 1984)

Taylor, L. and A. Willis, *Media Studies: Texts, Institutions and Audience* (Oxford: Blackwell, 1999)

Thompson, E.P., *The Making of The English Working Class* (Harmondsworth: Penguin, 1963)

—, 'Preface from the Making of the English Working Class',

in J. Storey (ed.), *Cultural Theory and Popular Culture: A Reader* (Hemel Hempstead: Harvester Wheatsheaf, 1994), 65–68

Thornton, S., *Club Cultures: Music, Media and Subcultural Capital* (Cambridge: Polity, 1995)

Tidball, D.J., *Who are the Evangelicals?: Tracing the Roots of Today's Movements* (London: HarperCollins, 1994)

Tomlinson, D., *The Post-evangelical* (London: Triangle, 1995)

Toynbee, J., *Making Popular Music: Musicians, Creativity and Institutions* (London: Arnold, 2000)

Tuttle, C., 'Foundations of Praise and Worship', in R. Sheldon, *In Spirit and in Truth: Exploring Directions in Music in Worship Today* (London: Hodder & Stoughton, 1989), 131–50

Walker, A., *Telling the Story: Gospel Mission and Culture* (London: SPCK, 1996)

—, 'Thoroughly Modern: Sociological Reflections on the Charismatic Movement from the End of the Twentieth Century', in S. Hunt, M. Hamilton and T. Walter (eds.), *Charismatic: Christianity Sociological Perspectives* (Basingstoke: Macmillan, 1997), 76–92

—, *Restoring the Kingdom: The Radical Christianity of the House Church Movement* (Guildford: Eagle, 1998)

Walker, T., *Open to God* (Nottingham: Grove, 1975)

Walser, R., *Running With the Devil: Power, Gender and Madness in Heavy Metal Music* (Hanover: New England and Wesleyan University Press, 1993)

Ward, P., *Worship and Youth Culture* (London: Marshal Pickering, 1993)

—, *Growing Up Evangelical: Youthwork and the Making of a Subculture* (London: SPCK, 1996)

—, 'Alpha the McDonaldisation of Religion?', in *Anvil* 15.4 (1998), 279–86

Watson, D., *You Are My God* (London: Hodder & Stoughton, 1983)

Weber, M., *The Protestant Ethic and the Spirit of Capitalism* (trans. Talcott Parsons; London: Allen & Unwin, 1930)

Wells, D.F., *No Place for Truth or Whatever Happened to*

Evangelical Theology? (Leicester: Inter-Varsity Press, 1993)

Williams, R., *Culture and Society 1780–1950* (Harmondsworth: Penguin, 1958)

—, *Keywords: A Vocabulary of Culture and Society* (London: Fontana, 1976)

—, 'The Analysis of Culture', in J. Storey (ed.), *Cultural Theory and Popular Culture: A Reader* (Hemel Hempstead: Harvester Wheatsheaf, 1994), 56–63

Willis, P., *Common Culture* (Milton Keynes: Open University, 1990)

Wilson-Dickson, A., *A Brief History of Christian Music* (Oxford: Lion, 1992)

Woodward, K., 'Introduction', in K. Woodward (ed.), *Identity and Difference* (London: Sage, 1997), 8–13

— (ed.), *Identity and Difference* (London: Sage, 1997)

Songbooks

Combined Sound of Living Waters – Fresh Sounds (London: Hodder & Stoughton, 1977)

Songs for Jesus (New Malden: MGO, 1972)

Songs and Hymns of Fellowship (Eastbourne: Kingsway, 1985)

Songs of Fellowship Volume 1 (Eastbourne: Kingsway, 1981)

Songs of the Vineyard Volume 1 (Eastbourne: Kingsway, 1987)

Sound of Living Waters Songs of Renewal (London: Hodder & Stoughton, 1974)

The Graham Kendrick Songbook Volume 2 (Eastbourne: Kingsway, 1987)

The Survivor Songbook (Eastbourne: Kingsway, 2001)

The Survivor Songbook 2 (Eastbourne: Kingsway, 2002)

The Way of the Cross: The New Wine and Soul Survivor Song Book (Chorleywood: New Wine, 1996)

Youth Praise Book One (London: Falcon Press, 1966)

Youth Praise Book Two (London: Falcon Press, 1969)

Magazines and Publications

Buzz (published monthly Oct 1965–Sep 1987)
Cross Rhythms (published bi-monthly May 1990–May 1995)
Worship (Encore) (published quarterly Spring 1987 –Autumn 1989)
Congregational Worship and Copyright (Christian Copyright Licensing, 1998)
Music Photocopying Report (Christian Copyright Licensing, 1998)
Reference Manual (Christian Copyright Licensing, 1998)
Come Together Booklet (Jimmy and Carol Owens, 1972)
Soul Survivor Magazine (published bi-monthly from October 1995)
Worship Together (published bi-monthly November/December 1996–July/August 1997)
Church of England Newspaper 29 May 1998

Videos and Compact Disc Recordings

Redman, Matt, *Passion for Your Name* (Eastbourne: Kingsway, 1995)
Soul Survivor Passion for Your Name (Eastbourne: Kingsway, 1995)
Soulzone The Soul Survivor Video 1997 (London: LBC Video, 1997)

Songs Index

A new commandment (*SLW* 66) 130

Abba, Father (*SF* 1) 140

According to the working (*YP* 114) 125

All Around the World (*SS* 1) 162

All around your throne (*SS* 2) 162

All heaven waits (*GK* 9) 141

Alleluia (*SLW* 25) 128

Amazing Grace (*SLW* 5) 58

Are the Prayers of the Saints? (*SS* 5) 162

As I Close my Eyes (*SV* 1) 145

Be the Centre (*SS* 82) 2–3

Behold I stand (*YP* 68) 123

Behold I stand (*YP* 68) 123

Big Man (*GK* 30) 144

Bring Forth the Fruit (*YP* 110) 126

Burdens are Lifted at Calvary (*YP* 104) 124

Calypso carol (*SLW* 118) 131

Can it be true? (*YP* 36) 27, 125

Change My Heart, O God (*SV* 3) 147

Christ be My Leader (*YP* 97) 126

Christ Triumphant (*YP* 10) 125

Come and go with me (*SLW* 87) 133

Come and praise Him, Royal Priesthood (*SF* 14) 139

Come Bless the Lord (*SF* 15) 138

Come Bless the Lord (*SF* 16) 138–9

Come now, let us reason together (*GK* 11) 143–5

Come Walk with Me (*SF* 17) 136, 139

Come, Holy Spirit (*SV* 4) 149

Consider How he Loves you (*SV* 5) 148

Crazy Mixed Up Generation (*YP2* 272) 32

Do you not believe it? (*GK* 12) 141

Every Breathe that I Take (*SV* 6) 145, 148

Everyday (*SS* 17) 153, 162

Faithful One (*SF* 89) 7

Father, I place into your hands (*SF* 21) 140

Father, we adore you, You've drawn us (*SV* 7) 148

Fear not! rejoice and be glad (*SLW* 59) 132

For we see Jesus (*SF* 26 137

For Zion's Sake (*GK* 13) 143

For, I'm building a people of power (*SF* 25) 140

Go tell everyone (*SLW* 93) 133

God has spoken (*SLW* 95) 133

God himself is with us (*SLW* 22) 129

God is building a house (*SLW* 60) 130

Hallelujah for the Lord Our God (*SF* 30) 137

He is Lord (*SF* 37) 136

He lives (*YP* 52) 125

He shall teach you all things (*SLW* 41) 132

Hear My Cry, O Lord (*SF* 33) 139

Heart of the Father (*SS* 25) 153

Here comes Jesus (*SLW* 49) 131

Here I am once again (*SS* 31) 153

Here I am, a sinner free (*SS* 29) 158

His hands were pierced (*YP* 116) 125

Ho! everyone that thirsteth (*SLW* 88) 133

Hold me Lord (*SV* 10) 148

Holy, holy (*SLW* 19) 57, 129–30, 131–2

How lovely is your dwelling place: Better is one day (*SS* 36) 160

Hungry: Falling on my knees (*SS* 37) 153–4, 161, 208

I am a Wounded Soldier (*SV* 15) 149

I am Yours (*SV* 16) 145–6

I Bless you Lord (*SV* 17) 145

I come running: Only you (*SS* 40) 162

I come to you: Here with me now (*SS* 41) 159

I come, wanting just to be with you (*SS* 42) 159

I fix my eyes on you (*SS* 45) 158

I get so excited, Lord (*SF* 4) 138

I Give you all the Honour (*SV* 18) 147

I have come to love you, Lord (*SS* 46) 161–2

I hear the sound of rustling (*SF* 48) 140–1

I just want to love (*SS* 49) 202–3

I Lift my Hands (*SV* 21) 145

I lift you high, you must increase (*SS* 51) 156

I love you (*SS* 52) 153, 162

I love you, Lord (*SF* 49) 136–7

I Love you, Lord: Joy (*SS* 54) 159

I Only want to Love you (*SV* 23) 145

I Receive you (*SV* 20) 145, 147

I sing a new song (*SV* 24) 148

I still remember (*SS* 65) 161

I want to walk (*YP* 121) 126

I want to walk as a child of the light (*SLW* 34) 133

I will enter his gates (*SF* 62) 138

I will love you for the Cross (*SS* 78) 157

I will magnify (*SV* 28) 145

I will offer up my life (*SS* 80) 158

I will worship you (*SV* 29) 145, 148

I'll be a fried to Jesus (*YP* 109) 124–5

I'll be a friend to Jesus (*YP* 109) 125

I'm giving you my heart (*SS* 56) 154–5, 157–8

I'm singing for you Lord (*YP* 7) 200

I'm Yours (*SV* 22) 145, 148

If I tried (*YP2* 245) 31

If My People who Bear my Name (*GK* 16) 142

If you want joy (*YP* 72) 122

It is no longer I that liveth (*SF* 56) 137

It's your Blood (*SV* 27) 145

Jericho road (*YP* 80) 125

Jesus (*SLW* 57) 128

Jesus Christ: Once again (*SS* 83) 157, 159

Jesus Died for me (*YP* 42) 124

Jesus is Changing Me (*SF* 70) 138

Jesus is King (*GK* 17) 144

Jesus is Knocking (*YP* 73) 123

Jesus is Lord (*SF* 71) 137

Jesus is the Saviour (*YP* 61) 123

Jesus is the Saviour (*YP* 61) 27

Jesus my desire (*SS* 87) 162

Jesus, come closer to me (*SF* 67) 136

Jesus, how lovely you are (*SF* 68) 137

Jesus, I love you (*SV* 30) 148

Jesus, lover of my soul: It's all about you (*SS* 86) 162

Jesus, we enthrone you (*SF* 86) 137

Just a Closer Walk (*YP* 101) 126

Just Like you promised (*SV* 31) 145, 147–8

Let God arise (*GK* 3) 143

Let us give thanks (*SLW* 8) 127

Life is wonderful (*YP* 46) 122, 200

Light of the world: Here I am (*SS* 95) 208, 209

Living Lord (*YP* 126) 125

Long ago (*SV* 33) 145–6

Lord, Hear the Music of My heart (*SS* 97) 154

Lord of the cross (*YP* 11) 124

Lord who left the Highest Heaven (*YP* 89) 125

Lord, I am not my own (*SS* 98) 162

Lord, I love you (*SV* 36) 145, 147

Lord, I want to be (*SV* 35) 145, 147

Lord, I'll seek after you (*SV* 34) 146–7

Lord, the light of Your Love (Shine, Jesus, Shine) (*GK* 20) 144

Lord, you have my heart (*SS* 104) 152–3, 160, 203

Make up your mind (*YP* 76) 123–4, 126

Make Up your Mind (*YP* 76) 126

Make Way (*GK* 1) 142

Many are the words we speak: Now we live the life (*SS* 105) 156

May I sing a song of Love (*SS* 106) 155

May the fragrance (*GK* 22) 144

Morning has broken (*SLW* 9) 58, 127

My Heart Overflows (*SF* 91) 140

My Jesus, my saviour (*SS* 113) 155

My Lord, you are so good to me (*SF* 94) 137

No one but you (*SV* 38) 145

No one ever cared for me like Jesus (*YP* 58) 123, 126

Nothing in the World (*SS* 116) 154

O Come all you Thirsty Nations
   (*SF* 13) 140
O Holy Spirit, giver of life (*YP*
   112) 126
O Let the Son of God Enfold you
   (*SV* 39) 147–8
O Lord Most Holy God (*SF* 98)
   139
O Lord you are the truth (*SV* 40)
   145
O Lord, Have Mercy on Me (*SV*
   41) 145
O Lord, the clouds are gathering
   (*GK* 25) 142
O sacred King (*SS* 121) 155
Oh, lead me (*SS* 125) 159
One thing I ask (*SS* 128) 160
One thing my Heart is set upon
   (*SS* 129) 161
Open your eyes (*SV* 42) 145
Peace is flowing (*SLW* 91) 205
Perfect Love (*SF* 102) 138
Praises: At the foot of the cross
   (*SS* 135) 158
River of God (*SS* 137) 161
Search me, O God (*SS* 139) 154
Silver and gold have I none (*SLW*
   50) 132
Sing to the Lord (*SS* 141) 156
Sing to the Lord: Awaken the
   dawn (*SS* 144) 156
Sometimes when I feel your love:
   I love your love (*SS* 142)
   161–2
Spirit divine (*SLW* 33) 132
Spirit of the living God (*YP* 108;
   SLW 29) 126, 132
Spirit of the Living God (*YP* 108)
   126
Tell me, why do you weep? (*GK*
   28) 142

Thank you (*YP* 13) 127–8
Thank you for being (*SV* 45)
   145–6
Thank you for the blood (*SS* 147)
   157
Thank you Jesus, Praise you
   Jesus (*SF* 117) 138
The body song (*SLW* 111) 130,
   183
The canticle of the gift (*SLW* 2)
   127, 131
The cross has said it all (*SS* 148)
   157
The Earth is the Lord's (and
   everything in it) (*GK* 4) 142
The foot washing song (*SLW* 125)
   131
The Holy Ghost medley (*SLW* 77)
   132
The King of Love (*YP* 63) 27
The kingdom of God (*SLW* 61)
   130
The Lord who left the highest
   heaven (*YP* 89) 127
The name of Jesus is higher than
   any other (*SF* 37) 136
The promised land (*SF* 126)
   141
There is a Name (*YP* 43) 124
There you died for me (*YP* 38)
   124
This is my commandment
   (*SLW* 70) 130
We are the Lord's Own Army
   (*SF* 142) 140
We believe (*GK* 5) 143
We bow down at your throne,
   O Lord (*SS* 164) 160
We bow our hearts (*SS* 165) 160
We declare that the kingdom of
   God is here (*GK* 2) 143

We Dwell in the Courts (*SF* 145) 139

We Fall Down (*SS* 167) 160

We see the Lord (*SLW* 23) 129

What a friend I've found: Jesus friend for ever (*SS* 175) 161–2

When the music fades: The heart of worship (*SS* 181) 152, 156, 209

When the road is rough (*YP* 96) 123

When the Road is Rough (*YP* 96) 126

Within the Veil (*SF* 155) 138

You are here (*SV* 47) 145

You are the King who Reigns (*SV* 48) 145, 148

You are the Mighty King (*SV* 50) 145

You are the Vine (*SV* 49) 145

Author Index

Adey, L. 4, 206
Albrecht, D.E. 40
Barclay, O. 21, 22
Baughen, M. 25
Bax, J. 190
Bebbington, D.W. 13, 14, 15, 16, 17, 18, 20, 21, 24, 26, 40, 42, 55, 100
Bellamy, J. 89
Bicknell, J. 105
Borlase, C. 100, 170, 171, 172, 175, 176, 177, 189, 190
Bowater, C. 171, 174, 178, 179
Butler, J. 14, 17
Carpenter, J.A. 17
Coates, G. 51, 72, 193, 194
Coutts, F. 17
Cox, H. 17
Cray, G. 166, 167
Cummings, T. 67, 68, 69, 76, 77, 81, 83, 84, 91, 92, 93, 94
Doerkson, B. 7
Dorsett, L.W. 17, 19
Dudley-Smith, T. 21, 22
Dunstan, A. 23
Eddison, J. 20, 22
England, E. 201

Enroth, R.M. 36, 37, 39
Ericson, E.E. 36, 37, 39
Everett, P. 27, 28
Fellingham, D. 78, 169, 175
Finney, C.G. 14
Ford, C. 36
Forster, R. 72, 193, 194
Graham, B. 39, 168
Green, L. 72, 193, 194
Gunstone, J. 170, 171, 186, 201, 202
Hambrick-Stowe, C.E. 14, 17
Hamilton, M. 42
Hastings, A. 17, 19, 40, 57
Hatch, N.O. 17, 18
Henderson, S. 54
Hollenweger, W.J. 17
Hunt, S. 42, 103
Hylson-Smith, K. 19
Jaspers, T. 38, 45, 53, 56
Johnson, D. 20, 22
Jones, C. 23
Kendrick, G. 46, 71, 72, 73, 85, 173, 174, 176, 189, 190, 193, 200
Law, S. 80, 81, 82
Leaver, R. 25, 26
Leech, K. 38, 42, 43, 45

Leher, M. 32
Lives, E. 80, 81, 82
Lyon, D. 110
Maries, A. 184, 185, 186, 189
Marsden, G.M. 17, 19
Martin, W. 19
Marty, M. 17
McDannell, C. 37
McGrath, A.E. 13, 20, 21
Millar, S. 101
Moore, R.L. 17
Murray, I.H. 22
Negus, K. 88, 93
Noll, M. 13, 14
Owens, C. 51, 52
Owens, J. 51, 52
Palms, R.C. 36, 39, 168
Payne, D. 28, 29
Percy, M. 146, 147, 148
Peters, C.B. 36, 37, 39
Pilavachi, M. 100, 170, 171, 172, 175, 176, 177, 189, 190
Plowman, E.E. 38
Pollock, J.C. 22, 23
Poulton, J. 201
Price, C. 99
Pulkingham, G.W. 57
Pytches, D. 98, 99, 100, 101, 104, 105
Rawlyk, G.A. 13

Redman, M. 100, 101, 179, 180, 190
Richards, N. 78
Sansom, H. 57, 94
Saunders, T. 57, 94
Saward, M. 13, 20, 24
Scotland, N. 180, 187, 188
Sheldon, R. 166, 169
Springer, K. 99
Steven, J. 169, 188
Steven, J.H.S. 109
Stout, H. 17, 19
Sweet, L.I. 11, 19, 116
Sylvester, N. 23
Thomas, W.T.H. 50
Tidball, D.J. 13
Tuttle, C. 168, 176, 189
Wainwright, G. 23
Walker, A. 40, 41, 42, 71, 72, 99, 100, 135
Walker, T. 58
Walter, T. 42
Ward, P. 5, 12, 19, 20, 23, 24, 25, 54, 55, 59, 102
Watson, D. 21, 58, 200
Weber, M. 11
Wells, D.F. 17
Wilson-Dickson, A. 186, 193
Yarnold, E. 23

General Index

Alliance Music 94, 113
Alpha 97–8, 101–3, 111–12, 114, 191
Authentic Media 113, 192
Barnett, Doug 61, 66, 70
Baughen, Michael 24–5, 33
Big House Audio 90
Blessitt, Arthur 38, 42–5
Bonnke, Reinhard 89
Boone, Pat 51
Bowater, Chris 171, 174, 178
British Youth For Christ (BYFC) 61, 63–5, 70, 77
Buzz magazine 12, 28–31, 32–3, 43–4, 46, 49–53, 55, 64–6, 68, 70, 89, 111, 113–14, 167, 192
Calver, Clive 63–4, 70, 78
Cambridge-Inter Collegiate Christian Union 21–2
Children's Special Service Mission (CSSM) 6, 23–4, 26
Christian Copyright Licensing Scheme, The 75, 81–8, 85–7
Christian Music Association, The 86, 89
Church Pastoral Aid Society (CPAS) 25

Churches Youth Fellowships Association 20, 24
Clifton, Dave 102
Coates, Gerald 51, 73, 78, 194
Coltman, Nigel 67–8, 75, 81
Come Together 7, 30, 49–53, 55–7, 130
CopyCare 75, 81
CSSM Chorus Books 23–4, 26
Dales Bible Week 41, 72, 80
Delirious? 114–16
Delve, Eric 55, 64, 70
Dudley-Smith, Timothy 21, 25
Fellingham, Dave 78, 1269, 174, 187
Feltham, Don 90
Festival of Light 43–5, 53
Filey Bible Week 30, 68
Fisherfolk, The 56–8
Forster, Roger 73, 194
Fountain Trust, The 40, 42, 45, 57
gospel beat groups 12, 27–29, 32–3, 75, 167
Graham Kendrick Somgbook Volume 2, The 135, 141–5, 215
Graham, Billy 22, 39, 79, 89
Green, Lynn 73, 194

Green, Michael 168, 202
Greenbelt Festival 7, 49, 53–6, 76, 89, 91, 106, 112
Hadden, David 92
Harper, Jeanne 57
Harper, Michael 40, 57–8
Harvestime 84–5, 92
Holy Trinity, Brompton 97, 99, 101, 103, 110–11
International Christian Communications (ICC) 90–5
Inter-Varsity fellowship 20, 22
Ishmael 65, 102
Jesus Family, The 53–5, 89
Jesus Movement 4, 33, 35–47, 49–50, 53, 167
Jesus People, The 36–9, 44–5, 49, 54, 168
Kaufman, Helmut 90–2
Kendrick, Graham 45, 46, 51, 62–5, 70–3, 77–9, 85, 136, 141–5, 173–4, 176, 190, 194, 200
Keswick Convention 111
Key Records 33, 62, 65
Kingsway Music 1, 61, 66–71, 78–80, 84, 92–4, 105–6, 191–2
Make Way 69, 72–4, 77, 135, 142, 191, 194, 205
March for Jesus 69, 72–4, 142, 191, 193–4
Meadows, Peter 28, 46, 63, 65–6, 70, 114
Mechanical Copyright Protection Society 81–3
Mission Praise 79, 193
Music Gospel Outreach (MGO) 4, 11–12, 27–33, 35, 43–6, 49–50, 59, 61–3, 65–7, 75–6, 89, 103, 167, 205
New Wine 103–5, 107, 109, 111, 151

Norman, Larry 31, 37–8, 42, 44–6, 49, 54, 76
Owens, Jimmy 30, 51, 53, 179
Owens, Carol 51, 53, 129
Performance Rights Society 81, 83, 85
Phonographic Performance Licensing Company 81–3
Piercy, Andy 102–3, 115
Pilavachi, Mike 77–8, 100, 105, 170–7, 189
Pope, Dave 51, 64, 70, 92
Premier Radio 105, 114
Pytches, David 77, 98–9, 101, 104, 108–9
Redman, Matt 77–8, 98, 100–1, 105, 115, 152, 180, 190, 209,
Richard, Cliff 32, 45, 62–3
Send the Light Ltd 113
Shearn, Geoff 28, 56, 65–8, 71, 75, 83, 85–6
Smith, Martin 98, 115–16
Snell, Adrian 64
Songs For Jesus 46
Songs of Fellowship 7, 61, 67–9, 72, 78–9, 93, 115, 121, 133, 135–41, 143, 145, 151, 193
Songs of the Vineyard 69, 135, 145–9
Soul in the City 112, 205–6
Soul Survivor 1, 7, 69, 87, 97–8, 103, 105–12, 115–17, 151, 161, 172–3, 181, 191, 202, 205
Sound of Living Waters 7, 50, 56–9, 121–2, 127–33, 183, 205
Soundtree Studios 92–3
Spring Harvest 1, 47, 61, 68, 70–2, 74, 76, 79–80, 91–2, 95, 97, 111, 117, 181, 191–2
St Andrew's, Chorleywood 77, 98–9, 101, 103–5

Stott, John 21–2, 25, 33
Spring Harvest 1, 47, 61, 68,
    70–2, 74, 76, 79–80, 91–2, 95,
    97, 111, 117, 181, 191–2
Survivor Songbook, The 3, 5, 115,
    121, 151–2, 155, 158
Toronto Blessing, The 107, 109
Thankyou Music 1, 65–7, 69, 78,
    80, 85–6, 106
The Tribe 113
Vineyard
    churches/fellowships 3, 69,
        94, 97, 99, 107–9, 116, 168,
        179, 199
    Music/songs 2–3, 97–8, 108–9,
        113, 116–17, 145–9, 153

Virgo, Terry 78, 99–100
Watson, David 21–2, 25, 57–8,
    98–9, 114, 200–2
Wigwam Acoustics 89–90
Wimber, John 40, 69, 98–101,
    106–7, 112, 135, 145, 180
Word 30, 52–3, 76, 86, 94, 111,
    113
World Wide Message Tribe 95,
    113, 118
Youth Praise 5, 7, 11–12, 23, 25–7,
    31–3, 58, 121–9, 130, 132, 138,
    151, 167, 186, 200, 207
Youthwork magazine 114, 117

Also Published By Paternoster

Liquid Church
Pete Ward

ISBN: 1-84227-161-X
RRP £9.99

The church must be like water – flexible, fluid, changeable. This book is a vision for how the church can embrace the liquid nature of culture rather than just scrambling to keep afloat while sailing over it.

Ward urges us to move away from the traditional understanding of church as a gathering of people meeting in one place at one time to a dynamic notion of church as a series of relationships and communications. In the Liquid Church, membership is determined by participation and involvement. Liquid Church is continually on the move, flowing in response to the Spirit and the gospel of Jesus, the imagination and creativity of its leaders, and the choices and experiences of its worshippers.

In this provocative, insightful, and challenging book, Pete Ward presents his vision of a Liquid Church that addresses the needs of the isolated consumer-Christian by providing connection and community, located in common cause and similar desire for God.